New Evidence of Trotsky's Conspiracy

By Grover Furr

Erythros Press and Media, LLC

Corrected Version August 2020

New Evidence of Trotsky's Conspiracy
April 2020; corrected version August 2020

Published by Erythrós Press and Media, LLC
PO Box 294994
Kettering, OH 45429-0994
media@erythrospress.com

Published and printed with permission of the author, who assumes all responsibility for the content herein.

ISBN: 978-0-578-64976-4

270 pp. Includes index.

1. Trotsky, Leon, 1879-1940. 2. Revolutionaries - Russia- Biography. 3. Stalin, Joseph, 1878-1953. 4. Soviet Union – History – 1925-1953. 5. Trials (Conspiracy).

Table of Contents

Acknowledgements and Dedication

I wish to express my gratitude to Kevin Prendergast, Arthur Hudson – Arthur, may you enjoy your well-deserved retirement! -- and Siobhan McCarthy, the skilled and tireless Inter-Library Loan librarians at Harry S. Sprague Library, Montclair State University. Without their help, my research would simply not be possible. With their continued help, I can persevere.

I again extend my heartfelt thanks to my skilled, wonderful Moscow colleague Vladimir L'vovich Bobrov, for all his tireless and brilliant help during the twenty-one years of our research together.

* * * * *

I would like to recognize Montclair State University for giving me a sabbatical leave in the fall semester of 2015, and special research travel funds in 2017 and 2019, which have been invaluable in my research on this book.

* * * * *

Dedication

I dedicate this book to Ellen and John Murray, of Oakland, CA, and Raj Sahai, of Berkeley, CA.

You have been infallibly supportive of my work, in every way. Encouragement and help such as yours can never be repaid. But it can be acknowledged, and I gladly do so here, with thanks and humility.

Introduction

This book is a study of Soviet-era documents, recently declassified, that bear on Leon Trotsky and his conspiracies against the Soviet government and Party during the 1930s. These documents are: Yuri Piatakov's statement to Nikolai Ezhov, chief of the NKVD, of December 19-20, 1936; the transcript of the trial of Marshal Mikhail N. Tukhachevsky and seven accomplices of June 11, 1937; and a collection of investigative materials from the former NKVD archive concerning the First and Second Moscow Trials of August, 1936, and January, 1937.

I obtained Piatakov's statement to Ezhov some years ago from my Moscow colleague and skilled historian Vladimir L. Bobrov, from the FSB (formerly NKVD) archive in Moscow. It has since been declassified and published online from the Russian State Archive of Social-Political History (RGASPI), also in Moscow. The texts are the same, though they were typed at different times and have different pagination.[1]

The 172-page text of the trial of the "Tukhachevsky Affair" defendants was silently declassified from the Russian State Archive of Socio-Political History (RGASPI) in May, 2018, and posted on the Russian historical site istmat.info. It is in printed form, perhaps to be circulated in a limited manner.

The third set of documents are from the two-volume work *Politbiuro i Lev Trotskii (sbornik dokumentov), 1923-1940*[2], edited by Oleg V. Mozokhin and published in 2013 in Prague, Czechoslovakia, by Sociosféra-CZ. This two-volume work is essentially unobtainable. As of November, 2019, the Worldcat meta-database of world re-

---

[1] I have given the pagination for both versions in the text of Piatakov's statement printed in the Appendix to this book.
[2] English translation: :"The Politburo and Leon Trotsky (collection of documents), 1923-1940."

search libraries contains an entry for this work which states that "no libraries with the specified item were found."[3]

In 2017 a one-volume version of this work was published in Russia. But this volume omits some of the most interesting documents from the two-volume work.[4] My colleague Vladimir Bobrov obtained a copy of the two-volume, 2013 work at the FSB archive. I have used this copy for the present book.

Mozokhin is a historian employed by the FSB, the successor to the KGB and NKVD, and author of many books and articles on the "special services." The two-volume 2013 work is cited on his personal page. But there is no information about why it was published in Czechoslovakia rather than in Russia, or why it is unobtainable.[5]

In the present book we will consider only the documents in volume 2 of the two-volume 2013 work (hereafter referred to as PiLT2). The first document in volume 2 dates from November 3, 1932. The latest is from August 24, 1940, and is an announcement of, and copy of the *Pravda* article on, Trotsky's assassination on August 20, 1940.

Our study of the documents published in PiLT2 yields some important results concerning Trotsky's conspiracies during the 1930s. The documents in this volume also touch on many other important issues with which we are not concerned here.

A. Introduction – Conclusion: The Results of This Study

What follows is a brief summary of the conclusions to be drawn from the evidence under examination in this book:

---

[3] https://www.worldcat.org/title/politbiuro-i-lev-trotskii-sbornik-dokumentov-1923-1940/oclc/889406153&referer=brief_results

[4] https://www.worldcat.org/title/politbiuro-i-lev-trotskii-1922-1940-sbornik-dokumentov/oclc/1050151524&referer=brief_results I have compared the Tables of Contents of the 2013 and the 2017 works.

[5] See http://mozohin.ru/photos/image/Politbjuro-i-Lev-Trockij.html

Trotsky Did Conspire with Germany and Japan against the USSR

The information in these documents that are examined in the present book constitutes additional strong evidence that Leon Trotsky did indeed enter into conspiratorial relations against the Soviet Union with both Nazi Germany and fascist Japan. It corroborates a large body of other evidence of Trotsky's conspiracies with the fascist powers. We located, identified, and studied some of that evidence in a previous work [6]

Much more evidence of Trotsky's German-Japanese collaboration is being disclosed as more documents from former Soviet archives are being released. We will collect and examine it in future studies.

The Statements and Confessions of Moscow Trials Defendants Reflect What The Defendants Chose To Say

All the documents under examination in the present book relate to the First and Second Moscow Trials of August, 1936, and January, 1937. Today we have a great deal of evidence that, in the cases of the three famous Moscow Trials of 1936-38, the NKVD did *not* force those under interrogation to confess to crimes they had not committed.

During his tenure as chief (People's Commissar) of Internal Affairs Nikolai Ezhov did frame, or simply murder, hundreds of thousands of innocent Soviet citizens. We have discussed this horror, the *Ezhovshchina*, in a separate study.[7]

In the first twelve chapters of *Trotsky's 'Amalgams'* we checked many statements by Moscow Trials defendants against independent evidence now available. In *The Moscow Trials As Evidence* we published an updated version of this study. On the basis of this ex-

---

[6] *Leon Trotsky's Collaboration with Germany and Japan.* Kettering, OH: Erythrós Press & Media, LLC, 2017).
[7] *Yezhov Vs. Stalin: The Truth About Mass Repressions and the So-Called 'Great Terror' in the USSR.* Kettering, OH: Erythros Press & Media LLC, 2018 (2016).

amination we concluded that the testimony in the Moscow Trials proves to be truthful in those instances where we can independently check it. The interrogations published in PiLT2 provide a great deal of additional corroborative evidence that the Moscow Trials testimony was genuine – meaning, that those under interrogation answered the way they chose to answer.

Documents from the Harvard Trotsky Archive help to show that many of those interrogated here told the truth. We can also independently check a number of statements made in these interrogations against other independent sources, such as Mark Zborowski's reports to his NKVD handlers; Anton Ciliga's memoirs about his years in the Verkhneural'sk political isolator along with Trotskyists and other oppositionists; and Valentin Astrov's testimony.[8]

Our hypothesis that the prisoners' confessions in PiLT2 are genuine has been confirmed. Whenever we can check them by internal or external evidence they turn out to be genuine. There is no disconfirming evidence at all – no evidence that any of the confession statements were the result of compulsion of any kind. Therefore we must conclude that the statements made in the confessions contained in PiLT2 that we cannot now directly confirm are also genuine and, consequently, may be used as evidence.

The implications of this finding go far beyond the documents in PiLT2. The contents of these interrogation-confessions are consistent with those in the First and Second Moscow Trials. We have other evidence that confirms the genuineness of the testimony in these trials. Together with our analysis of the confession statements in PiLT2 we have even stronger evidence that the testimony of the defendants in the Moscow Trials is genuine – that is, not forced upon the defendants by the Prosecution or the OGPU-NKVD interrogators.

---

[8] See Furr, Amalgams, Moscow Trials, and Trotsky's Lies, for studies of the evidence from Zborowski, Ciliga, and Astrov.

We should consider the contents of the confessions to be *truthful* unless we have evidence to the contrary. In a few cases, like that of I.N. Smirnov, we know that those under interrogation lied to the interrogators. We know Smirnov lied because we have evidence from Leon Sedov himself, found in the Harvard Trotsky Archive, that Smirnov was indeed the leader of the Soviet-based clandestine Trotskyist group.

The evidence is clear that the arrested oppositionists testified what they chose to say. In some cases they deliberately lied, or did not tell the whole truth, in order to deceive the prosecution. Swedish researcher Sven-Eric Holmström has discovered compelling evidence that at least one more prominent Soviet figure aided Piatakov in this Norway trip. If Holmström is correct, Piatakov remained silent about this person, no doubt to protect him.

Another example is Grigori Sokol'nikov's claim during the January, 1937, Moscow Trial that he had not received any communications from Trotsky. We know that in fact he did, because the Harvard Trotsky Archive preserves a return receipt from a letter Trotsky sent him. The NKVD evidently did not know about this, so Sokol'nikov's statement went unchallenged by the prosecution. It would be interesting to know what Trotsky said to Sokol'nikov in that letter. Probably it was similar to the letter he sent to Radek and whose contents Radek described at trial, since it was sent during the same period of time.

Ivan Nikitich Smirnov, Leader of the Clandestine Trotskyists in the USSR, Lied

The PiLT2 documents give us more information about the First Moscow Trial. We see I.N. Smirnov, who claimed at trial that he no longer "did any work" in the Trotsky conspiracy, lying to the investigators as soon as he is arrested. We know this now because many others testify to Smirnov's leading role in the conspiracy.

The Trotskyists Conspired to Murder Sergei Kirov

The PiLT2 documents give us important evidence that the Trotsky-ists, and therefore certainly Trotsky himself, were indirectly in-volved in the assassination of Sergei Kirov on December 1, 1934. The Trotskyists were planning similar assassinations and were in touch with the Zinovievists who in fact murdered Kirov.

One Trotskyist told another that it was "their people" who had killed Kirov.[9] This was not in fact true – Kirov was murdered by a clandestine Zinovievist group -- but it shows that the Trotskyists were aiming at the same thing.

Valentin Ol'berg Was Guilty of Collaborating with Trotsky and the Gestapo

We learn a lot more about Valentin Ol'berg, one of the leading de-fendants in the First Moscow Trial of August, 1936. PiLT2 contains much more information about Ol'berg and his background, includ-ing testimony from his brother and his wife, and from others who knew and helped him. Ol'berg claimed to have been on a mission from Leon Sedov, coordinated with the Nazi Gestapo, to assassi-nate Stalin. We now have confirmation of his accusation from co-conspirators who knew about it.

Since the publication of PiLT2 in 2013, more evidence concerning Ol'berg and of those associated with him, including his wife, brother, and associates, has been declassified and made available to researchers. We will study this evidence in a future book.

Trotskyists Within the USSR Collaborated with Fascists, Ukrainian Nationalists, and Nazi Agents

We have more details about the ties between the German secret police, the Gestapo, and the Trotskyist conspiracy. As far as the

---

[9] Interrogation of Ivan Aleksandrovich Maslennikov, April 26, 1936. PiLT 2, 249.

Trotskyist conspirators are concerned, it appears that some of them, at least, did not take the initiative to contact the Gestapo but instead were persuaded to work with the Gestapo as a result of being under arrest. Their trust in Leon Trotsky and their intense hostility towards Stalin and the Soviet government made their Gestapo collaboration voluntary.

We learn more about these contacts from the testimony related to the Second Moscow Trial. Once Trotsky had made it clear to his followers that he was instructing them to collaborate with all who opposed the Soviet government, the Trotskyists formed alliances with other Soviet oppositionists and dissidents; with Soviet citizens who had joined fascist anti-Soviet groups; with Ukrainian nationalists; with German technicians who, while working in the Soviet mining industry, were also German agents; and with the Gestapo.

We have corroborating evidence about Trotskyist and fascist sabotage in the Kuzbass mining region, a topic that is featured in the Second Moscow Trial.

Trotsky Also Collaborated with Great Britain and France

The single interrogation of Grigori Sokol'nikov in this volume corroborates his own confession at trial concerning his contacts on Trotsky's behalf with the Japanese and British. His contact with the French is also briefly mentioned. Other confessions by Sokol'nikov had recently become available. We will examine them in a future study.

Piatakov Did Meet with Trotsky in Norway in December, 1935

The testimony in PiLT2 corroborates Piatakov's testimony in his Statement to Ezhov of September 19-20, 1936. This is particularly important since Piatakov was more closely in touch with Trotsky than any other conspirator whose materials we now possess. The details in PiLT2 also confirm the genuineness of Piatakov's testimony concerning his secret visit to Trotsky in Norway in December 1935.

B. Evidence and Denial

The "Anti-Stalin Paradigm"

> The bourgeoisie turns everything into a commodity, hence also the writing of history. It is part of its being, of its condition for existence, to falsify all goods: it falsified the writing of history. And the best — paid historiography is that which is best falsified for the purposes of the bourgeoisie.
>
> - Friedrich Engels, "Notes for the 'History of Ireland.'" (1870)

According to the only acceptable model of Soviet history of the Stalin period – we call it, for convenience, the Anti-Stalin Paradigm -- Stalin was guilty of many horrific crimes, principally mass murder, and the fabrication of false charges against innocent persons followed by their punishment (often death). In mainstream historiography of the Soviet Union it is considered illegitimate to challenge any charge of a serious crime against Stalin. It is *a fortiori* considered taboo to conclude that Stalin did *not* commit any crime that he has been accused of.

Researchers of Soviet history of the Stalin period are constrained to adhere to the Anti-Stalin Paradigm regardless of the evidence. The ASP, therefore, is not a way of learning what really happened. Rather, it is a way of *not* learning what really happened. It is a way of telling historians: "Your task is to come to acceptable, anti-Stalin, anticommunist conclusions, and, where necessary, to back those conclusions up with phony evidence and fallacious reasoning." Or, at best, "your job is to confine yourself to drawing conclusions that do not challenge or threaten to disprove the ASP."

The Trotskyist Paradigm

A similar paradigm controls Trotskyist writing, which must conclude that "Trotsky was right" and "Stalin was wrong," regardless of the evidence.

Today we have a great deal of evidence that corroborates the charges leveled against Trotsky in the Moscow Trials of conspiring to murder Soviet leaders, sabotage Soviet industry, undermine the Soviet military, and collude with Nazi Germany and fascist Japan for the defeat of the USSR in war. But no Trotskyist historian can deal objectively with this evidence, or they will no longer be welcome in the ranks of Trotskyists.

Likewise, no academic historian of the Soviet Union can approach the evidence objectively and conclude that Stalin was not guilty of this or that crime of which he has been charged, or they will not be published, with serious consequences for their academic careers.

The Anti-Stalin Paradigm and the Issue of Denial

Whatever the subject of research, it is always appropriate, and in fact essential, to discuss questions of evidence. In this larger sense, there is nothing special about the need for such discussion in the field of Soviet history of the Stalin period.

However, the role of bias – anticommunist, and specifically anti-Stalin bias – is so great that it poisons the entire field of Soviet history, and so it must be confronted. Likewise, the issue of denial and evasion – the refusal to objectively consider evidence that sharply contradicts the prevailing Anti-Stalin Paradigm[10], is so pervasive that we must say something about it.

---

[10] Or the Trotskyist paradigm, which is, in effect, one variety of the Anti-Stalin Paradigm (ASP).

The Role of Denial and Evasion

> President Trump and many congressional Republicans
> now treat anything other than partisan hackery for their
> own side as partisan hackery for the other side.

– David Leonhardt, *New York Times*, November 18, 2019

We predict that the result of this research will be ignored by mainstream Soviet historians, and of course by Trotskyists. The reader should understand the reasons for this denial and evasion.

The fact is that the academic field of Soviet history of the Stalin period exists primarily to promote falsehoods about that history. The truth about Stalin and the history of the Soviet Union during Stalin's time, and about Trotsky and his conspiracies, including with the Nazis, is simply too threatening to be honestly confronted. The evidence supporting these conclusions is too strong, and there is too much of it, for it to be mentioned, much less discussed. The only way to "save" the Anti-Stalin and Trotskyist paradigms of Soviet history is to ignore the evidence and to continue to repeat fact-claims that we can now prove false.

It would be excellent if some mainstream historians of Soviet history would subject the evidence in this book, and in my other books and articles, to scholarly critique. I would expect to learn that I had made some errors – after all, some degree of error is inevitable in all human endeavor. I would also hope to learn that I had overlooked some evidence and/or counter-evidence. That would be beneficial to me in my research. It would also contribute to the project of learning the truth about Soviet history of this Stalin era and about what Leon Trotsky was really up to, as opposed to what his acolytes *claim* he was doing.

I do not expect this to happen. Willful ignorance, and personal attacks on me for daring to contradict the prevailing "wisdom" – that is, falsehoods – about Stalin and Soviet history of this period, have been the only response to my research. I expect that "mainstream" historiography will continue to deny and evade the truth.[11]

My goal is to discover the truth. I do not "defend" or "apologize for" Stalin. If Stalin committed crimes, I want to know what they were. The only way to know this is to do honest research. However, persons who perpetuate falsehoods in the service of a political agenda assume that *everyone* does as they are doing – that everyone, like they themselves, is bending, ignoring, or inventing evidence in the service of their own biases. *Dishonest persons justify their own dishonesty by assuming that everyone else is also dishonest.* This is why I am called a "defender of" or "apologist for" Stalin.

Techniques of Evasion and Denial: Logical Fallacies

Argument Ad Hominem

Example A: A Prominent Trotskyist

A prominent American Trotskyist – I will refer to him as W.A. -- has called me a conspiracy theorist. Readers should recognize this as a logical fallacy, the *argumentum ad hominem* – an attack on the person making an argument rather than on the matter at hand.

> **Ad hominem** (Latin for "to the person"), short for **argumentum ad hominem**, typically refers to a fallacious argumentative strategy whereby genuine discussion of the topic at hand is avoided by instead attacking the character, motive, or other attribute of the person making the argument, or persons associated with the argu-

---

[11] For my extended analysis of one highly-praised study by a professional scholar of the Stalin period, see Grover Furr, *Stalin. Waiting for ... the Truth. Exposing the Falsehoods in Stephen Kotkin's* Stalin. Waiting for Hitler. 1929-1941. New York: Red Star Publishers, 2019.

ment, rather than attacking the substance of the argument itself.[12]

W.A. did not explain what he means by this remark. This is "name-
calling." In itself it is without substance and requires no refutation.
But it is nonetheless telling in the present context.

Wikipedia has a useful definition of *Conspiracy theory*:

> A conspiracy theory is an explanation of an event or
> situation that invokes a conspiracy by sinister and pow-
> erful actors, often political in motivation, when other ex-
> planations are more probable. The term has a pejorative
> connotation, implying that the appeal to a conspiracy is
> based on prejudice or insufficient evidence. Conspiracy
> theories resist falsification and are reinforced by circular
> reasoning: both evidence against the conspiracy and an
> absence of evidence for it, are re-interpreted as evidence
> of its truth, and the conspiracy becomes a matter of faith
> rather than proof.[13]

According to this definition, Leon Trotsky himself was a conspiracy theorist. Trotsky claimed that Stalin was conspiring -- plotting
– to wipe out personal enemies and any potential threat to his own
power. There was not then, nor is there now, any evidence at all to
support Trotsky's notion that Stalin was conspiring to do away
with personal rivals and enemies.

Trotskyists and Cold-War anticommunists may claim that the Soviet – "Stalin's" – accusations against the oppositionists in the
USSR – Zinovievists, Trotskyists, Rightists, and others – also constitute a conspiracy theory. But this is false. We now know that the
Soviet investigators and prosecution did *not* base their conclusions
on "prejudice or insufficient evidence." They had a great deal of
evidence! More and more of such evidence continues to be made
public. We also have significant *non-Soviet* evidence that could not

---

[12] See https://en.wikipedia.org/wiki/Ad_hominem
[13] See https://en.wikipedia.org/wiki/Conspiracy_theory

possibly have been coerced or planted by "Stalin" – i.e., the Soviets.[14]

W.A. adheres to the Trotsky cult -- he "believes" Trotsky. If anyone were to simply "believe" whatever Stalin wrote or said, he would be ridiculed, and rightly so! "Belief" can never aid the search for truth. Karl Marx himself said that "Question everything!" (*De omnibus dubitandum*) was his favorite slogan. In this important sense, Trotskyists are not Marxists.

There is no evidence whatsoever to support the Trotskyist accusations. We have exposed and discussed a number of the lies that Trotsky concocted to create and sustain his anti-Stalin conspiracy theory. *None* of it is evidence. (Furr, *Trotsky's 'Amalgams'; Trotsky's Lies*).

This makes W.A. himself a conspiracy theorist in that, in defiance of the evidence and logic, he continues to uncritically believe Trotsky's charges against Stalin. It is a clever, though dishonest, rhetorical ploy to call someone you disagree with a "conspiracy theorist" when in reality the term applies to you yourself.

Example B: Stephen Cohen

Stephen Cohen, a senior scholar of the Stalin period and defender of the Anti-Stalin Paradigm, has called me "a Stalin terror denier or apologist;" "a pseudo-scholar who disregards or falsifies overwhelmingly evidence — plain facts, to put the matter plainly," and "who has no standing ... among serious scholars here or in Russia."[15]

Cohen is "blowing smoke." *Neither he nor any of the "serious scholars" of Soviet history of the Stalin period have any evidence, much less "plain facts", that Stalin planned the "terror."* On the contrary: *all* the evidence supports the opposite conclusion. Cohen simply

---

[14] See Furr, *The Moscow Trials as Evidence.*
[15] Personal communication dated July 2, 2019 from a colleague with an email from Stephen Cohen dated May 25, 2019.

asserts that there is "evidence" that I am "disregarding" or "falsifying." But he cites no examples. No wonder: he *can't* do so, because no such evidence exists.

Appeal to Authority

When Cohen refers to "standing ... among serious scholars" he is committing the logical fallacy of "appeal to authority." The fact that others disagree with me is not evidence that I am wrong. Any more than the fact that *they* do not agree with *me* evidence that *they* are wrong!

Only primary source evidence counts, not the "authority" of scholars who, instead of pursuing the truth "and letting the chips fall where they may," choose to uphold the Anti-Stalin Paradigm out of whatever motive – careerism, anticommunism or loyalty to Trotsky.

Cohen is loyal to Nikolai Bukharin. In 1973 Cohen published a biography, *Bukharin and the Bolshevik Revolution*, that was to become famous. In the tenth chapter – the chapter that takes Bukharin's life from 1930 to his trial and execution in 1938 -- Cohen relies heavily on Khrushchev-era materials about Stalin. In 2010 my colleague Vladimir L. Bobrov and I published an article in which *we demonstrate that every anti-Stalin statement Cohen writes in that tenth chapter is provably, demonstrably false.*

We also prove that Cohen deliberately lied. In his book Cohen quotes the memoir of Jules Humbert-Droz, a former communist and friend of Bukharin's. Humbert-Droz reveals that Bukharin told him in 1927 or 1928 that he and his followers were already conspiring to murder Stalin. This was before collectivization, the first Five-Year Plan, the famine of 1932-33, possibly even before Trotsky had been expelled from the Party (November 12, 1927) and, as far as we know today, before Trotsky himself was plotting to kill Stalin.

But Cohen *withholds* this information. He does not tell his readers that Humbert-Droz, whose memoir he cites in his Bukharin book, stated this. To do so would have undermined Cohen's desire to portray Bukharin as an innocent "victim of Stalin."[16]

Those who uphold the Anti-Stalin and Trotskyist paradigms do so in defiance of all the evidence we now have. What are they afraid of? We should be clear: they fear the overthrow of the Anti-Stalin Paradigm and the complete dismantling of the "Trotsky Paradigm," the Trotskyist cult which is structured around Leon Trotsky's lies and deceptions.

Fallacy of Personal Incredulity

The problems of logical fallacies and preconceived bias persist even among Marxists. Here is an example of fallacious thinking by the editors of *Science & Society*, a scholarly Marxist journal of worldwide reputation for eighty years. First, they announce in positive tones the publication of a commentary article of mine:

> We are glad to be able to present Grover Furr's critical commentary on Gerald Meyer's article, "Joseph Stalin: Revisionst Biography," ...

Then there follow these words:

> **Furr is well known for his resolute defense of Stalin** and his rejection of the entire *corpus* of literature, from both the capitalist mainstream and the left, depicting Stalin as an authoritarian and repressive figure, and one who was guilty of major crimes against humanity.

This is false. I do not "defend Stalin." I defend the truth, as demonstrated by the best primary source evidence. I work hard to be objective, to question and doubt my own biases and preconceived ideas, because failure to do so leads inevitably to Confirmation Bias and forfeits any chance of discovering the truth. If Stalin

---

[16] See Grover Furr and Vladimir L. Bobrov, "Stephen Cohen's Biography of Bukharin:A Study in the Falsehood of Khrushchev-Era "Revelations". *Cultural Logic*, 2010. At https://ojs.library.ubc.ca/index.php/clogic/article/view/191531

committed crimes I want to know about them. I want to find the truth, whatever it is and "let the chips fall where they may."

The *Science & Society* editors correctly state:

> Furr argues, to the contrary, that almost all of these claims, from the Khrushchev "revelations" to the mountains of establishment scholarly works on the subject, are false.

That is true – though the editors neglect to say that I base my conclusions upon *evidence* and study of that evidence with firm *objectivity.* Then they state:

> We need to be clear: the great majority of the S&S Editorial Board and Manuscript Collective do not accept Furr's position.[17]

This is an example of the *fallacy of personal incredulity. On what basis* do the editors say this? Not from studying the evidence, let alone studying it in a strictly objective manner. They just "do not accept" – that is, do not *believe* - it.

In reality, the *S&S* editors have no basis either to agree or to disagree with me. The "great majority" of the board is basing their "non-acceptance" of my "position" – by which they mean the results of my research – on bias and preconceived notions, no doubt bolstered by the "authority" of some person or persons unnamed.

This stance is not compatible with a materialist, scientific approach to history. Materialists decide questions of truth or falsehood on the basis of primary source evidence and solid, objective reasoning. Once again, this demonstrates the power of the Anti-Stalin Paradigm. Yet *S&S* is one of the foremost Marxist journals in the world today. How sad!

---

[17] "Editorial Perspective. In This Issue." *Science & Society* 82, No. 4 (October, 2018), p. 475.

C. Objectivity – The *sine qua non* of discovering the truth

But how *can* we learn the truth? How can we avoid being blinded by our own biases and preconceived ideas? It is a basic tenet of materialism that one's conclusions about reality, including historical reality, must be firmly based on *evidence*. This is the only way to discover the truth in history. The primary source evidence must be identified, located, collected, studied, and conclusions drawn from it that are based on the evidence alone, not on preconceived ideas, biases, prejudices, without faults in logic and reasoning.

The materialist researcher must work hard to be thoroughly *objective*. She must be aware and suspicious of her own biases and preconceived ideas. Everyone possesses biases, prejudices, and preconceived ideas. So the materialist researcher must adopt a method that is closely similar to that used in the "hard" sciences like physics or chemistry.

The objective historian must be self-aware. It is her own preconceived ideas and biases, not those of anyone else, which are most likely to mislead her and to poison her research.

* She must take special pains to look with increased suspicion at any evidence or argument that tends to *confirm* her own preconceived ideas. This is the threat of Confirmation Bias.[18]

* She must also force herself to look with an additional dose of sympathy and interest at any evidence or argument that tends to *disconfirm* her own preconceived biases.

This is the only way to operationalize – to put into practical use – the ideal of objectivity. If a researcher fails to be objective, she will never discover the truth, or even recognize it if she sees it.

---

[18] "Confirmation bias is the tendency to search for, interpret, favor, and recall information in a way that affirms one's prior beliefs or hypotheses." https://en.wikipedia.org/wiki/Confirmation_bias

D. Why Is There No German or Japanese Evidence of Trotsky's Collaboration?

> "Most conspiracy theorists don't understand this. But if there really were a C.I.A. plot, no documents would exist."[19]

> Instructions on concrete organization questions regarding preparation for underground conditions must be given only verbally. . . At the very least it should have been specified that these names and addresses be given strictly orally. . . [20]

In the course of this study we will show that there is a large amount of mutually-corroborative evidence of Trotsky's German-Japanese collaboration from the Soviet side.

In addition we have important evidence from German and Japanese sources of collaboration by members of the Soviet opposition, including some who themselves claimed to have been working with Trotsky. Here are a few examples:

* The late Alvin D. Coox discovered and discussed the oral evidence he collected from former Japanese officers confirming that Genrikh S. Liushkov, an NKVD general who defected to the Japanese in June, 1938, told them rather detailed information about anti-Stalin military conspiracies in the Far Eastern Army and confirms that the Rightists – specifically, Aleksei Rykov – were involved in the conspiracy. In turn, Rykov and others implicated Trotsky.

* We also have evidence that Japanese General Hajime Sugiyama was in contact with Soviet oppositionists. This story was reported

---

[19] Gerald Posner, "author of an anti-conspiracy account of the Kennedy assassination, on efforts to obtain C.I.A. documents relating to the assassin." *The New York Times'* "Quotation of the Day" of October 17, 2009.
[20] O. Weber. "How Not to Prepare For Underground Conditions of Revolutionary Work." *The Communist International.* July 1, 1932, 417.

in Soviet newspapers and reprinted in the *New York Times*. We have confirmed it by obtaining the original Japanese newspaper article.

No evidence of German or Japanese collaboration with Trotsky has been discovered outside the former USSR. There are a number of possible explanations for this fact:

* Trotsky never collaborated with the Germans or Japanese. All the Soviet evidence is fabricated.

If Trotsky did collaborate the following possibilities exist:

* Many of these archives were destroyed during the war.

* Nobody has looked for it. At least, we are not aware anybody has done so.

* These archives too might have been "purged," as the Harvard Trotsky Archive has certainly been.

But, as suggested in the quotations above, the most likely explanation is that conspiratorial information of this kind is never written down. Therefore, there never was any "archival evidence" of this collaboration

We know that some purging of the Soviet archives was done by Nikita Khrushchev.[21] Elsewhere we have discussed the "purging" of the Trotsky archive at Harvard of incriminating materials.[22] We know of two cases in which archival materials have disappeared.

In addition, most Soviet archives are not open to researchers. Given the evidence that we have discovered in the relatively few

---

[21] See Furr, *Khrushchev Lied*, Chapter 12: "There is general agreement that after he took power Khrushchev had the archives searched and many documents removed and doubtless destroyed. The same scholars agree that these documents probably had to do with Khrushchev's own role in the massive repressions of the late 1930s." See references there.
[22] See Furr, Amalgams, Chapter 6, and Moscow Trials, Chapter 6: "Non-Soviet Evidence: -- The Trotsky Archive Purged."

archival documents that have been published to date it seems likely that further evidence implicating Trotsky may be contained in archives that are still classified.

We now have a great deal of evidence that the military commanders led by Marshal Mikhail Tukhachevsky did indeed collaborate with the German General Staff. We have indirect confirmation of this from German sources, and more direct confirmation in a document from the Czech National Archive. We have massive evidence from former Soviet archives of the guilt of Tukhachevsky and his co-defendants. The German and Czech evidence confirms the Soviet evidence.[23]

In discussing their espionage for Germany several Soviet defendants said they had dealt directly with German General Kurt von Hammerstein-Equord. Rumor of this collaboration has survived in Hammerstein's family. Although to our knowledge no written record of that collaboration exists, it appears that no one has actually looked for such records.[24] Nor has anyone ever undertaken to survey the surviving papers of the other German generals allegedly involved in this conspiracy and named by Soviet defendants.

But absence of evidence is only "evidence of absence" when evidence should indeed be present. We believe that the single most likely reason is simply that no one should expect a conspiracy like this to be documented anywhere, ever, much less in archives. The demands of secrecy and security require that such information be exchanged only by word of mouth.

The Kremlin Affair: Conspiracy and Evidence of Conspiracies

In 2000 Russian historian IUrii N. Zhukov published the only serious study that has yet appeared devoted to the Kremlin Affair of

[23] For the document from the Czech National Archive see Furr, Amalgams, and Furr, Trials, Chapter 7: "The Mastny-Benes Note of February 9, 1937."
[24] Hans Magnus Enzensberger. *Hammerstein oder der Eigensinn. Eine deutsche Geschichte.* Berlin: Suhrkamp, 2008, pp. 234; 213-215.

1935. His conclusion is that, on the evidence, the "Kremlin Affair" was not a fabrication, but the uncovering of a real conspiracy.

> Therefore, at the present time – until there is a substantial widening of the evidentiary base, until the declassification of the materials in the Central Archive of the FSB, we consider the following to be beyond doubt. Of all the possible hypotheses that can be formulated to explain both the "Kremlin Affair" and the Enukidze case, the only one that can account for all the known facts without exception is that which assumes that the conspiracy against Stalin and his group really existed.[25]

Zhukov cites powerful evidence in support of his hypothesis. He has some important things to say about evidence generally that is relevant to our purposes.

> It goes without saying that in this hypothesis the lack of evidence should make us wary – either direct or indirect evidence, but indisputable evidence. **And for this we must decide the question as to whether evidence is to be expected in general in such cases.** Could such evidence be found in the investigation of the "Kremlin Affair" and if so, what kind of evidence? Plans for the arrest of the members of the "narrow leadership"? A list of the future Politburo and government, or something similar. Or lists of conspirators, perhaps confirmed by their signatures? Or, perhaps, declarations, decrees, orders intended for publication immediately after the seizure of power and prepared in advance? **Hardly, because any normal conspirator who was also preparing a coup d'état would do everything possible to be certain that no evidence of this kind existed.**

---

[25] IU. N. Zhukov, "Tainy 'Kremlevskogo dela' 1935 goda i sud'ba Avelia Enukidze" (The Secrets of the 'Kremlin Affair' of 1935 and the fate of Avel' Enukidze). *Voprosy Istorii* No. 9 (2000), 83-113, at p. 109.

It would be just as futile to hope to find while searching the homes of the conspirators, let us say, plans of the Kremlin, on which were noted the apartments and offices of Stalin, Molotov, and others, the routes of their usual walks. The conspirators – if they were indeed such – would not need them either. Both Peterson and Enukidze, who had lived and worked in the Kremlin, would have long known these things.

We could not expect to find evidence of any other kind that definitively reflected the criminal plots that have been uncovered. **Unless the conspirators suffered from dementia, they would never commit their plans to paper. Everything, absolutely everything, would be only in their heads.** (Zhukov 110-111)

Zhukov cites an example of the kind of evidence that he finds convincing and reasonable to expect.

Now let us consider an alternative hypothesis, the most paradoxical one. Let us suppose that the conspiracy really existed. Are there any facts to confirm this? Yes, although they appeared only two years later, and also are of a very specific and unconvincing character – only confessions of suspects at interrogation. On the day of the arrests of Enukidze, February 11 [1937] in Khar'kov, and of Peterson, April 27 [1937] in Kiev they gave to different investigators confessions of guilt that are identical down to the details. They related how they were preparing a coup and the arrest or murder in the Kremlin of Stalin, Molotov, Kaganovich, Voroshilov and Ordzhonikidze.[26] (108)

---

[26] Zhukov discussed these specific confessions and the conclusions he draws from them in more detail in a meeting with Vladimir L. Bobrov on December 6, 2002. (Email letter "LETTER_V3o.doc, rec'd 12.08.02 doc" from Vladimir L. Bobrov to Grover Furr.)

The Conspiracy to Arrest Lavrentii Beria

How likely is it that agreements of espionage and conspiracy would have been written down in the first place? Anything written down at some point would surely have been hidden securely or, more likely, destroyed as soon as read. As long as such written evidence remained it would pose a terrible threat to any conspirator.

We can be certain of the existence of one such conspiracy in Soviet history – that among members of the Presidium to get rid of Lavrentii Beria – because it succeeded on June 26, 1953. Yet no prior written record of that conspiracy has ever come to light, and no single, reliable account of it exists even now. There are a few accounts by those who were involved (or claimed to have been involved). But these accounts do not agree. We know nothing certain about the conspiracy except that it succeeded. We also know nothing about Beria's fate – whether he survived to be tried and executed in December, 1953, as the official story runs, or whether he was killed, perhaps accidentally, on June 26.

This conspiracy must have involved at least half a dozen men. Accounts of it by its participants do not agree in details except in this: it was all planned and carried out through oral communication. There is no mention of it in writing. What does exist in the archives is the outline of a speech to be delivered by Georgii M. Malenkov at the Presidium meeting of June 26, 1953. It was at this meeting, we know, that Beria was either arrested or killed. Malenkov was certainly a party to whatever occurred. Yet Malenkov's archive contains only an outline of his speech, according to which Beria was to be removed as head of the MVD (Ministry of Internal Affairs, including the internal police force) and made Minister of the Petroleum Industry.[27]

---

[27] The outline of Malenkov's speech is in *Lavrentii Beriia. 1953. Stenogramma iiul'skogo plenuma TsK KPSS i drugie dokumenty.* Ed. V. Naumov, IU. Sigachev. Moscow: MDF, 1999, pp. 69-70.

Rehabilitations

It is often assumed that, if a person convicted of a crime during the Stalin period has been "rehabilitated," his or her innocence can be assumed to be established. But this is false.

A leading anticommunist researcher on Soviet history, Marc Junge, has written:

> Mit der vorliegenden Arbeit wurde das Ergebnis der Studie des Utrechter Historikers van Goudoever bestätigt, daß Rehabilitierungen in der Sowjetunion grundsätzlich ein politisches und nicht juristisches oder gar ethisch-moralisches Phänomen darstellten.

> With the present work the result of the study of the Utrecht historian van Goudoever was confirmed that rehabilitations in the Soviet Union in principle represented a political and not juristic or even ethical-moral phenomenon.[28]

In *Khrushchev Lied* we studied all the "rehabilitation" reports available in 2000, when a major collection of documents was published.[29] None of them provide any evidence of any convicted person's innocence. They are simply *declared* to be innocent.

In succeeding years we studied other "rehabilitation" reports. For example, in the case of the 1988 report on the remaining (as yet un-rehabilitated) defendants of the Third Moscow Trial of March 1938, the "Bukharin-Rykov" trial, we showed that the rehabilitation report lied about an important document that was published in 2006.

---

28 Marc Junge, *Bucharins Rehabilitierung. Historisches Gedächtnis in der Sowjetunion 1953-1991. Mit einem Dokumentenanhang.* Berlin: BasisDruck Verlag, 1999, p. 259.
29 *Reabilitatsiia: Kak Eto Bylo. Mart 1953 – Fevral' 1956 gg. Dokumenty Prezidiuma TsK KPSS i Drugie Materialiy.* Moskva: Mezhdunarodniy Fond "Demokratiia", 2000.

This 1988 report remains unpublished at the time of this writing (November, 2019).[30] To demonstrate that the Soviet Prosecutor and the Supreme Court were deliberately lying would cast doubt upon all the thousands of "rehabilitations' issued during the Gorbachev years. The so-called "revelations" of these years played, and continue to play, a huge ideological and legal role in the attacks on Stalin and on the Soviet government and Party during the Stalin years, and have been used uncritically by two generations of scholars of Soviet history since that time. There is a great deal at stake in perpetuating the falsehood that the Khrushchev-era and Gorbachev-era "rehabilitations" were honest and prove that the "rehabilitated" persons were innocent.

It may well be that some persons "rehabilitated" during the Khrushchev and Gorbachev years, and since the end of the Soviet Union, were in fact innocent of the crimes for which they were condemned. But, as Junge notes, the mere fact of "rehabilitation" cannot establish whether the "rehabilitated" persons were guilty or innocent.

Primary Sources

Only primary source evidence is acceptable evidence. Secondary sources – normally, studies by scholars who themselves use primary sources – are *not* evidence, though they can be very useful for other purposes: for example, in identifying primary source evidence and in providing interpretations of primary source evidence that can help in one's own interpretation of them.

No primary source evidence is "proof positive" or "a smoking gun." In historical study all primary sources are created by human beings, who have biases, prejudices, and memories that change over time. All primary source evidence must be carefully examined in

---

[30] In Russian only: Ferr (Furr), Grover, Vladimir L. Bobrov, *Pravosudie Stalina. Obzhalovaniu nt podlezhit!* Moscow: Eksmo, 2010, Chapter 2: "'Reabilitatsionnoe' moschenichesto," cc. 64-84.

the context of other primary source evidence. This essential practice is called source criticism.

Soviet Primary Sources

Cold-war anticommunists and Trotskyists sometimes claim that evidence originating from Soviet police, investigation, prosecution, or judicial sources should not be used because it *may* be false – obtained by threats to the arrestee, to his family or friends, or by promises, perhaps false ones, of lenient treatment.

However, all academic and Trotskyist researchers into Soviet history of this period, use Stalin-era sources all the time. It is in principle invalid to use Stalin-era Soviet sources when they appear to prove what the researcher wants to find but to reject them when they tend to dismantle the Anti-Stalin Paradigm by providing evidence that Stalin did not commit some crime of which he has been accused.

Trotskyists often recommend the many volumes on Soviet history of the Stalin period by the late Vadim Rogovin, a committed Trotskyist historian who made no attempt to be objective. Rogovin's sources are almost exclusively Soviet documents from the Stalin period.

Many people believe that *any* statement – confession, accusation, whatever – obtained while in police custody is useless as evidence. Marxist historian Roger Keeran has written:

> [Furr refers to] the well-known confessions and interrogations of the condemned ... Furr never acknowledges that confessions, particularly when given under duress, are pretty useless as historical evidence.[31]

---

31 "Khrushchev Lied But What Is The Truth?" (review of Furr, *Khrushchev Lied*). *Marxism-Leninism Today* November 23, 2011. At
https://mltoday.com/khrushchev-lied-but-what-is-the-truth/

French Marxist economist Frédéric Boccara has said:

> I do not believe evidence obtained from persons in po-
> lice custody.[32]

Many people are confused by, or even agree with, statements like these. It is important to examine such statements in order to point out how and why they are incorrect.

Anyone, at any time, can either be telling the truth; attempting to tell the truth (i.e. as they remember it or believe it to be) but be mistaken; or be lying. This is the case whether or not a person is under arrest.

* No evidence should ever be "believed." "I don't believe it" is not a category of scholarly analysis. Rather, it is an admission that one does not have any idea how to evaluate historical evidence.

* It is essential to discard the false notion that persons under ar-rest are "more likely to be lying" than persons not under arrest. All statements, made under any circumstances, by all persons, must be critically studied and compared with other statements.

* The fact that a person claims to be telling the truth at one time, and then at some later date claims that their first statement was false and that they are telling the truth now, is not evidence that either statement is true (or false). It is a basic error to accept the last statement a person made as true and all the previous state-ments as false, or vice versa.

Corroborating Evidence

When we find statements – fact-claims – made by different per-sons, at different times, in different places, that agree with each other, it becomes more and more likely that the statements are either true or reflect what the persons making the statements be-lieved to be true.

---

[32] Personal communication, November 2, 2019.

"Forced" Confessions?

In 2007 Stephen G. Wheatcroft, a historian specializing in the Stalin period, wrote that a statement by Mikhail Frinovskii, one of Nikolai Ezhov's top lieutenants, was "forced":

> According to Frinovskii's **forced statements** taken after his arrest...
>
> Of course there are grave doubts as to how we should treat these **forced depositions** ...[33]

Wheatcroft does not explain why he thinks that Frinovskii's confession statements are "forced" or what he means by "forced." Nor does he explain why he thinks that there are "grave doubts" about how to deal with them, what those "grave doubts" might be, or in fact *how* to "treat" them. He simply quotes them, and states that they may or may not be truthful.

In reality, there is no evidence that Frinovskii's statements were "forced" – assuming that this means false *and* obtained through torture, threats, promises, etc. Does Wheatcroft assume that persons under arrest do not make any statements that incriminate themselves unless they are "forced" to do so? That would be stupid. Persons under arrest may make truthful statements, including self-incriminating statements, for any number of reasons.

But why, then, does Wheatcroft call Frinovskii's confession statements "forced" in this case? I surmise he does this because Frinovskii's statement tends to exculpate Stalin of guilt for Ezhov's mass murders and repression in the so-called "Great Terror." This evidence threatens to dismantle the Anti-Stalin Paradigm, which controls research on Soviet history.

---

[33] Wheatcroft, "Agency and Terror: Evdokimov and Mass Killing in Stalin's Great Terror," *Australian Journal of Politics and History*: Volume 53, Number 1, 2007, p. 42.

In this same confession statement Frinovskii admits that Ezhov and he himself, Ezhov's second-in-command, did indeed have NKVD men torture false confessions from defendants:

> The investigative apparatus in all departments of the NKVD was divided into "investigator-bonebreakers", "bonebreakers", and "ordinary" investigators. ...
>
> With such methods the investigations supplied the names.
>
> In my opinion I would speak the truth if I declared, in general, that very often the confessions were given by the investigators, and not by those under investigation.
>
> Did the leadership of the People's Commissariat, that is I and Ezhov, know about this? We knew.
>
> How did we react? Honestly speaking – not at all, and Ezhov even encouraged it.[34]

These confessions from Frinovskii's statement have often been quoted by mainstream researchers as evidence that many innocent defendants were tortured into signing false confessions. But the *rest* of Frinovskii's statement includes his confessions that the defendants in the Moscow Trials really were guilty. *These* parts are *never* quoted.

Like all evidence, the fact-claims in Frinovskii's statement must be carefully identified and, where possible, checked against other

---

[34] "TO THE PEOPLE'S COMMISSAR FOR INTERNAL AFFAIRS OF THE UNION OF SOVIET SOC. REPUBLICS – COMMISSAR OF STATE SECURITY 1ST DEGREE BERIA L.P.From the arrested suspect FRINOVSKY M.P.STATEMENT. *Lubianka. Stalin I NKVD – NKGB – GUKR "SMERSH". 1939 – mart 1946.* Moscow, 2006, p. 46. English translation at
https://msuweb.montclair.edu/~furrg/research/frinovskyeng.html Russian original at https://msuweb.montclair.edu/~furrg/research/frinovskyru.html Choose text encoding Cyrillic (Windows).

evidence we now possess. When that is done, it is clear that Frinovskii was not lying.

The Fallacy of "Torture"[35]

The claim is sometimes made that someone was tortured into
making a false confession. However, a claim unsubstantiated by
evidence is not itself evidence. Even if we could verify that a person was tortured and subsequently confessed to a crime, that
would not establish that the confession was false or that the person was innocent of that crime. Torture has historically been employed to extract truth as well as to elicit false testimony.

In theory, torture is outlawed in all legal systems so that the police
and investigators will actually do some investigating, solve crimes,
and catch criminals, instead of simply torturing innocent persons
into confessing to the crimes they are supposed to solve. Torture
of defendants is also outlawed to protect the individual suspect, so
that he or she is not forced to falsely confess to crimes they did not
commit.

But historians are not involved in a judicial process. No one's free-
dom is at stake. In the case of the history of the Stalin period in
Soviet history, all the historical actors are dead. Dead persons have
no rights that need defending. Works of historical research are not
trials. Historians' conclusions are not verdicts.

The Fallacy of "Everyone Knows It"

Arch Getty, a prominent American scholar of Soviet history, has
stated:

> Had he [Oleg Khlevniuk] focused on the source base of
> Jansen and Petrov's book, for example, he would have
> noted that their most sensational revelations, compris-
> ing more than one in seven of the footnotes, are from the

---

[35] See also Furr, *Khrushchev Lied*, Chapter 10: "Torture and the Historical
Problems Related To It."

NKVD interrogations of Ezhov and his henchmen. **As everyone knows, these stories were invented by the police and beaten out of the accused.**[36]

This statement is false. Getty does not "know" this. *No one* "knows" this. There is no evidence to support this statement, and a good deal of evidence to disprove it. Ezhov did renounce his confessions after the end of the investigation and at trial. But that does not prove he was lying first and telling the truth later, any more than it proves the reverse.

What researchers supposedly "know" – and, according to Getty, ought to say – is that Ezhov's confessions of guilt are false. Why? I think it is because in them Ezhov is very clear that he was deceiving Stalin and the Soviet leadership. For example, in a confession statement of August 4, 1939, Ezhov stated:

> **The [Soviet] government, understandably, had no conception of our conspiratorial plans** and in the present case proceeded solely on the basis of the necessity to prolong the operation without going into the essence of how it was carried out.

> In this sense, of course, we were deceiving the government in the most blatant manner.[37]

Getty's statement is an example of the logical fallacy of "argumentum ad populum,"[38] This is the fallacy that because many people –

---

[36] J. Arch Getty, "To the Editors." *Kritika: Explorations in Russian and Eurasian History* 5, 1 (Winter 2004), p. 233.

[37] "From the transcript of the interrogation of the accused Ezhov Nikolai Ivanovich. 4 August 1939." Nikita Petrov, Mark Jansen. *"Stalinskii pitomets"* – *Nikolai Ezhov.* Moscow: ROSSPEN, 2008, p. 368. English translation at https://msuweb.montclair.edu/~furrg/research/ezhov080439eng.html Russian text at https://msuweb.montclair.edu/~furrg/research/ezhov080439ru.html (choose Text Encoding Cyrillic (Windows).

[38] See https://en.wikipedia.org/wiki/Argumentum_ad_populum

in this case, presumably, historians of the Soviet Union -- believe a statement is true, then the statement must be true, or at least is "more likely" to be true. (It might also be classified as an example of the fallacy of "argumentum ad lapidem," or "appeal to the stone"[39] -- dismissing a claim as absurd without demonstrating proof of its absurdity.)

The evidence we now have substantiates the essence of Ezhov's and Frinovskii's confessions and those of others of Ezhov's men. This evidence is consistent with the hypothesis that the mass murders of July, 1937, through approximately September, 1938, misnamed "the Great Terror," were the result of Ezhov's own conspiracy against the Soviet state. These murders were a conspiracy not *by* but *against* Stalin. We discuss this evidence more fully in *Yezhov vs. Stalin*.[40]

Argument by Scare Quotes

Sometimes the denial of evidence that is inconvenient for the Anti-Stalin Paradigm is expressed in the use of scare quotes. A good example is Matthew Lenoe's book *The Kirov Murder and Soviet History* (Yale University Press, 2010). I examine and critique Lenoe's faulty use of evidence and incorrect conclusions in *The Murder of Sergei Kirov. History, Scholarship and the Anti-Stalin Paradigm*. A detailed examination of the fallacy of "argument by scare quotes" may be found there in Chapter 4, pages 87 ff.

In the edition of his translation of one of Marshal Mikhail N. Tukhachevsky's confession statements, Steven J. Main writes:

> The large part of this article consists of a translation - to the best of this author's knowledge for the first time in English- of what is purported to be Tukhachevsky 's **'testimony'**, concerning his alleged role in the so-called

---

[39] See https://en.wikipedia.org/wiki/Appeal_to_the_stone
[40] Grover Furr, *Yezhov vs. Stalin. The Truth About Mass Repressions and the So-Called 'Great Terror' in the USSR*. Kettering, OH: Erythrós Press & Media, LLC, 2016.

anti-Soviet Trotskyite military organization, the **'existence'** of which allowed Stalin the excuse to launch his
bloody purge ...

The **'evidence'** against the Red Army's top personnel
began to accumulate ...

Using the recently gathered **'evidence'**, Voroshilov ...

Tukhachevsky's alleged **'guilt'** ... Tukhachevsky's alleged
'confession' ...

Regardless, however of whether, or not, the **'confession'**
was genuine, the **'plot'** had been unmasked ...

'Testimony' of M.N. Tukhachevsky[41]

Apparently the scare quotes are supposed to alert us to the fact
that he, Main, does not accept this testimony, evidence, existence,
etc., as genuine. But Main makes no effort to try to verify his suspi-
cions by studying Tukhachevsky's statement in the context of
other evidence we now have. Like Wheatcroft, Main uses the confession while at the same time implying that it is not reliable. But
in fact he has no idea at all how reliable (or unreliable) it is. He
does not try to verify it or to disprove it.

The reader is left to wonder: *Why* does Main think Tukhachevsky's
confession might be false? He does not claim outright that it is
false, that the evidence it presents is phony. He only suggests, repeatedly, that it *might* be false. But to concede that the statement
might be false, is also to concede that it *might not* be false – that it
might be true. But to concede that would be a violation of the Anti-
Stalin Paradigm – violation of a virtual taboo.

If Tukhachevsky's statement is true – and today we have a great
deal of evidence to corroborate it -- that would go a long way to-

---

[41] Steven J. Main, "The Arrest and 'Testimony' of Marshal of the Soviet Union M.N.
Tukhachevsky (May-June 1937). *The Journal or Slavic Military Studies*, Vol. 10,
No.1 (March 1997), pp. 151-155 and *passim.*

wards overturning the Anti-Stalin Paradigm. It would mean that, in arresting, trying, and executing Tukhachevsky and his high-ranking military accomplices, Stalin prevented the Soviet Union from militarily allying with Nazi Germany, fascist Italy, and milita-rist-fascist Japan. Such an alliance would have completely changed the balance of power in the world in favor of the Axis powers and had an incalculable effect on world history.

* * * * *

All text in **boldface** is the author's, unless otherwise specified.

Chapter 1. Documents published in

Politbiuro i Lev Trotskii, Kniga 2

(Prague, 2013)

This essay examines a collection of documents that has important implications for the study of Leon Trotsky's activities during the decade of the 1930s; for our understanding of the Moscow Trials of 1936-1938; and for the history of the Soviet Union during the period of Joseph Stalin's leadership.

Politbiuro i Lev Trotskii is a two-volume collection of documents from former Soviet archives. Almost all are published, and thus made available to researchers, for the first time. These volumes were published in a very small printing and are very hard to obtain. They are from the Central Archive of the FSB, the Russian successor to the NKVD, as the commissariat (= ministry) was called during most of the period in question.

There are no grounds to doubt that these documents are genuine. The editor, Oleg B. Mozokhin, is the chief researcher for the FSB. He has published a number of important collections and studies of documents from the former NKVD, including important studies of the repression and violence perpetrated during the 1930s by this agency of the Soviet government. We don't know why these specific documents were chosen for publication, out of the many thousands still in the archive.

The significance of these documents is as follows.

* They constitute yet more important evidence that the pretrial interrogations in the 1936 and 1937 Moscow Trials were not "fabricated" in any way by the NKVD, were not forced upon the defendants. Instead, all the evidence we now have supports the hypothesis that these trials were genuine, in that the Prosecution be-

lieved the charges they brought against the defendants, while the defendants testified what they wanted to testify.

* They are confirmed by evidence from outside the USSR, particularly evidence from Trotsky's own papers in the Harvard Trotsky Archive.

* They confirm, and are confirmed by, other evidence from former Soviet archives.

The purpose of this article is to demonstrate the truth of these conclusions, and to draw further conclusions from them that allow us to understand certain historical questions related to Trotsky's conspiratorial activities.

Direct Evidence that Defendants' Confessions Were Not Coerced

Confession of I.N. Smirnov of January 15, 1933

I.N. Smirnov was the leader of the Trotskyists within the USSR. This is confirmed by Sedov's letter to Trotsky of sometime in 1932 (hereafter referred to as "Sedov's 'bloc' letter") discovered by Pierre Broué in the Harvard Trotsky Archive in 1980.

> La lettre à l'encre sympathique de Léon Sedov fait apparaitre l'existence des groupes suivants : le groupe trotskyste d'U.R.S.S. (« notre fraction »), les « zinoviévistes », le groupe d'I. N. Smirnov, le groupe Sten-Lominadzé, le groupe « Safar(ov)-Tarkhan(ov) », « les droitiers » et « les libéraux ». (Broué 1980 p.7)[1]

In the following statement, apparently the first he made after his arrest, Smirnov denies any oppositional activity whatever. He claims that he only retained doubts about the success of collectivi-

---

[1] I.N. Smirnov is identified as the source of the information in the Sedov to Trotsky bloc letter in Documents Nos 1 and 2, reprinted in Broué 1980, pp. 34-36 from the Harvard Trotsky Archive.

zation and industrialization and spoke about these doubts with a few "former" Trotskyists now reinstated in the Party, as Smirnov himself had been, and with a few others who had not been reinstated. When asked about the large archive of Trotskyist materials found at his home Smirnov replied that he had kept them only because they contained some letters from Trotsky and from other "former Trotskyists" and that he had intended to burn them. (20)

Thanks to Sedov's "bloc" letter we know that Smirnov was lying to conceal his clandestine Trotskyist activities. Therefore it is clear that this statement was not coerced – Smirnov made it voluntarily. At the August 1936 Moscow trial Smirnov claimed that he "did no work" in the Trotskyist underground.

> *Smirnov:* I listened to those instructions and communicated them to the centre. The centre accepted them but I did not take part in its work
>
> ... I did not officially resign from the *bloc*, but actually I did no work. (Report 1936, 81, 85)

Smirnov's trial testimony is what he chose to say. It was not forced upon him. We shall cite much more evidence that the defendants testified *as they chose to do*.[2] This is evidence that the confessions at the First Moscow Trial were not fabrications, faked or otherwise forced upon the defendants by the prosecution. There would be no reason for the prosecution to "force" Smirnov to *deny* that he had continued to lead the underground Trotskyists. If the prosecution were "forcing" confessions at all, they would have forced Smirnov to say that he had indeed continued to lead the Trotskyist underground.

This collection of documents, together with the testimony at the First Moscow Trial, does provide much evidence that Smirnov remained in the leadership of the underground Trotskyists in the USSR, and thus that his claim that he "did no work" was false. It

---

[2] For an extended study of this question see Furr, Moscow Trials.

follows from this that Smirnov's testimony at that trial represented what he wanted to say.

More Evidence That Confessions Were Not "Forced"

A. Konstantinov

According to a report to the Politburo dated January 20, 1933 by
Genrikh Iagoda, Assistant Chairman of the OGPU (predecessor to
the police function of the NKVD), A.A. Konstantinov, a member of
Smirnov's underground Trotskyist group, opposed forming a bloc
with the Rights because he and others felt that the Rights could not
be trusted.

> (Iagoda) Recently we received information that not long
> before the liquidation of the "Union of Marxist-Leninists"
> a question stood before the Smirnov group about a bloc
> with the Rights. On December 2 of this year Konstanti-
> nov ... stated that
>
> "The question of a bloc with the Rights did stand be-
> fore us, but we, of course, were decisively against a bloc
> with the Rights. On the one hand, the Rights are not a
> resolute group, they are cowardly and will not stick it
> out to the end, and on the other hand, they only have a
> temporary need of us as a group that would be able to
> help them in underground work. And generally, in the
> event of victory they will crush us...." (38)

We know that Trotsky approved of such a group at exactly this
time, 1932 (Sedov "bloc" letter). The OGPU[3] would have no reason
to invent a *lack* of willingness by Trotskyists to bloc with the
Rights. This confession, therefore, reflected what Konstantinov
wanted to say. It was not forced on him nor fabricated.

---

[3] In July, 1934, the OGPU became part of the new NKVD, or People's Commissariat
for Internal Affairs.

B. Aleksandr Ivanovich Shemelev

Trotskyist Aleksandr Ivanovich Shemelev confessed on April 5, 1936 that his group had heard from Sedov, through Gorovich (who had met with Sedov in Berlin) that Trotsky wished to "*ustranit'*" or "*ubrat'*" – "remove" -- Stalin. We know that this discussion did take place because it occurs in the Sedov-Trotsky correspondence in the Harvard Trotsky Archive. But Shemelev said the exact words might have been "liquidate" rather than "*ustranit'*" or "*ubrat'*."

It is significant that Shemelev refused to claim that Sedov's order was to forcibly remove (i.e. to kill) Stalin. Shemelev states only that he understood Sedov's order in that way. (221) This would make no sense if the NKVD had been trying to "frame" – generate false accusations against – either Shemelev or Sedov. Had the NKVD been "framing" the Trotskyists they would have tried to force Shemelev to claim that Sedov had ordered Stalin killed. So the NKVD did not force Shemelev to make this statement. Therefore, this interrogation reflects what Shemelev wanted to say.

C. Nikolai Isaakovich Gordon

In an interrogation of October 20, 1936 Trotskyist Nikolai Isaakovich Gordon said that he had been told by Aleksandr Georgievich Beloborodov, a leading Trotskyist in Smirnov's group, that Smirnov was the person who had direct contact with Trotsky on behalf of the group. (321) This is confirmed by the Sedov "bloc" letter.

Gordon also revealed the following:

> ... the Trotskyists and Zinovievists in Rostov were united into one organization which, upon the instruction of the united Trotskyist-Zinovievist center, were preparing terrorist acts against the leadership of the VKP(b) and the Soviet government. (320)

Thanks to the Sedov bloc letter and the other letters from the Harvard Trotsky Archive that were published by Broué in 1980, we know that Gordon's testimony here is accurate. Smirnov did lead the Trotskyists, and the bloc consisted of Trotskyists, Zinovievists, and some other oppositionists that were not firmly in either of these two camps.

This, in turn, suggests that his further statement about its terrorist aims is also accurate. We will explore the issue of Trotskyism and terrorism below.

D. The Verification of Mikhail Sergeevich Ivanov

Document No. 291 (385-386) is a request dated December 19, 1938 of a certain Sobol'ev, a political officer of the border guards of the NKVD concerning one of his men named Mikhail Sergeevich Ivanov. According to Sobol'ev, Ivanov had expressed Trotskyist ideas in 1923-24 and was now being investigated for having signed the joint oppositionist "Platform of the 83" in 1927. Ivanov claimed that he was not the "Mikhail Sergeevich Ivanov" – a common Russian name -- who had signed this opposition statement. In Document No. 292 dated December 22, 1938, Aleksandr N. Posk-rebyshev, head of Stalin's chancery, certified that NKVD man Ivanov was correct: the "M. Ivanov" who had signed the "Platform of the 83" was a different person.

Serious Investigation, Not a Rush to Judgment

This is evidence that a serious investigation had taken place. A person accused of being a hidden Trotskyist was not simply fired from his job, much less arrested or imprisoned. Rather, the allegation was investigated and, in this case, disproven.

This was important, for by this time Trotskyism had been outlawed within the USSR as a terrorist and espionage organization rather than a political tendency. Documents in this volume contain plenty of evidence to confirm this charge. We will examine some of them below.

Confirmation by Evidence from Outside the USSR

Many statements made in the interrogations and defendants' statements in this volume can be confirmed by other evidence we now possess. The NKVD could not have fabricated this evidence because it originated from outside the USSR.

Statements Confirmed by Documents in the Harvard Trotsky Archive

A. "Remove Stalin" – *ubrat'*, *ustranit'*, *ustranenie*

Towards the end of 1932 Sedov and Trotsky discussed the slogan "remove Stalin." Broué discusses this in his 1980 article, in the subsection titled "Trotsky et le mot d'ordre 'Chasser Staline'" (20-22), and Broué identifies the relevant documents in the Trotsky Archive.[4] Broué's convenient summary notes that Trotsky rejected this demand at that time.

The documents in PiLT2 show that discussion and disagreement over this slogan – in Russian, *ubrat'*, *ustranit'*, *ustranenie* – took place in Opposition circles in the Soviet Union at the same time. Party member Vasilii Ivanovich Dzhoev's statement of ca. January 2, 1933 says that Gassiev, another Trotskyist, declared that "this leadership must be removed (*"ubrat'"*) (25).

Iagoda's Report

In a report to Stalin dated January 20, 1933 OGPU chief Genrikh Iagoda reported, *inter alia*, that a new letter from Trotsky had been received by Smirnov's group in mid-October (either October 17 or October 15). In it -- unexpectedly for Iagoda -- Trotsky said "The slogan ' *ubrat'* Stalina" is not our slogan. 'Down with the personal regime' – that is not right." (37)

---

[4] 10248. These are excerpts from letters sent to Sedov. The author possesses copies, obtained from the Trotsky Archive at the Houghton Library, Harvard University.

This statement in Iagoda's report agrees completely with the documents found by Broué in the Harvard Trotsky Archive (TA). We have discussed this in *Trotsky's 'Amalgams'.*[5]

> At the January 1937 trial Karl Radek testified that, in his letter of the Spring of 1932, Trotsky had said that once "union" with the Zinovievists had been achieved "the question of removing the leadership" would have to be raised. This term – "remove Stalin" – can be partially traced in both the Trotsky-Sedov correspondence of late 1932 and in Astrov's confession and confrontation with Bukharin of January 1937.

> We say "partially traced" because, in reality, only excerpts – called "vyderzhki" or "vypiski" at the top of each document – from the correspondence on this subject remains in the Trotsky-Sedov correspondence in the Harvard Trotsky Archive. Evidently these excerpts – all have been retyped in a uniform manner – were prepared by a secretary, probably Jean van Heijenoort, for possible use at the Dewey Commission hearings in Paris, which took place later than those in Mexico.

> The full texts of these letters is not in the Archive. They have been removed at some time. This is further evidence of what Getty called the "purge" of the Trotsky Archive, involving incriminating materials.

> Broué outlines the discussion between Trotsky and Sedov concerning the use of this slogan in several of his published works. In the documents we have, Sedov appears to have been the more ardent partisan of the slogan "remove Stalin." Trotsky agreed with the concept but **in October 1932** told Sedov that they should not

---

[5] See the sections in Chapter Five, "The Slogan 'Remove Stalin'," 131-135, and "The Slogan 'Remove Stalin' in the Trotsky Archive," 135-141; also see Furr, Moscow Trials, 108-118.

adopt it as yet, in order not to alienate other potential allies.[6] Broué concedes that "we do not know which one convinced the other" (Léon Sedov 81). Writing in Russian Rogovin puts quotation marks around the phrase: "*ubrat' Stalina.*"[7]

Rozenfel'd

Many other passages confirm that the same slogan was later interpreted to mean "kill Stalin." Boris Rozenfel'd, Kamenev's nephew (the son of his brother) said that his father and Kamenev had told him that the only way the opposition could come to power was by the "removal (*ustranenie*) of Stalin." (185) This sounds like a reference to the same interrogation of the young Rozenfel'd.[8] In this previously published interrogation Rozenfel'd uses the term *ustranenie* and also the word "terror" (*terror*) to describe his own convictions and those of his father and others about Stalin.

Dmitriev

On April 5, 1936, F.M. Dmitriev, a Trotskyist, confessed that Shemelev, a fellow Trotskyist, had said to him "at the beginning of 1935" that "one of the leaders" of the Trotskyist organization had recently told him that "the leadership of the [Trotskyist] organization considered essential the forcible removal ("*ustranenie*") of Stalin. (225) Shemelev also testified that the directive to use "terrorist" methods to "remove" (*ustranenie*) Stalin came from Smirnov as well. (281, 282).

Birkengof

We find yet more striking confirmation of the truthfulness of the interrogations contained in this volume in an interrogation of clandestine Trotskyist Aleksandr Il'ich Birkengof of May 23-25, 1936. Birkengof testified that he had been in direct touch with Yuri

---

[6] Broué, Trotsky et le bloc 20-22; Broué, "Liova le 'fiston'" 15.

[7] Rogovin, *1937.* Ch. 44.

[8] Published in the collection Lubianka 1922-1936, pp. 628-631

Gaven, who had himself met with Trotsky personally. Birkengof testified that in December 1932 Gaven communicated the following to him:

> Gaven informed me that he had established contact with I.N. Smirnov, leader of the Trotskyist organization in the USSR, that the situation in the organization was tense since Smirnov had reason to think that arrests were imminent, and Gaven specifically told me that Smirnov himself expected to be arrested. ... By the way, I.N. Smirnov really was arrested soon thereafter. (298)

This corresponds exactly to what Sedov reported about Smirnov and his group to Trotsky in his "bloc" letter. Sedov referred to Gaven with a pseudonym. Broué discovered that Trotsky had lied when he denied that he no contact with Gaven.

> Gaven est « Sorokine, comme Holzman est « Orlov »,. et Smimov « Kolokoltsev », dans la correspondance de Sedov et de son père. [9]

> Gaven is «Sorokin," as Holzman is "Orlov", and Smirnov is "Kolokoltsev", in the correspondence between Sedov and his father.

We discuss Gaven and his testimony in more detail below.

No Fabrication

The NKVD interrogator tried to get Birkengof to admit that by "removal" Birkengof meant "terror," i.e. assassination. But Birkengof refused to admit this and this refusal was reported in the interrogation transcript. (300). This is good evidence that Birkengof was not forced to confess. Nor did the NKVD forge or fabricate a false interrogation.

---

[9] Broué, "Compléments à un article sur les trotskystes en U.R.S.S." CahLT 24 (1985), Here, Broué concludes that Sedov had met with Gaven.

B. The Bloc of Trotskyists and other Oppositionists

We know about the bloc of Trotskyists, Zinovievists, Rightists, and other oppositionists from the Sedov "bloc" letter and the Sedov-Trotsky correspondence in the Harvard Trotsky Archive. Pierre Broué dates this exchange to 1932. The Sedov "bloc" letter refers to the bloc as something that had been in the planning for some time.

This bloc is mentioned in numerous documents published in PiLT2. In late 1932 or very early January 1933 Vasilii Ivanovich Dzhoev informed the GPU of a conversation he had had with childhood friend and current Trotskyist Ilia K. Gassiev. Gassiev informed Dzhoev about the Trotskyists' desire to "remove" (*ubrat'*) the Party leadership.

Dzhoev stated that Lominadze, one of the "other" oppositionists, was also a member of the group and that Zinoviev and Kamenev were leading the "Trotskyist" (sic) group. Each of these details is confirmed in the Sedov-Trotsky correspondence in the TA originally identified by Broué in the Sedov "bloc" letter:

> Le [...] (15) est organisé. Il comprend les zinoviévistes, le groupe Sten-Lominadzé et les trotskystes (anciens « ... ») ... La declaration de Z. et K. (18) sur la faute très grave qu'ils ont commise en 27 a été faite lors de pourparlers avec les nôtres sur le bloc, juste avant la deportation de Z. et de K. (Broué 1980, p.36)

> [The bloc] has been organized. In it have entered the Zinovievites, the Sten-Lominadze group and the Trotskyists (former "[capitulators]".... The declaration of Z. and K. concerning their enormous mistake in '27 was made during negotiations with our people concerning the bloc, immediately before the exile of Z and K.

Dzhoev added that Rykov had been "partly" drawn into it, but Bukharin had "not yet" been drawn in. He also stated that the bloc was working in the military, and that their goal was a *coup d'état*.

Dzhoev repeated many of these claims in an interrogation of January 7, 1933, also included in this volume. (25-28)

When arrested and interrogated Gassiev admitted the existence of the underground organization, Lominadze's participation, Rykov's participation in its leadership along with "perhaps" that of Zinoviev and Kamenev (30-31). As we saw above, Lominadze is named in the Sedov-Trotsky correspondence. In his 1980 article Broué speculates that the "droitiers" (= "Rightists") would probably be Bukharin, Rykov, and Tomsky.[10]

In the light of the much later "Tukhachevsky Affair" it is noteworthy that Gassiev testified that Semion Mikhailovich Budyonny and Mikhail Nikolaevich Tukhachevsky, both later promoted to marshal of the Soviet Union, were "close to us" in their sentiments. (30) When arrested and interrogated in May-June 1937 Tukhachevsky testified at great length about his conspiracy with Trotsky and his followers. We have a great deal of other evidence of his, and the military conspiracy's, ties to the Rights. Thus Gassiev's testimony is confirmed in part by Sedov and Trotsky, while Tukhachevsky's later admissions are confirmed in part by Gassiev. In another chapter in the present book we examine the role of Trotsky in some of the confessions and statements by Tukhachevsky and his co-defendants.

Iagoda's introductory letter to Stalin of January 20, 1933, in which Iagoda revealed that Trotsky had at that time rejected the slogan *"ubrat' Stalina"* (see above) also stated that "Smirnov's group" – that is, the underground Trotskyists – had also been discussing a "bloc with the Rights." (38) The Sedov-Trotsky "bloc" correspondence confirms this.

Naumov-Lekakh

In an interrogation dated October 4, 1934 David Borisovich Naumov-Lekakh, a Trotskyist, said that the Trotskyists were trying

---

[10] Broué, 1980, pp. 12-13. In document No. 2 in his Appendix Broué quotes a letter from Trotsky to Sedov that refers to the "droitiers."   (35-6)

to unite all oppositionists of whatever stripe who were disillusioned with the Party's political line. (144) He revealed that the bloc with the Rights had been discussed since 1930. The "bloc" exchange between Trotsky and Sedov in the Trotsky Archive confirms that by 1932 the bloc had been under discussion for some time.

Naumov-Lekakh also discussed the Trotskyists' cooperation with Ukrainian Nationalists, who he said were stronger in Ukraine than were the Trotskyists. Collaboration of underground Trotskyists with Ukrainian nationalists is also discussed in Ivan Serov's 1956 report to the Molotov Commission, a document we study closely in Furr, Collaboration, Chapter 4.

In a subsequent interrogation of December 26, 1934 Naumov-Lekakh mentioned among other matters that the Trotskyists in Moscow were working with the organization of Rights, specifically with Riutin. (141-145).

Bervitskii-Varfolomeev

Trotskyist Aleksandr Arsen'evich Bervitskii-Varfolomeev, interrogated on October 26, 1934, revealed that during the first half of 1932 he and an associate had discussed the need for "representatives of the Right-Left bloc to establish concrete contacts with Syrtsov." (159)

Lominadze

Lominadze, also mentioned in Sedov's "bloc" letter, is named many times in these documents. His associate oppositionist Ian Sten's name crops up once, in an interrogation of the Trotskyist Aleksandr Gavrilovich Kolodin of March 8, 1936. Kolodin identifies Sten as a "close acquaintance" of G.F. Dmitriev, leader of Kolodin's Trotskyist group. Dmitriev told Kolodin that Sten, a former Comintern worker, was in agreement with them. (214) Sedov also names Sten in his "bloc" letter to Trotsky.

> Le [...] est organisé. Il comprend les zinoviévistes, le
> groupe Sten-Lominadzé et les trotskystes (anciens « ... »)

[The bloc] has been organized. In it have entered the Zi-
novievites, the Sten-Lominadze group and the Trotskyists (former "[capitulators]". (Broué 1980,

Terror

On February 28, 1936 Trotskyist Ivan K. Fedotov testified that
"terror" – assassination – was the tactic chosen by the Trotskyist
underground in the USSR. Fedotov said that he had heard from
fellow Trotskyist Kurt Miuller about Trotsky's directive for the use
of "terror" against the Party leadership (206). The goal of assassi-
nating Stalin, Molotov, Voroshilov, and Kirov was to clear the path
for the return of Trotsky, Zinoviev and Kamenev to leadership of
the country. According to Fedotov, Furtichev had informed him in
early 1934 that the bloc was to act in Leningrad, where the bloc
was the strongest. Fedotov understood that this meant an attempt
to kill Kirov. (207). Kirov was indeed murdered on December 1,
1934.

Interrogated on April 26, 1936 Trotskyist Efrem Mikhailovich Bocharov testified about the activities of the Trotskyist-Zinovievist
group. In 1930 the Zinovievist Bakaev told him that the goal of the
Trotskyist-Zinovievist group was to take power "and bring Trotsky, Zinoviev and Kamenev to the leadership of the country." (253)

On October 17, 1936 Dmitri Ignat'evich Matveev, a Rightist, testified that in the Spring of 1932 Uglanov, one of the leaders of the
Rights, had been carrying on discussions with Kamenev about
forming a bloc between the Rights and the "Trotskyist-Zinovievist
organization" for "joint struggle against the leadership of the
VKP(b)." This confirms the Sedov-Trotsky correspondence which
Broué dated to 1932. In the "bloc" letter Sedov reported that the
bloc with the Zinovievists was confirmed but that the Rights had
not yet entered it. (315)

Sokol'nikov

This volume includes one interrogation of Grigorii Iakovlevich
Sokol'nikov, who was to be one of the two major defendants in the
January 1937 Moscow Trial. There is much of interest in this

document, which mainly concerns Sokol'nikov's contacts with British representatives on behalf of the Trotskyist-Zinovievist-Rightist conspiracy. In it Sokol'nikov confirms that this organization planned to bring to power a government consisting of Rykov and Bukharin, (Rightists); Kamenev and Zinoviev (Zinovievists); and Piatakov and himself, Sokol'nikov (Trotskyists). Trotsky would take charge of the Party, though possibly not immediately after the seizure of power since Trotsky was "politically compromised in the eyes of the broad masses," but that Trotsky would assume the Party leadership "as soon as the situation is solidified." (325)

Sokol'nikov's description of the existence and leadership of the Trotskyist-Zinovievist-Rightist conspiracy is confirmed in general terms by the Sedov-Trotsky correspondence about the "bloc" as well as by other evidence. It is yet another example of the general truth that we have no evidentiary reason to believe that the statements made by defendants in the Moscow Trials were fabricated and every reason to conclude the opposite – that they represent what the defendants wanted to say.[11]

These are the kinds of statements that have been widely dismissed as fabrications by those who contend that the Moscow Trials were frame-ups. In reality, all the evidence we now have tends to confirm that the interrogations and statements made by arrested suspects are genuine and represent what the persons making them wanted to state.

Political Activity Continued in Political Isolators

In his 1980 article announcing the existence of the bloc of Trotskyists, Zinovievists, and other oppositionists, the Sedov "bloc" letter and Sedov's correspondence with Trotsky about the bloc, Pierre Broué claimed that the bloc was "ephemeral" and came to an end early in 1933 when the leaders of the Trotskyist movement were

---

[11] We discuss the important question of Moscow Trial testimony in more detail in Furr, *Amalgams*.

arrested to be imprisoned in the Verkhneural'sk political isolator. But Broué had *no evidence* that the bloc had come to an end, nor that political activity was not possible in the political isolators.

We know that Broué was incorrect. In fact, years later Broué himself admitted that political activity continued in this political isolator. In his obituary of Ante Ciliga, published in 1993 in his own journal *Cahiers Léon Trotsky* Broué wrote:

> Arrested in 1930 he was imprisoned in the isolator at Verkhneuralsk where he participated in the life of the 'Bolshevik-Leninist collective.'[12]

A number of Rights and Trotskyites, I.N. Smirnov among them, were imprisoned in this same isolator at the same time as Ciliga. Ciliga was imprisoned at Verkhneural'sk from November 1930 to July 1933. Chapters 4 through 11 of his memoir *The Russian Enigma* testify to the very lively political life there and the privileges the prisoners enjoyed. As Broué himself noted, Ciliga testifies that the factions among the prisoners, including the Trotskyists, continued their activities there.

The documents in PiLT2 show evidence of this political activity. In a report to Stalin dated January 1- 3, 1933, Genrikh Iagoda, at the time Vice-Chairman of the OGPU, quotes Trotskyist M. Novikov testifying to the political activity at Verkhneural'sk even before the arrival there of I.N. Smirnov and the Trotskyists arrested and imprisoned at the same time. (32) This corresponds with what Ciliga writes.

In an interrogation dated December 17, 1934, Trotskyist Isai Davidovich Fal'kevich testified about the words of a certain Rappoport, who had recruited him to the Trotskyist organization at the end of 1931:

> He also told me that in the political isolator itself the Trotskyists were always fully informed on questions

---

[12] Broué, "Ante Ciliga (1898-1992)," *Cahiers Léon Trotsky* no. 50, 1993, 121-122.

about new instructions from Trotsky and about the activities of Trotskyists in various places. (124)

Interrogated on April 29, 1936, Trotskyist Mikhail Georgievich Saf'ianov testified that at the end of 1935 he and others had been told by Shemelev, who had recruited him in 1933, that "terror" was now necessary against Stalin:

> Shemelev set before us in the most frank manner the question of the transition to terrorist forms of struggle against the leadership of the VKP(b) and in the first place against Stalin... He said that this directive came from I.N. Smirnov, who was a supporter of terrorist means of removing [*ustraneniia*] Stalin. (281)

Smirnov had been in the Verkhneural'sk political isolator since early 1933. At the August, 1936, First Moscow Trial Smirnov claimed that he had "done no work," not participated in, the activities of the Trotskyist bloc while in prison.

Therefore we now have a good deal of evidence that Broué was wrong to assume that the bloc of Trotskyists, Zinovievists, and other Oppositionists ended when many of its members were arrested at the beginning of 1933. In fact, there never was any evidence at all to support Broué's contention. Why, then, did he insist upon it?

It appears that Broué's assertion was a "tell." A loyal, lifelong Trotskyist, Broué showed considerable courage in revealing the existence in the Trotsky Archive of the Sedov-Trotsky correspondence that proved that the "bloc" of Trotskyists, Zinovievists, and other oppositionists, had indeed existed, and that therefore Trotsky and Sedov had lied, over and over again, by denying that there was or could have been any such bloc with "capitulators."

Broué could have stolen or destroyed the evidence that Trotsky had lied, and especially the very damning evidence that the "bloc" of Oppositionists had really existed. It was Arch Getty who discovered the evidence that someone had "purged" the Harvard Trotsky

Archive of material that incriminated Trotsky. Since then, we have identified more evidence of the "purging" of the archive.

On the basis of the evidence now available, we concluded in *Trotsky's 'Amalgams'* that the person who did the "purging" was probably Jean van Heijenoort.[13] Broué and van Heijenoort were close friends. In publishing the documentary evidence that the "bloc" had existed despite Trotsky's and Sedov's repeated and fervent denials Broué was not only calling Trotsky and Sedov liars, but also his friend van Heijenoort.

Broué certainly knew, and must have feared, the serious implications of this discovery for his commitment to Trotskyism. If "Stalin" – the Soviet prosecution in the Moscow Trials – had been telling the truth about the bloc while Trotsky was lying, anyone might wonder: What else was Trotsky lying about? What other charges made by the Soviet prosecution were true? Did the Soviet prosecution perhaps tell the truth about the bloc's terrorist conspiracies and fascist ties? If Trotsky and Sedov had been lying about the bloc, could they have been lying about these charges too?

For a historian to make a definitive assertion of fact about an historical question of vital importance to himself without any evidence to base it on is a sign that he is facing some critical issue. We assume that Broué asserted that the bloc came to an end with the arrest of I.N. Smirnov and a number of other underground Trotskyists in early January 1933 because he wished to salvage his image of Trotsky and the Soviet Trotskyists as the innocent victims of a frame-up.

Phony Capitulations

Pierre Broué accepted the Soviet contention that I.N. Smirnov and other Trotskyist oppositionists had falsely renounced their oppositionist views and had falsely vowed that they would support the Party's positions – a process that Trotsky and others called "ca-

---

[13] Furr, Trotsky's 'Amalgams', Chapter Six, pp. 149-156.

pitulation." Broué even wrote that "everybody" knew that these capitulations were fraudulent, a tactic to continue oppositional activity from a position within the Party itself. (POS 104)

In this instance too Broué failed to trace the implications of his position. For one thing, it means that there is no reason to doubt the admissions by Zinoviev, Kamenev, and many others that they had falsely capitulated. Statements and interrogations in PiLT2 confirm many more false capitulations.

Prior to arresting I.N. Smirnov, leader of the Trotskyist underground in the USSR, and a number of other Trotskyists, Iagoda sent a report to Stalin that includes the following:

> According to facts uncovered by our agents, among the former Trotskyists who declared their break with the Opposition at one time or another the group headed by Ivan Nikitich Smirnov, comprising about 200 former active Trotskyists, merits special attention.
>
> This group is essentially the ideological and organizational center of those who supposedly abandoned the Trotskyist opposition and, upon their return from exile and political isolators renewed their counterrevolutionary activity.
>
> The group of Smirnov began its formation at the moment of his declaration of break with the Opposition which he signed together with M. Boguslavskii. This document, despite the fact that it was changed twice by Smirnov after discussion with the Party Control Commission, still remained a convenient cover for Trotskyist hypocrites [literally, "two-faced persons"] ... [T]his document does not contain any qualification of all previous activity of the Trotskyists as counterrevolutionary and contains a number of "rubber" formulations by which a Trotskyist-hypocrite can easily include his disagreements with the Party.

M. Novikov, a former active worker of the underground technique of the Moscow Trotskyist center (exposed as a hypocrite) in his confessions given to the OGPU on April 19, 1930 explained the massive exodus from the Opposition of those Trotskyists imprisoned in the Verkhneural'sk political isolator in this way:

"In arguments with a group of supporters of the Radek-Smilga declaration we were stronger ideologically. After that group was freed, there was complete unanimity in the isolator.

The draft of I.N. Smirnov's declaration that we received made a great impression. We thought that Ivan Nikitich was following this political line with L.D.'s (Trotsky's) agreement and we were all eager to take the same line.

I.N. Smirnov organized the exiled Trotskyists to renounce [the opposition] by means of signing this declaration, and openly agitated for a hypocritical capitulation.

In one of his documents Smirnov directly advocated the necessity of making a declaration of renunciation [of the opposition] on the grounds that the longer it was postponed, the more difficult it would be to do.

'We must sign this declaration. This is the most correct document; there are no others. When people start to write individually, who knows what they will write. For example, Grinchenko (former member of the Moscow Trotskyist center) wrote that the social composition of the opposition was non-proletarian. By doing this he slandered the whole movement as petty-bourgeois. Undoubtedly, it wasn't..." (32)

Novikov went on to explain that the Smirnov statement did not admit that its own views were anti-Party, but that the Party had begun to carry out the program of the Trotskyists. (32-33)

Instead of composing individual letters of their own, dozens of Trotskyists signed the Smirnov letter. Novikov's – that is, Smirnov's -- explanation of this curious fact makes sense. If each Trotskyist had been required to compose a convincing letter to explain his or her political views and how they had changed, to explain why they had joined the Trotskyist opposition and then give their reasons for renouncing it, the Party Control Commission (PCC) – "Stalin" – would have obtained a great deal of information about the Trotskyist movement. They would have been able to compare these many accounts with one another. They would probably have learned many things, including names that the leaders of the Trotskyist movement preferred to keep secret and other details.

So it appears that Stalin and the Party leadership showed considerable leniency in accepting a collective document instead of insisting upon individual statements and individual decisions about reinstatement to Party membership. With the benefit of hindsight, we can now see that this was a serious error on their part. It greatly facilitated false capitulations, renewed Party membership, and an easy continuation in conspiracy for the Trotskyist underground.

In an interrogation of February 11, 1934, Trotskyist Anna Pavlovna Lifshits admitted that she had given a statement of breaking with the opposition to the PCC in 1931 and said: "This break of mine was not sincere." She met with two others who also knew that her break with the opposition had been hypocritical. (102) Later in the same interrogation Lifshits again mentions her fraudulent renunciation of Trotskyism. (111)

Evidently some Trotskyists did make individual dishonest "breaks" with Trotskyism, perhaps unknown to other Trotskyists. At an interrogation of November 27, 1934, Trotskyist Boris Samoilovich Rappoport-Dar'in stated:

> My break with the Trotskyists in the isolator in 1930 was hypocritical, with the goal of continuing counter-revolutionary Trotskyist activity. (177)

This tactic may have been designed to create another, more secret level of Trotskyists – those believed by other phony capitulators to have really capitulated.

On March 8, 1936 Aleksandr Gavrilovich Kolodin, a Trotskyist formerly exiled and then allowed to return, stated the following:

> Question: After your release from exile did you continue to carry out your Trotskyist activity?
>
> Answer: Yes, even after my exile was over I continued to remain a convinced enemy of the VKP(b) and of Soviet power and remained with my Trotskyist convictions. I hated the leaders of the VKP(b) and the Soviet government and conducted active Trotskyist work. I rejoined the Party for hypocritical purposes. (212)

All this evidence of false capitulations, which even Broué agreed did take place, discloses a lie or "amalgam" by Trotsky himself. Throughout the 1930s Trotsky continued to proclaim that those who had "capitulated" were his enemies and that he refused to have anything to do with them. Therefore, Trotsky claimed, the Soviet prosecution, press, and representatives generally were lying when they claimed that many of his followers had capitulated dishonestly.

To explain their claims of false capitulation Trotsky resorted to asserting that they had been either tortured or threatened into saying these things. In fact we see that these statements fit the facts, and it was Trotsky, not the Trotskyist defendants at the Moscow Trials, who was lying. Trotsky's lies fooled the Dewey Commission and many others, and still do.

Yuri P. Gaven

In 1985 Broué announced the discovery in the Harvard Trotsky Archive of evidence that in late September or October 1932 Sedov had indeed met with Yuri Gaven.[14] Broué had discovered evidence in the TA that Trotsky, who had denied any contact with Gaven, had in fact met secretly with him and had probably given him a message for the Trotskyists within the USSR. (POS 105) This was one of the accusations made during the First Moscow Trial. Trotsky and Sedov always firmly denied this and claimed that the Soviet prosecution was lying about this.

PiLT2 contains one interrogation of Gaven dated April 23, 1936. In it Gaven admits to meeting with Sedov in Berlin at the end of 1932, to receiving a letter from him signed by Trotsky, and to handing this letter on to I.N. Smirnov. In this interrogation the NKVD investigators did not ask Gaven about the contents of the letter, only to whom he distributed it. But the NKVD did not fail to do this. As of October, 2019, we have one further interrogation of Gaven in which he describes this letter to Smirnov as containing only instructions for Trotskyists within the USSR to rejoin the Party, in order to obtain influence in it. We will examine it in a future study.

In an interrogation of May 25, 1936, A.I. Birkengof had quite a lot to say about his contacts with Gaven in Trotskyist work. It was evidently from Gaven that Birkengof had learned about the arrests of I.N. Smirnov and many other underground Trotskyists in early 1933. Birkengof admitted that Gaven had told him that the only way out of the current situation was the "removal" (*ustranenie*) of Stalin. He refused to speculate about what "removal" meant.

We would like to know the contents of Trotsky's letter which was given to Gaven by Sedov and which Gaven then handed on to I.N. Smirnov. In an interrogation of April 29, 1936 Mikhail Georgievich Saf'ianov, a Trotskyist, stated that Gaven had transmitted Trotsky's directives to carry out the "forcible removal" of Stalin.

> Question: Did you receive instructions of a terrorist nature from anyone else, other than Shemelev?

---

[14] Broué, "Compléments à un article sur les trotskystes en U.R.S.S." *Cahiers Léon Trotsky* 24 (1985), 63-72.

> Answer: In 1934 Gidlevsky informed me about his visit to Gaven and informed me that Gaven considered the "forcible removal" of Stalin to be absolutely essential, as the most expedient means of struggle under current conditions. Gidlevsky told me that these instructions were received by Gaven from abroad and came from Trotsky. (282)

This does not necessarily mean that the letter Gaven carried to Smirnov in 1932 advocated Stalin's "forcible removal." We have seen that in 1932 Trotsky was hesitant to advocate this. It does appear to mean that by 1934 Gaven, on instructions from Trotsky, was advocating terror against Stalin.

In a report to Stalin of September 9, 1936, Iagoda told Stalin that Trotskyist Gidlevsky had told another Trotskyist (Saf'ianov) that instructions had been received from Trotsky through Yuri Gaven that Stalin must be "removed by force " (*nasil'stvennogo ustraneniia*) (278; 282).

If Gaven or Birkengof had been tortured or forced to falsely confess, why would the text of their interrogations not say that they were advocating terror? This is yet more evidence that the NKVD was not forcing false confessions on the arrested oppositionists.

Matveev's Interrogation

PiLT2 includes one interrogation of Dmitrii Ignat'evich Matveev of October 17, 1936. Matveev was not a Trotskyist but a Rightist. In it, after initially denying everything, Matveev admits that in the fall of 1932, at the Moscow apartment of Uglanov, another Rightist, a meeting was held where Uglanov and others stated that they could no longer rely on economic difficulties to bring the Soviet government down and therefore had decided to resort to terror. Throughout the interrogation Matveev stoutly denied that he himself agreed with terror, claiming that he left the meeting because he rejected it. The interrogator did not believe Matveev's disavowal of terror but Matveev persisted in his refusal to confess that he supported terror.

We can check this confession in at least two ways. Matveev does affirm that he heard in the spring of 1932 about the negotiations "between the Rightists and the Trotskyist-Zinovievist organization for joint struggle against the Party leadership." He then said that he knew when the bloc had been formed:

> Question: From whom did you learn about the bloc of the Rights with the Trotskyist-Zinovievist organization?
>
> Answer: Uglanov told me about the meeting with Kamenev and about the establishment of contact with the Trotskyist-Zinovievist organization during the same spring of 1932. (315)

This is confirmed by the contents of the Sedov "bloc" letter and to Broué's analysis of the Sedov-Trotsky correspondence during 1932. (Broué, 1980)

We can also check the accuracy of Matveev's interrogation by comparing it to the statement by fellow Rightist, a resident not of Moscow but of Leningrad, Valentin N. Astrov. In an important interrogation of January 11, 1937, Astrov said that, together with other young Rightists, Matveev had advocated terrorist methods against the Party leadership since 1931.

> MATVEEV said that the main task was to remove (*ubrat'*) Stalin by any means, including terror. (Lubianka 1937-1938 20).

We have studied this statement of Astrov's in some detail in *Trotsky's 'Amalgams'* and in *Trotsky's Lies*. Astrov lived into the post-Soviet period, until the summer of 1993. Astrov twice wrote that he was treated respectfully by the NKVD and that they had not forced him to invent anything. Moreover, the only statement in his interrogation that he retracted was his assertion that Bukharin had *explicitly* called for the murder of Stalin.

Astrov's retraction of this accusation may well have been false. It was certainly unpopular in the late 1980s, during the "Bukharin boom" when Gorbachev was using Bukharin to portray Stalin as a

murderer of innocents, to claim that it was really Bukharin who
had been advocating terror. Yet thanks to the memoirs of Jules
Humbert-Droz, a Swiss communist and close associate of Bukharin's in the 1920s, we know that Bukharin and some of his supporters were conspiring to murder Stalin as early as 1928 [15]

To sum up: In October, 1936, Matveev agreed that in 1932 the
Rightists were talking about killing Stalin. But Matveev denied that
he himself advocated or agreed with this tactic. On the basis of accusations by his fellow Rightists the NKVD believed Matveev was
lying and really had been advocating terror. Matveev stuck to his
denial in this interrogation, and the NKVD went on to another subject. Matveev was not compelled in any way to confess to advocating terror. This is yet more evidence that the suspects testified as
they chose (whether truthfully or not) and were not forced to
make false statements to incriminate themselves and/or others.

Yet Astrov claimed that Matveev had been explicitly advocating
terror as early as 1931. And when he had the chance, Astrov refused to recant his statements to the NKVD, with the exception of
his statement that Bukharin had explicitly advocated terror.

Trotsky and Terror

In the early 1990s, not long after the demise of the USSR, Oleg
Tsarev and John Costello obtained access to the NKVD file of Alex-
ander Orlov, who had been the resident head of the Soviet NKVD in
Republican Spain during the Spanish Civil War, and to certain
other NKVD materials. Among those other materials were at least
some of the reports sent back to his NKVD handlers by Mark
Zborowski, a young NKVD agent who had managed to become a
close confident and coworker of Leon Sedov. In reports from
1937-38 Zborowski reported that Sedov had urged the assassination of Stalin even while he and Trotsky were publicly denouncing

---

[15] See Furr, Trotsky's 'Amalgams', Chapter 8, or Furr, Moscow Trials, Chapter 8,
for a detailed discussion of Humbert-Droz's remarks.

"terror" as a political strategy that Trotsky had never and would never countenance.[16]

The reports and confessions in PiLT2 contain many references to Trotskyists' plans for "terror" – assassination – against Stalin and Bolshevik leaders. In this section we will examine the claim that instructions to carry out terror came from Trotsky himself.

The February 28, 1936, interrogation of Trotskyist Ivan Kuz'mich Fedotov is important in this connection. Fedotov's interrogation is the first mention of the tactic of "terror" of all the confessions and statements of Trotskyists in this collection. He said that in 1935 he had been in touch with Valentin Ol'berg before the latter's arrest and knew about Ol'berg's intention to kill Stalin. Ol'berg was one of the defendants in the first Moscow Trial of August 1936.

> Valentin Ol'berg told me that one of his tasks was to get in touch with the Trotskyist organization [in the USSR] and to really [*real'no*] prepare and carry out the murder of Stalin upon Trotsky's order. (205)

But Fedotov said that the Trotskyists had been making terrorist plans before this. He testified that he had worked from November 1933 to the end of January 1934 with a certain Miuller. Miuller was a Trotskyist who was demoted from leading work in the German Communist Party because of his Trotskyist views but had somehow managed to come to the USSR and was working in an automobile factory in Gorky, where Fedotov met him.

Miuller said that he was in touch with the leadership of the Trotskyist movement in Berlin and was leading Trotskyist work within the USSR. Then Fedotov said:

> Miuller told me that the removal (*ustranenie*) of the leadership of the VKP(b) could only be accomplished through terror, and that the transition to terrorist strug-

---

[16] Zborowski's reports on Sedov are studied in Furr Amalgams, Chapter 13, and Furr, Trotsky's Lies, Chapter 2.

gle against the Party leadership was begin carried out **according to a directive that came straight from Trotsky.**

Fedotov continued:

> I in turn told Miuller that there was a Trotskyist terrorist organization in Gorky comprised of reliable persons. (206)

Previous defendants had testified, and even Broué agreed, that Trotsky and Sedov advocated the "removal" (*ustranienie*) of Stalin and the Party and government leadership. But they had refused to state that this meant *forcible* removal. That admission is made for the first time in these documents. Since Fedotov said that he had told Miuller that a Trotskyist terrorist organization already existed in Gorky we know that the "turn to terror" had taken place some time earlier than November 1933 – January 1934.

Fedotov said that Furtichev, a prominent Trotskyist with whom he had talks during February-March 1934, had seconded Miuller's views about the necessity of terror against the Party leaders in order to bring Trotsky, Zinoviev, and Kamenev to the leadership of the country. (208)

Later in the same interrogation Fedotov returned to the subject of Valentin Ol'berg's role, which he said he learned of from Ol'berg himself in August 1935.

> Ol'berg put before me his plan of action.

> He said that Trotsky considers that our people in the USSR are very busy with propaganda of Trotskyist views. That this will not decide the outcome of our struggle with the Party leadership.

> The most basic and most important thing to do is to carefully organize and carry out the murder of Stalin. This will be the alarm that will raise the masses to decide all the other questions and will permit us to con-

cretely decide the question of the return of Trotsky to the leadership of the country. (209)

Miuller's name comes up again in the interrogation of Iakov Abramovich Furtichev dated May 4, 1936. When asked about his discussions with Fedotov concerning terrorist activity Furtichev replied:

> For Fedotov terrorist plans were not new. He told me that when he was still working at the automobile factory he had met a certain Kurt Miuller, who had at one time been a leader of the German Komsomol but had been removed from this work because of his Trotskyist views. According to Fedotov Miuller gave Fedotov a directive of Trotsky's concerning the necessity of preparing terrorist acts against the Party leaders and in the first place against Stalin. (271)

Kurt Miuller features in a number of additional interrogations of Trotskyists that have been made public recently.

Shemelev

In his interrogation of April 5, 1936, arrested Trotskyist Aleksandr Ivanovich Shemelev mentioned Trotsky's instructions for terror several times.

> I wish to inform the investigation that during previous interrogations I concealed some substantive matters concerning the instructions which I received from Sedov (through Gorovich) and from I.N. Smirnov and A. Safonova (through Adish) ... When I gave my previous confessions about the instructions that Gorovich received in Berlin from Sedov I concealed from the investigation the following: When he returned from Berlin in 1932 Gorovich told me that in Sedov's opinion, along with diligent work to gather our cadre, it was essential to set and to carry out the main task, which consisted of the removal (*ustranenie*) of Stalin, and that this was Trotsky's directive.

Shemelev was careful to qualify exactly what he heard:

> Let me say that I will not guarantee that the word "re-
> move" (*ustranit'*) was used. It is possible that he used the
> word "liquidate," "remove" (*ustranit'*) or "get rid of"
> (*ubrat'*). But I remember very well: that the meaning
> was the necessity of the forcible removal (*na-
> sil'stvennogo ustraneniia*) of Stalin. (221)

This testimony of Shemelev's confirms the reports of Mark
Zborowski that Sedov was privately advocating terror against Stalin at the same time that he and Trotsky were denying, repeatedly
and in the strongest terms, that they would ever consider adopting
the tactics of terror. Here Shemelev claims that Sedov was advocating violence as early as 1932, though perhaps without being
completely explicit. If this is true, it would be another issue about
which Sedov and Trotsky were lying, to be added to those that
Broué, Getty, and I have discovered.

It is significant that Shemelev did not insist that he had heard any
specific word, much less that "terror" or assassination was explicitly mentioned. Instead, he insisted that these were understood
but not spoken. If the NKVD had been compelling him to incriminate Trotsky or Smirnov, why would they not have forced him to
be more direct? This is yet more evidence that, in this case, Shemelev's testimony was what he wanted to say, rather than some lie
that the investigators were forcing upon him.

Shemelev testified that in February or March, 1933, he had had a
talk with another Trotskyist, Dmitriev, in the latter's apartment.

> Dmitriev of course understood about whom "abroad" we
> were talking, although I did not explicitly tell him that I
> meant the contact with Trotsky. He was very interested
> in my declaration about "occasions" abroad, got quite
> excited, and asked: "What do they think abroad?" I reply
> to him more or less as follows: "'Abroad they think that
> the main thing is to liquidate Stalin." Dmitriev very
> openly answered that he thought the same thing and

that he and his group (*ego edinomyshlenniki,* those who agreed with him) had arrived at an analogous conclusion. It was completely obvious for us both that we were talking about the forcible removal (*nasil'stvennogo ustraneniia*) of Stalin. (222)

Shemelev also talked about his contact with the Trotskyist Adish:

Adish was the contact man for the members of our organization of [I.] N. Smirnov and A. Safonova. ... But I concealed from the investigation that Adish transmitted to me Smirnov's and Safonova's evaluation of the situation in the Party and country, and speaking about the perspectives of illegal work told me that Safonova assigned me to transmit the view of I.N. Smirnov that if we could find a man (or a group of men) prepared to deal with Stalin, then under the present circumstances that would be the best outcome, and an act both politically and historically justified. (222-223).

Shemelev then said that he went to meet with Dmitriev again, "with the knowledge that Dmitriev and his group were precisely what we needed in order to carry out Sedov's and Smirnov's directive."

From my talks with Dmitriev, especially from the last one, it was completely clear to me that he correctly understood the essence of the directives of Sedov and Smirnov in relation to the liquidation of Stalin. (223)

Gurevich

On May 18, 1936 Trotskyist Khaskel' Gesselevich Gurevich was interrogated. According to the accompanying report to Stalin by Iagoda Gurevich had been named by Valentin Ol'berg.[17]

Gurevich's story is an interesting one. He had been arrested in Berlin by the Gestapo, whom Gurevich told that he was a Trotskyist and was going to the USSR to plan terrorist acts against the Party leadership. Hearing this the Gestapo released him on the condition that he inform them about developments in the Trotskyist organization's terrorist plans. This made Gurevich an agent of the Gestapo and, in the eyes of Soviet authorities, a German spy.

Some writers have dismissed the possibility that any Jew could have been a Gestapo agent, either because no Jew would agree to be one or because the Gestapo would never recruit a Jew. Gurevich's story demonstrates how this kind of thing could happen: blackmail, plus a mutual interest in opposing the Soviet government, could produce this kind of alliance. Karl Radek, though of Jewish background and a professed internationalist, was so enamored of Germany that, in the words of Nazi diplomat Gustav Hilger, "We could always count on him to help us when it was a question of dealing with difficult situations in our dealings with the Soviet regime.[18] Radek even famously told the violent Nazi Gauleiter Erich Koch "There are some fine lads in the SA and SS."[19]

Gurevich claimed that he had received instructions directly from Leon Sedov in Berlin:

---

[17] This interrogation of Gurevich has recently been published in facsimile – http://istmat.info/files/uploads/60578/rgaspi._f.17._op.171._d.224_protokoly_d oprosov_gurevicha.pdf

[18] "... konnten wir immer auf ihn rechnen, wenn es darum ging, uns in schwierigen Situationen bei unseren Verhandlungen mit der Sowjetregierung zu helfen." Gustav Hilger, *Wir und der Kreml: Deutsch-Sowjetische Beziehungen 1918-1941 : Erinnerungen eines deutschen Diplomaten*. Berlin: Athenaum, 1955, 80.

[19] Gerhard Reitlinger, "Last of the War Criminals." *Commentary* 27, 1 (January,1959), 33.

Frida Grebe[20] knew that I was in contact with the Trotskyist organization in Berlin and in Leipzig, and knew about **my contact with Leon Sedov**, and also knew that Mikhail Bykhovskii and I had an assignment from the Trotskyist organization to prepare and to carry out in the Soviet Union terrorist acts against the Party leaders.

... Yes, I must admit that ... at the beginning of June [1933] **one of the Gestapo workers** questioned me concerning the question of my Trotskyist activities and contacts in Germany. I admitted at this interrogation that **I was a member of the Trotsky organization and was in contact in my activity with Sedov, Ol'berg, Fridman, Bykhovskii, and others,** and that **I was assigned by the organization to go to the USSR in order to prepare terrorist acts against the leaders of the Party**. (289)

In the same interrogation of October 20, 1936 N.I. Gordon stated that in 1933 he had heard directly from Beloborodov, one of the leaders of the Trotskyist group in the USSR whose senior leader was I.N. Smirnov, that Trotsky had urged a "transition" to terrorist acts against Stalin and those associated with him:

According to Beloborodov, Smirnov, Mrachkovskii, and Ter-Vaganian formed the Trotskyist center and were in direct contact with Trotsky. **Smirnov maintained the contact with Trotsky.** Beloborodov said that Trotsky firmly insisted upon the transition to decisive actions in the struggle against Stalin. I asked Beloborodov what that means – that is, how should these active measures find expression? Beloborodov answered: "It means the transition to terrorist acts, first of all against Stalin, and then also against his closest associates." At the same time Beloborodov said that although this really is the most extreme form of struggle, we had no other way out,

---

[20] Gurevich's wife.

because **we could not rely on the masses**, and any further delay would mean the strengthening of Stalin's position. (321)

Smirnov was arrested during the first few days of January, 1933.
This means that Trotsky had begun to advocate the murder of Stalin by sometime in 1933 at the latest.

This corresponds with what Gaven had told Birkengof in early
1933. It also corresponds with what Radek testified at the January,
1937, Moscow Trial about the letter he received from Trotsky in
February early March, 1932. Birkengof refused to say that Gaven
had specifically recommended "removing" Stalin by violence.
Radek testified that in his letter Trotsky did not explicitly mention
violence, but that he, Radek, understood that violence was what
was meant since there was no other way of getting rid of the Party
leadership.

Trotskyist Involvement in the Murder of Sergei Kirov

When Sergei Mironovich Kirov, the First Secretary of the Leningrad city and oblast' Party, was murdered on December 1, 1934,
the crime was soon traced to an underground Zinovievist group.
These men were quickly arrested, interrogated, tried, convicted,
and shot. In January, 1935, Zinoviev, Kamenev, and others in Moscow were tried and convicted of knowing about the existence of
this Leningrad Zinovievist group and not informing the authorities. They were sentenced to prison.[21]

At the end of December 1934 Trotsky published some articles in
which he claimed that his name had come up because the Soviet
government was trying to pin the blame on him since he, Trotsky,
was the more important figure. We have studied Trotsky's writ-

---

[21] See Furr, *The Murder of Sergei Kirov*, for a thorough discussion of this and related conspiracies.

ings about the Kirov murder in detail in *Trotsky's 'Amalgams'* and *Trotsky's Lies.*

We know Trotsky lied in these writings because we know from Sedov's "bloc" letter that he was already in a bloc with the Zinovievists, among others. Yet Trotsky always publicly denied it. At that time (1934-1935) the Soviet authorities did not accuse Trotsky of direct complicity in the murder of Kirov. Nor did they yet know about the bloc that had been formed in 1932. The Zinovievists did not reveal that they were in a bloc with the Trotskyists.

The question arises whether the Trotskyists, and Trotsky himself, were involved in the planning of Kirov's murder and if so, to what extent. This was one of the charges at the first Moscow Trial, the "Zinoviev-Kamenev" trial, of August, 1936. Until the publication of this collection we did not have other evidence that the Trotskyists and Trotsky himself were accomplices to Kirov's murder.

Trotskyist Ivan Aleksandrovich Maslennikov, interrogated on April 26, 1936, testified that he knew from another Trotskyist that the Trotskyists in Leningrad were in touch with the Zinovievists who murdered Kirov and that the Trotskyists had been planning similar acts.

> I did not know about any plans to carry out terrorist acts. I knew only that the Trotskyist organization had set for its goal the murders of members of the Politburo and of Stalin above all ... As soon as December 1934, just two or three days after the murder of S.M. Kirov, in the room of the Dean of the Faculty of Natural Sciences, Nilender told me that Kirov's murder had been organized by "our people" (i.e. the Trotskyists).

> ... [F]rom my talk with Nilender I understood that the preparation of the terrorist act against S.M. Kirov had been known to Nilender.

> Question: What specifically did Nilender tell you about the contact of your Trotskyist counterrevolutionary or-

ganization with the participants in the murder of S.M.
Kirov?

Answer: Nilender did not tell me anything about this directly, but from his words I very clearly understood that
our terrorist organization was in contact with the Leningrad group. (249-250)

In his interrogation of May 4, 1936, Furtichev testified about the
connection between the Trotskyists and Zinovievists in the murder of Kirov:

...In the spring of 1934 Bocharov told me that he had
heard from Bakaev that the Trotskyist-Zinovievist organization was planning to murder Stalin in Moscow and
Kirov in Leningrad, and were forming special terrorist
groups for this purpose. (272)

On May 27, 1936, Moisei Naumovich Iakovlev, a Zinovievist, confessed that the Zinovievists had ties with the Trotskyists. In June
1934 (305), Kamenev had told him that the Zinovievist and Trotskyist groups were united.

Kamenev said that the union of the Zinovievist organization, headed by me, with the Trotskyist group of Zaidel'
fully corresponded with the plans of the Moscow Zinovievist organization. At the same time Zinoviev told me
that on this same basis, terrorist struggle against the
Party leadership, the Zinovievist center had long since
united with the Trotskyist organization of I.N. Smirnov –
Mrachkovskii.

Question: Did Kamenev tell who personally was in the
united Zinovievist-Trotskyist center?

Answer: Kamenev said that in the united center of the
Zinovievist-Trotskyist organization were Zinoviev, him-
self – Kamenev, Bakaev, Smirnov, Ter-Vaganian and
Mrachkovskii. (306-307)

In the interrogation cited above (October 20, 1936) Gordon said the following:

> In 1934 I met twice with Glebov-Avilov ... In an outburst of anger Glebov-Avilov told me that the Stalin regime could not be removed (*ustranit'*) by democratic means, some other determined measures were necessary. And then Glebov told me that direct orders had been received from the Trotskyist-Zinovievist center in Moscow to prepare terrorist acts against the Party leaders and that we should start with Stalin. (322)

Thus we now have a good deal of testimony that the Trotskyists were accessories to the murder of Kirov. This confirms the testimony at the First Moscow Trial of August 1936, where it is one of the main charges against the defendants. It was also a major charge against some of the defendants in the Second Moscow Trial or Trotskyist trial of January, 1937.

Trotskyists and Terror

We have already noted that the first confession in these documents in which a Trotskyist acknowledges that the goal of the Trotskyists in the USSR was "terror" – the assassination of Soviet leaders – is that of Ivan K. Fedotov of February 28, 1936. However, there must be earlier confessions by Trotskyists, for Nikolai Ezhov's draft report to the Central Committee plenum of June 1935, "On the CEC Apparatus and Comrade Enukidze"[22] had already stated that this was the Trotskyists' goal.

---

[22] An earlier draft of this report with the same title dated April 3, 1935 was printed in 2003 in a volume of documents. (Lubianka 1922-1936 No. 518) This document was not called a "report" but rather a communication to all members and candidate member of the Party, and bore the names of Stalin, Molotov, and Kaganovich as well as that of Ezhov. It concerned only the terrorist groups, including Trotskyists groups but also Zinovievists, in the Kremlin, the "Kremlin Affair" of 1935. None of the quotations cited above are in this earlier version, which is therefore really a different document despite its identical title.

Concerning the direct participation of the Trotskyist center abroad in the organization of terrorist work in the USSR speak the confessions of the leader of the Trotskyist terrorist group of military workers Cherniavskii. Cherniavskii who, as we stated above, during his trip abroad established contact with active Trotskyists, confessed during the investigation about the task which he received from the Trotskyist Raskin:

"...Raskin stated that in the USSR the Trotskyists have valuable cadre and that inside the country there is a favorable situation for the development of Trotskyist work.

In 1933 Raskin told me that for Russia the Trotskyists had the task of the largest possible development of separate groups of sympathizers.

Together with that work it was necessary to create cadres of persons capable of the most determined and extreme forms of struggle with the Party. He explained to me that he considered that it was essential to create terrorist groups for the murder of Stalin and other leaders of the Party, that this activity could be the most practical means for the return of Trotsky to the helm of state (*k kormilu pravlenia*)." (185)

Ezhov quotes another Trotskyist, Novozhilov, who also quoted Cherniavskii on the necessity of murdering Stalin. (187)

Ezhov quotes other excerpts in this draft report from confessions of arrested Trotskyists about the goal of terror.

... [T]he Trotskyist Azbel' described the ideological plan of his organization in this way:

"All the dissatisfied elements in the country are frightened. It is possible to stimulate the dissatisfied elements to active struggle against the leadership of the Party only by means of terror. We saw all the evil was in Stalin and therefore we believed that by means of his murder, that of the most influential and deciding person in the country, we could cause confusion among the current leadership of the Party and stir up to the struggle all those elements dissatisfied with the existing regime." (186)

This report of Ezhov's is called a "draft" (*proekt*). We don't know whether a final draft based upon it was presented to the June 1935 CC Plenum. It does show that by June 1935 the NKVD had been told of terrorist plans by Trotskyist groups.

Valentin Ol'berg

According to Arch Getty,

> Sometime in the first days of 1936, Ezhov had received a mandate from Stalin to reopen the Kirov assassination investigation. He [Ezhov] later said that for Stalin something "did not seem right" about that investigation, and Ezhov was charged with taking a new look.

> ... His [Ezhov's] train of investigations began with the arrest on 5 January 1936 of V.P. Ol'berg, who within a month confessed to being a Trotskyist agent dispatched to the USSR by Trotsky to organize the assassination of Stalin. (189-190)

Here Getty is following the account in the Gorbachev-era journal *Izvestia TsK KPSS*, a journal devoted to Gorbachev's dishonest attempt to attack Stalin by declaring that no conspiracies ever existed.

Thanks to the publication of PiLT2 we now have additional information about Ol'berg and his activities that generally corroborates what Getty wrote. The first mention of Ol'berg and his conspiracy in this volume comes not from Ezhov but from Iagoda, at that time still the commissar of Internal Affairs (= head of the NKVD). These documents are from the NKVD archive, where materials gathered by Ezhov, who was not yet head of the NKVD, might not have been filed.

On February 28, 1936, Iagoda sent to Stalin an interrogation of Ivan Kuz'mich Fedotov, a Party member, clandestine Trotskyist, and head of the Gorky Pedagogical Institute. Fedotov confessed that he had hired Ol'berg as a teacher after Ol'berg had approached him in mid-August, 1935, and had made it clear to him that he had been sent by "the old man" (*starik*), the name Trotskyists called Trotsky, and had told Fedotov about the latter's ties with other Trotskyists.

Fedotov continued:

> When I asked him who he was this unknown person said his name was Valentin Ol'berg and told me that he had arrived in the USSR illegally on a false Honduran passport with **assignments from Trotsky, whose emissary he was.**
>
> To my question whether he had any contacts in Gorky V. Ol'berg told me that he had first sent his brother Pavel Ol'berg, an engineer and a Trotskyist, to Gorky at the end of 1934, in case he needed to explain his arrival in Gorky by the desire to visit his brother.
>
> Valentin Ol'berg told me that among his assignments was to contact the Trotskyist organization and **really** prepare and carry out the murder of Stalin as ordered by Trotsky. (205)

As we stated above, aside from Ezhov's report of June 1935 this is the first mention of terrorist goals in this collection of documents. It is also confirmation of Ol'berg's own confessions which apparently began "a month after his arrest."[23]

As we have already seen, Fedotov testified that he had learned in 1933 from Kurt Miuller that Trotsky had given the order to murder Stalin (206). We also saw above that Fedotov said that in 1933 he had told Miuller that there was a "Trotskyist terrorist organiza-

---

23 See Izv. TsK KPSS No.8, 1989, p. 82.

tion" in Gorky. The word "really" (*real'no*) which Fedotov said that Ol'berg had used probably reflects the fact that this organization had not yet done anything to fulfill its task of killing Stalin.

Getty continued:

> His [Olberg's] wife testified that Ol'berg had received money and false passports from Trotsky's son Sedov and other Trotskyists in Paris and Prague. (190)

Getty must have seen this in an archival document as it is not in the issue of *Izvestiia TsK KPSS* he cites in the same note. The present volume, PiLT2, contains a single interrogation of Ol'berg's wife Betti, dated April 26, 1936. It contains a number of important matters.

For one thing it states that Betti Ol'berg was a Honduran citizen. In fact she was a German citizen. Further interrogations of Betti Ol'berg and of other Trotskyists, revealed that she and her husband bought the false Honduran passports with the combined help of the Nazi Gestapo and of Trotsky's son Leon Sedov. Clearly the investigation had not discovered this fact at the time of this interrogation. We now have more interrogations of Valentin Ol'berg, Betti Ol'berg, and other Trotskyists, and will examine them in a future study.

Here are some excerpts from the interrogation of Betti Ol'berg in the volume. It is clearly not the one seen by Getty since it does not discuss the obtaining of false passports and money.

> In reality Kurt Rovel, whom I knew to be a Trotskyist, was also connected in Trotskyist work while still in Berlin with my husband Valentin Ol'berg, and had come to the USSR at the beginning of October, 1935, with Trotskyist assignments.
>
> Kurt Rovel was in contact at that time with me and with the Trotskyist Fella Slomowitz. Fella Slomowitz was in turn in contact with Sedov.

Fella Slomowitz was assigned by Sedov to send Kurt Rovel to the Soviet Union with instructions to contact my husband Valentin Ol'berg in Gorky, Karl Boshtedt in Moscow, and Gurevich in Leningrad. Kurt Rovel was supposed to alert all three men in Sedov's name to the necessity of carefully organizing and carrying out terrorist acts against Stalin in Moscow and Zhdanov in Leningrad.

The terrorist act against Stalin was to be prepared, according to Sedov's instructions, by the terrorist group in Gorky headed by Valentin Ol'berg and by persons connected to Karl Boshtedt in Moscow.

Gurevich and the terrorists connected to him in Leningrad were to prepare the terrorist act against Zhdanov.

The murders of Stalin and Zhdanov were intended for the May Day demonstrations of 1935. Kurt Rovel was supposed to alert Ol'berg, Boshtedt and Gurevich about this. (251)

In a confession of April 25, 1935, Mark L'vovich Elin, Party Secretary of the town of Dzerzhinsk in the Gorky region, admitted to obtaining a job for Ol'berg. Evidently this means that Fedotov had to get Party approval for Ol'berg since the latter was to teach the history of the revolutionary movement.[24]

This volume also contains one interrogation of Pavel Ol'berg dated May 5, 1936. He was Valentin Ol'berg's brother and a chemist also employed in Gorky.

Question: When did Valentin Ol'berg join the German Communist Party?

Answer: In about 1928.

---

[24] Russian Wikipedia page on Ol'berg at
https://ru.wikipedia.org/wiki/Ольберг,_Валентин_Павлович

Question: And the Trotskyist organization?

Answer: From 1929 to 1931-32, that is until he was expelled from the Party, he carefully concealed his contact with Trotsky and Sedov. He was expelled after it was discovered that he was a Trotskyist. ...

Question: What were Valentin Ol'berg's political views before joining the Communist Party, that is before he finished gymnasium in Brunswick (*Braunshveig*)?

Answer: He was a confirmed monarchist...

Question: How long did Ol'berg live in Prague?

Answer: He lived in Prague from the summer of 1933 to the end of 1934. About that time he obtained a Honduran passport and, as I have stated in my earlier confessions, he went to the USSR in order to organize a terrorist act against Stalin, upon the instructions that he had received from Leon Sedov.

Question: Did he go directly to the USSR from Prague?

Answer: No, at first he went to Berlin, where he remained for 2-3 months, and then from Berlin he went to the USSR ...

Question: According to your confession, first, V. Ol'berg did not return to Germany in 1933 because he feared repression. Second, he lived in Prague as a political emigrant from Germany. Why did he then go from Prague to Berlin again? We ask you to tell the truth.

Answer: I admit that my confessions were untruthful. I concealed from the investigation the fact that I knew that **Valentin Ol'berg had contact with the German secret police (Gestapo)**.

Question: Who told you about this?

Answer: Valentin Ol'berg informed me.

Question: Why did he tell you?

Answer: When Valentin Ol'berg arrived in the USSR in March, 1935, I asked him repeatedly in conversations with him why he was not fearful of returning to Berlin from Prague. At first he was silent about this, answered me with empty phrases such as "you will know everything in time." At that time, as I have said in previous confessions, I was actively helping V. Ol'berg to prepare a terrorist act, bringing him a weapon from Gorky to Moscow, and Valentin Ol'berg treated me with great trust. One time when I asked V. Ol'berg again how it was that he risked to go to Berlin and was not afraid for his wife Betti who was even then in Berlin, **he told me that he had ties to the Gestapo** ...

Question: Relate in detail everything that Valentin Ol'berg told you.

Answer: He told me the following: Soon after the fascists came to power in 1933 he was called to the Gestapo. During the fairly lengthy interrogation and after threats of a severe beating and of then being sent to a concentration camp Valentin Ol'berg confessed in detail about how Trotsky and Sedov were sending him to the USSR for underground work, they offered him to collaborate with the Gestapo, and he agreed.

Question: What assignment did Valentin Ol'berg receive from the Gestapo?

Answer: The Gestapo confirmed Leon Sedov's assignment about the necessity of travelling to the USSR to make contact with the Trotskyist underground. After he had completed this assignment Valentin Ol'berg was to receive further instructions from the Gestapo ...

Question: What else?

Answer: During his first trip to the USSR in 1933 Valentin Ol'berg was not able to contact the Trotskyist organization and get himself settled in the USSR. **Then he went to Prague, from where he confirmed his contact with the Gestapo. When he received the assignment from Sedov in 1934 to go to the USSR in order to prepare a terrorist act against Stalin, he informed the Gestapo about it.** Then he received an assignment from the Gestapo to accept this assignment [from Sedov] and before he went to the USSR to go to Berlin for instructions.

Question: Who helped V. Ol'berg obtain a Honduran passport in Berlin?

Answer: The Gestapo helped him get the passport. He received the money to buy the passport, the sum of 13,000 Czech crowns, from Leon Sedov. Besides that, before his trip to the USSR he also obtained money from the Gestapo. He did not tell me how much he received from the Gestapo. (274-5)

In his interrogation of May 18, 1936 already referred to above Gurevich admitted that he had told the Gestapo that he was a member of the Trotskyist organization and was in contact with Sedov, Ol'berg, and others. When the Gestapo questioned him about their plan to organize terror Gurevich told him that Ol'berg had already entered the USSR and that others were to follow. Then the Gestapo proposed that he also collaborate with them. (289)

Gurevich revealed that the underground Trotskyist group also planned to assassinate Andrei Zhdanov, who had replaced the murdered Sergei Kirov as First Secretary of the Leningrad Party.

I was cautioned by the Gestapo employee that as someone directly connected with the terrorist plot I must not have direct contact with the couriers who arrived in the USSR. This contact would be maintained through Frida Grebe. ... Through Grebe, and in connection with my as-

signments, I also gave to the Gestapo information about
the preparation of the Trotskyist organization in Leningrad for a terrorist act against Zhdanov. (290)

Trotskyist Terror

During 1936 the number of underground oppositionists uncovered and arrested by the NKVD increased dramatically as more
and more of those arrested named others. Many of these arrested
oppositionists admitted that they were involved in terrorist – assassination – conspiracies. We will cite some examples here.

As we have seen, it was in late May, 1936, that Birkengof confessed
that in February, 1933, Gaven had told him that the "forcible *ustranenie*" (removal) of Stalin was the only possible course of action. In the confession of May 27, 1936,[25] cited above Moisei N.
Iakovlev admitted that the Trotskyist and Zinovievist underground
were united in Leningrad. He further admitted involvement in terror plots:

> Kamenev came to Leningrad in June, 1934. Kamenev and
> I were connected by our mutual counterrevolutionary
> activity in the Zinovievist organization and I went to him
> to tell him about the situation in the Leningrad organiza-
> tion and to get from Kamenev directives for future work.

> Kamenev listened to me and discussed with me the
> situation in the Leningrad organization and then gave
> me the decision of the center about organizing struggle
> against the Party and government leaders by means of
> terror.

> He asked me what I thought about this and when he had
> received my positive reply he made a direct proposal
> about the necessity of preparing a terrorist act against
> Kirov in Leningrad and told me that at the same time the

---

[25] This interrogation is also printed in Lubianka 1922-1936, pp. 759-763.

> Moscow organization was preparing an attempt on Sta-
> lin ...

> Kamenev told me that under the present circumstances
> the only possible method of struggle against Stalin was
> terror. Any other avenue of struggle, Kamenev said,
> would inevitably mean that they would smash us. The
> only chance for success lay in terror. For this reason,
> while we still had the forces, we had to use this last re-
> maining means. (304)

Iakovlev went on to discuss the plan to kill Kirov, saying that
Kamenev had asked him directly whether he was in touch with the
underground Zinovievist group of Kotolynov-Rumiantsev in Leningrad. This was the group that did carry out the murder of Kirov
on December 1, 1934. (305)

On June 23, 1936, Efim A. Dreitser, later a defendant in the August,
1936, "Zinoviev-Kamenev" Moscow Trial, confessed that in 1934
Mrachkovskii, one of the Trotskyist leaders and also a defendant in
the same trial, had directed him to organize "battle groups"
(*boevikh grupp*) to prepare terrorist acts against Party leaders. The
trial transcript states that this happened in the spring of 1933, not
in 1934, but otherwise has all this information (August 19, 1936,
evening session). This may be the reason these confessions are not
included in the present volume.

We have cited a number of other terror confessions by Trotskyists
in other chapters in the present book.

Chapter 2. Trotsky and the Nazis, Fascists, and Ukrainian Nationalists

Introduction

We have seen that there is a lot of evidence that the documents in PiLT2 are not the result of fabrication but represent what those under interrogation chose to testify. Soviet authorities did not attempt to force these prisoners to lie.

In *Trotsky's 'Amalgams'* and *The Moscow Trials as Evidence* we have devoted a lot of attention to verifying the Moscow Trials testimony. We found that the Moscow Trials testimony is "genuine" – a shorthand way of saying that whenever we can check a statement made by a defendant in the Moscow Trials against independent evidence, it turns out that the defendant's statement represents what he chose to say. Usually they stated the truth. Where we can show that defendants lied, in each case they did so in order to make themselves appear *less* guilty, not more.

In the previous chapter we studied the materials in PiLT2 with a view to checking and verifying the statements made there whenever possible. The result was the same: these materials are "genuine" in that they reflect what those who made them wished to say. We have excellent evidence that the NKVD was not fabricating them in any way.

Therefore, to the extent that Piatakov's testimony in his Statement to Ezhov agrees with statements in PiLT2 we can conclude that Piatakov's statements in that document are also genuine – that they represent what Piatakov chose to testify. We analyze Piatakov's Statement separately in another chapter of the present book.

"Against Stalin All Means Are Good"

In his confession of October 17, 1936 D.I. Matveev said that at a meeting of the Rights in the fall of 1932 (314) Chesnokov, a fellow Rightist, had stated "against Stalin all means are good." (315) This is what Trotsky told Piatakov during their meeting in Norway:

> "Remember, **in this struggle all means are good** and every ally is useful. Here we must not sand on ceremony and live by old memories." (LD 270)

The Rights were in the political bloc with the Trotskyists.

Opposition Ties with German Firms by Trotsky's Order

In his confession of October 14, 1936 Aleksei Aleksandrovich Shestov, later a defendant at the Second Moscow Trial, the "Piatakov-Radek" trial, of January 1937, stated that he worked with only one German firm, Deilmann (Frölich-Klüpfel-Deilmann) "on director orders from Sedov and Smirnov." (331). Deilmann was to maintain contact between the Trotskyists in the Kuzbass, where Shestov worked as an engineer, and the Trotskyists abroad.

This was confirmed by the interrogation of Mikhail Stepanovich Stroilov of October 16, 1936, who had been told that the Deilmann firm "helped the Trotskyists abroad in their work." (350; 353) He had learned in Moscow that Iurii Piatakov favored the German firms "Borsig" and "Demag" even though their products were much more expensive than those of other firms.

> From talks in Berlin with different comrades: Zubkov of Soiuzugol' in the Donbass; Nekrasov of Soiuzzoloto; with an engineer from Solikamsk who was working under the direction of a commission from Glavkhim—I can't recall his name but I know him very well by his face – I learned that such German firms as "Borzig" and "Demag" for some reason enjoyed Piatakov's special favor. These firms received large orders for the delivery to the Soviet

Union of compressors, cranes, compacting machinery, pumps, etc., at prices no less than 25% above the bids of other, no less solid firms. The compressors of the "Borzig" firm were 20% more expensive than those of other German firms. They seemed very strange to many people, and some were even indignant.

In one official meeting in Piatakov's office in Berlin one of the officials said that "Borzig" and "Demag" were very expensive firms and couldn't we avoid them. Piatakov nervously interrupted him and with malice threw out the following phrase: "You do not understand a thing. You forget that the most important thing is quality."

I remember that one engineer from Solikamsk complained to me that the orders for lifting machines were given exclusively to the "Demag" firm by Piatakov's directive and that he very much regretted throwing the 20%-25% of the cost of the lifting machines out the window, and said: "I don't understand why Piatakov has this inexplicable and strange love for the "Demag" firm. (333)

This corresponds to what Piatakov revealed about the origins of this arrangement.

Also in 1931 about 3 weeks after my first meeting with Sedov I.N. Smirnov told me that despite the fact that we had agreed not to meet, Sedov wanted me to meet with him again and that he, Sedov, would await me the following day at the same place and time.

The next day I went to the same café. This time our talk was brief. Sedov immediately raised the question of money. At first he said, "You understand, Yuri Leonidovich, that for this work we need money. Can you get money?" I answered that I had no possibility at that time. Then Sedov said that he had such possibilities but that it would be hard to do it without my help. He wanted me to give as many orders as possible to the firms "Demag" and "Borsig" and not to fuss over prices; he himself would arrange with the firms about these conditions. **"Obviously you will have to pay too much, but the money will go for our work,** since we have some kind of agreement with representatives of these firms." I did this. (LD 245)

In *Trotsky's 'Amalgams'* and in *The Moscow Trials As Evidence* we quoted from American mining engineer John D. Littlepage's writings in his articles in the *Saturday Evening Post* and his book *In Search of Soviet Gold*. Littlepage refers to and thereby confirms Piatakov's confession. For example, Littlepage wrote:

Among other things, the commission in Berlin was buying several dozen mine hoists, ranging from 100 to 1,000 horse-power. . . . The commission asked for quotations on the basis of pfennigs per kilogram. After some discussion, the German concerns later mentioned in Pyatakov's confession reduced their prices between 5 and 6 pfennigs per kilogram. When I studied these proposals, I discovered that the firms had substituted cast-iron bases weighing several tons for the light steel provided in the specifications, which would reduce the cost of production per kilogram, but increase the weight, and therefore the cost to purchaser.[1]

Littlepage confirms Piatakov's "sweetheart deals" with the German firms. His account is the strongest kind of confirmation of Piatakov's testimony.

Trotsky and the Germans

Piatakov made it clear that Trotsky felt it was essential to make agreements with Germany and Japan if the Opposition was to have

---

[1] John D. Littlepage with Demaree Bess, "Red Wreckers in Russia," *SEP* January 1, 1938, p. 53 col. 4.

any chance either of retaining power, if it managed to seize power through its own efforts, or of taking power, if its own efforts proved insufficient to seize power.

> Trotsky said that in the struggle with Stalin we can in no way ignore relations between governments. Once we understand that Stalin's scheme of building socialism in one country is an empty and dangerous scheme, then we too in our struggle with Stalin must not slide to the position of "one country."

> This struggle inevitably is interconnected with our relations with capitalist states. It would be stupid to think that it is possible to assume power without securing a benevolent attitude of the most important capitalist governments, especially of the most aggressive ones, such as the present governments of Germany and Japan. It is completely essential even now to have contact and agreements with these governments. He, Trotsky, has taken the necessary steps in this regard. He demanded from Radek and Sokol'nikov, who had the requisite possibilities, to put out feelers for the essential contact along these lines with the official representatives of these powers, and to support whatever he, Trotsky, was carrying out in practice.

> In this connection, as I seem to remember, Radek told me about some kind of conversations of his with Germans (I cannot recall the names of these Germans), from whom it was clear that Trotsky had made some arrangements with the German government. (LD 258)

> Of course, to reach agreements with Germany alone would be risky, since without a corresponding English and French counterweight Germany would put feet on the table and it would be very tough for us. Therefore in his practical steps he, Trotsky, is carrying out simultaneous preparatory work in different directions.

> Concerning Germany, there matters are essentially set-
> tled:

> He, Trotsky, had secured a favorable attitude of the
> German fascist government in case the bloc comes to
> power.

> Of course this favorable attitude was not due to any spe-
> cial sympathy towards the bloc but to real interests.

> At the basis of the agreement lies an appeal to the Ger-
> man government to help the bloc come to power. On his
> part Trotsky promised in the event of coming to power
> to make very concrete concessions, stipulated in ad-
> vance, to Germany. (LD 267)

In his October 16, 1936 interrogation Stroilov testified that he had
worked with German agents since 1932. This work was coordinated with Shestov, for the Trotskyists.

> Sommeregger suggested that I put Shebesto in contact
> with the Trotskyist Shestov, who was supposed to give
> practical help to German diversionist agents on the
> spot... I did not personally tell Sommeregger and Fless
> about my talks with Shestov. It was Sommeregger who
> told me Shestov was a Trotskyist. (353)

On October 21, 1936, Vladimir Mikhailovich Andreev was interrogated by NKVD investigators. A former Tsarist officer and mining
engineer, Andreev was a member of a fascist organization that
worked with Trotskyists. He had been recruited into this fascist
organization by a certain Peshekhonov, an engineer whom Andreev identified as having been involved in the Shakhty affair. A
certain Peshekhonov is indeed mentioned three times in the pub-

lished materials on the Shakhty trial of 1928.[2] Andreev described Peshekhonov as a fervent admirer of Hitler.

> He told me that our organization was founded by the Germans and that all our subversive work was carried out under direct orders that came from Germany. Then he told me that the Germans did not only organize and direct our work but participated in it themselves actively and practically. "Who are working for the Germans," said Peshekhonov, "for today Germany is the only country we can rely on as a force opposing the communist dictatorship. We must do whatever we can to help turn this opposition into active invasion." (375)

In September, 1936, Peshekhonov told him about a setback suffered by his fascist organization:

> In our counterrevolutionary group were, in addition, the following persons: the director of the "Central" mine Noskov, the chief of the 6th section of the mine Shubin, and the chief of the 4th section, Kurov. ...
>
> Question: What did Peshekhonov tell you about them?
>
> Answer: He said that it would now be harder for me to do my work since a very hard blow had been dealt against our c-r group. I asked: What blow? Peshekhonov answered that while I had been on leave Noskov and Shubin were no longer in our group and Kurov had to temporarily stop all c-r work because he was also under suspicion. I was very surprised since, hearing the names Noskov, Shubin, and Kurov, I recognized them as members of the Party. **I said to Peshekhonov: "They are communists, aren't they?" Peshekhonov answered me: "They are not communists, but Trotskyists, and communists and Trotskyists are as different from**

---

[2] *Shakhtinskii protsess 1928 g. Podgotovka, provedenie, Itogi. Kniga 1.* M.: ROSSPEN, 2011, pp. 400, 407, 408.

one another as day from night." I still did not understand Peshekhonov and asked him to explain.

Then Peshekhonov told me that the Trotskyists played an especially active role in our organization. In their hostility and vengeance against the Party they would stop at nothing and were connected with our organization through Stroilov and together with us were carrying out an active role against the Party and against construction in the country. Then he told me that during my leave (I had been on leave between the beginning of June and the end of August the Trotskyist activity of Noskov and Shubin had been exposed and both had been expelled from the Party and removed from work. Kurov was also in danger and in the interest of self-preservation he had to temporarily remove himself from c-r work. (377)

Andreev went on to describe some of the sabotage carried out by this joint fascist-Trotskyist group, including the following:

Question: The explosion of September 23, as a result of which 9 miners were killed and 15 injured – was that committed by your fascist-Trotskyist group?

Answer: Yes, it's true, the explosion of September 23 was the act of our fascist-Trotskyist group. (379)

This is consistent with Piatakov's testimony about the Trotskyist activities in the Kuzbass:

3/ To Shestov, whom I did not know personally but had heard that he was a reliable person, I told Trotsky's policies, although I knew that he already knew everything from I.N. Smirnov.

To Shestov I entrusted the resurrection of the organization in the Kuzbass. I brought to Shestov's attention that there was one of Trotsky's loyal men – N.I. Muralov, that Vladimir Kossior was also there somewhere, and that he should, while observing the necessary caution, see who of the Trotskyists in Siberia could be drawn into the organization. I told Shestov that the basic thrust of his work in the Kuzbass was sabotage and that for this work he would have to attract not only Trotskyists but also persons of anti-Soviet orientation from the engineering and technical personnel. (LD 244)

The Trotskyists' Bloc with Ukrainian Nationalists

On November 15, 1934 Pavel Postyshev, first secretary of the Communist Party of Khar'kov city and oblast' (province) committee and second secretary of the C.P. of the Ukraine, and Vsevolod Balitskii, Commissar of Internal Affairs of the Ukrainian SSR, sent a letter to Stalin concerning Iurii Mikhailovich Kotsiubinskii, former official of the Council of People's Commissars, former Commissar of Agriculture, former Chair of the State Planning Agency of the Ukrainian SSR and – important in this context – supposedly a former Trotskyist. Kotsiubinskii was again under arrest and charged with still being a Trotskyist.

In this letter Postyshev and Balitskii quote from the interrogation of the Trotskyist David Borisovich Naumov-Lekakh, who stated that

> [T]he bloc of the Trotskyist organization in the Ukraine with the Ukrainian nationalist-deviationist elements meant that, in practice, from the very beginning of the Trotskyist organization, that the Trotskyists waged no struggle against the Ukrainian nationalist-deviationist elements, but rather supported and defended them as far as they could... (120)

This information is repeated in more detail by the Trotskyist Boris Samoilovich Rappoport-Dar'in, in an interrogation of December 21, 1934. What follows is a short passage from this lengthy testimony:

> In its practical work during the period 1931-1934, the counterrevolutionary Trotskyist organization was in a

> bloc with the Ukrainian-nationalist elements, with Right antiparty groups, and also used however it could the remnants of the Menshevist organization. (135)

Naumov went on to say that Kotsiubinskii had told him that collaboration between the Ukrainian nationalists in the Party and the Trotskyists had gone on since 1926-27. (136) The text of the interrogation of Naumov, attached to the letter, gives much more detail about this Trotskyist-Ukrainian nationalist bloc. (143-146). The Trotskyist bloc with the Ukrainian nationalists is also briefly discussed in the interrogation of Elia Aronovich Shteinberg of November 26, 1934. (165)

In his interrogation of February 28, 1936, Trotskyist Ivan Kuz'mich Fedotov said that in the Ukraine he had been in contact with a certain Mukhin, a member of a Trotskyist group in Kiev. According to Fedotov:

> Mukhin told me that he was a member in Kiev of a Trotskyist terrorist group that carried out work together with Ukrainian Nationalists. (209)

On May 3, 1936 Nikander Emel'ianovich Mil'gevskii, a Trotskyist, testified that he maintained contact with the Trotskyist group in Khar'kov through a certain Gofman.

> Question: What concretely did Gofman tell you about the work of the Trotskyist organization in the Ukraine?

> Answer: When I met with Gofman in the spring of 1935 he told me that between the Trotskyist organization and the Ukrainian nationalist organization headed by Nyrchuk there was an agreement on a platform of joint struggle against Soviet power. (277)

Piatakov testified that in 1931, after meeting with Sedov in Berlin and agreeing to return to clandestine Trotskyist activity, he had returned to the USSR and taken "concrete steps to resurrect a

Trotskyist organization in the Ukraine," forming a Trotskyist center, of which Kotsiubinskii was a member. (LD 243-4)[3]

During his secret visit to Trotsky in Norway in December, 1935, Trotsky had outlined to Piatakov the concessions that he, Trotsky, had been obliged to make in return for German support, one of which was as follows:

> In the event that the "nationalist forces" of the Ukraine should want to separate from the U.S.S.R. — not to oppose this. (LD 268)

In 1939 and 1940 Trotsky published three essays defending Ukrainian independence. We note them in the chapter in the present volume on Piatakov's Statement to Ezhov. Since at that time no left or socialist Ukrainian independence movement existed, it is obvious that Trotsky's essays were a signal to Germany, who sponsored the only Ukrainian nationalist movements of any kind – far-right, violently pro-Nazi organizations that committed atrocities on an enormous scale during and after World War 2 -- that he, Trotsky, could be counted on to preserve his pro-German stance on this issue.

Opposition Plans to Take Advantage of Economic Difficulties

On December 26, 1936, Naumov told investigators:

> At the end of 1931, Kotsiubinskii told me that he and the leading Trotskyists in Moscow with whom he was talking, believed that the economic difficulties which at that time were appearing in the areas of industrialization and agriculture ... confirmed the erroneousness of the Party's policy and the necessity of organizing the Trot-

---

[3] Passages marked "LD" plus a number indicate the page ("list dela", page of the file) of the copy of Piatakov's statement in the Central Archive of the FSB (= Federal Security Service), where NKVD materials are stored. Complete details at the beginning of the text of Piatakov's Statement to Ezhov in the Appendix.)

skyist forces for struggle against the Party, and there must be no delay in forming a Trotskyist organization. (143)

Naumov repeated this reliance of the Trotskyists and Ukrainian nationalists on economic difficulties several more times (145-6).

In an April 26, 1936, confession Zinovievist and member of the Zinovievist-Trotskyist bloc Efrem Mikhailovich Bocharov said that the bloc had counted on the USSR's economic difficulties in the early 1930s to cause the Soviet government to fall and return its leaders to power.

> While Bakaev was in Gorky the activists of the organiza-tion regularly met in his apartment – Furtichev, me, Bo-charov, Ol'khovskii, Gorokhov, and others. At these get-togethers we discussed, in a Trotskyist spirit, the politics and actions of the Party and Soviet government. We paid much attention to collectivization. We counted upon the failure of the Party's policies in the first place on this front. Bakaev put before the organization as the main task the unification and preparation of cadres of Trot-skyists and Zinovievists who, after the failure of the Party's policies, could take power into its own hands in an organized manner and bring Trotsky, Zinoviev, and Kamenev to the leadership of the country. (253)

Bocharov went on to say that by 1934 the success of the Party's economic program led the Zinovievist-Trotskyist bloc not to drop its opposition but instead to turn towards violence – "terror."

> In January 1934, when I was at Bakaev's he told me that the situation in the country had changed dramatically. Through a slanderous evaluation of the means by which the Party and Soviet government had achieved the reali-zation of the line it had laid out, Bakaev conceded that the basic difficulties had been overcome by the Soviet government and that now we cannot any longer hope for the failure of the Party and the Soviet government.

> Bakaev emphasized that the new situation did not mean
> that our organization should stop its activity. He said
> only that the methods of struggle against the Party must
> be changed. He said that the Zinovievists and Trotskyists
> could count on success only if the Party leadership was
> removed (*ustraneno*) by force. In this connection he
> proposed as the basic task of the Zinovievist-Trotskyist
> organization a terrorist struggle against the Party lead-
> ership. (254)

In his confession of October 20, 1936, D.I. Matveev echoed these
views:

> Until 1932, we, the leadership of the organization of
> Rightists (both the nationwide [*soiuznyi*] and Moscow
> centers) relied principally on the difficulties that the
> country was experiencing. We hoped that the leadership
> of the Party would not overcome these difficulties and
> on this basis we considered that our main task was to
> preserve our cadres through duplicity [i.e. false capitula-
> tion] so that we could then step forward when the right
> time came.
>
> I must admit, however, that even during this period cer-
> tain members of our organization manifested putschist
> attitudes.
>
> ... At the end of 1932, when the Rightists were convinced
> that reliance on difficulties was no good, that the Party
> had dealt brilliantly with all the difficulties, Uglanov, in
> the name of the central group, directly set before us, the
> members of the Moscow center of Rightists, the question
> of the necessity to turn towards terrorist methods of
> struggle against the Party leadership and against Stalin
> in the first place. (314)

This is the same reason cited by defendants at the First Moscow
Trial of August 1936. For example, Reingol'd, one of the defendants, testified as follows:

Reingold: In 1932, Zinoviev, at Kamenev's apartment, in the presence of a number of members of the united Trotskyite-Zinovievite centre argued in favor of resorting to terror as follows: although terror is incompatible with Marxism, at the present moment these considerations must be abandoned. There are no other methods available of fighting the leaders of the Party and the Government at the present time. Stalin combines in himself all the strength and firmness of the present Party leadership. Therefore Stalin must be put out of the way in the first place. Kamenev enlarged on this theory and said that the former methods of fighting, namely, attempts to win the masses, combinations with the leaders of the Rightists, **and banking on economic difficulties, have failed. That is why the only method of struggle available is terroristic acts** against Stalin and his closest comrades-in-arms, Kirov, Voroshilov, Kaganovich, Orjonikidze, Postyshev, Kossior and the others. (Report 1936, 55).

To judge from the confessions quoted above it was sometime in early 1932 that the Oppositionists realized that the Soviet government's economic program of collectivization and industrialization was not going to lead to collapse, the discrediting of the leadership, and the demand to return the former Opposition leaders to power.

In his statement to Ezhov of September 19-20, 1936, Piatakov stated that Trotsky had already come to this same conclusion by the summer of 1931, when his son Leon Sedov met with Piatakov. Trotsky had concluded that the Opposition would now have to rely upon other strategies such as terror and the help of foreign capitalist states.

After that Sedov went on to outline what he called "the new methods of struggle."

Trotsky rules out any possibility at the present stage of any mass anti-Stalin movement. Stalin has succeeded in surviving the difficulties and we must frankly admit that we have missed the time.

"If we waste time now we will definitively lose all our cadres, and that will be the death of us.

For that reason now at the tip of the needle must be put

1) the terrorist struggle of tacitly conspiratorial groups against the main leaders of the party and government 2) active opposition against all the practical work of the party and government and 3) the discrediting in every possible way of Stalin's undertakings, especially on the economic front ... Just as Smirnov had done, Sedov again mentioned briefly one fundamental position of Trotsky's ... "We cannot," Sedov transmitted Trotsky's views, "regard our struggle in an isolated manner. To keep our struggle in one country is just as absurd as Stalin's desire to build socialism in one country. Therefore we cannot swear off questions of relations between states and relations with capitalist states."

... At that time Sedov did not go into more detail about this question. It is possible that Trotsky specially instructed Sedov to only mention this but not to go into any details. (LD 241-2. Emphasis added)

Nikolai Ivanovich Muralov

A leading Trotskyist in the 1920s, Muralov had been expelled from the Party in December, 1927, presumably in connection with his participation in the Opposition demonstration on the tenth anniversary of the Bolshevik Revolution, and a letter to the Congress, which he cosigned with Khristian Rakovsky and with which Karl Radek associated himself, in which the signatories both renounced factionalism and insisted that they would continue to argue for their views within the Party. (XV s"ezd 1247, 1317, 1338)

According to the biographical information now available Muralov wrote Stalin twice, in December, 1935, and January, 1936, renouncing Trotskyism and asking for reinstatement in the Party. Documents in PiLT2 show that by February, 1936, Muralov was already named as a leading Trotskyist in the Kuzbass. On February 21, 1936, Vasilii Nikolaevich Rakov, a Trotskyist, stated in a confession that after his release from a political isolator he had spoken with Muralov in August, 1935, to get further instructions in Trotskyist activity. (234) As we have seen, the Opposition's political activity continued unabated in the political isolators.

In an interrogation of March 15, 1936, another Trotskyist, Viktor Ignat'evich Demchenko, also said that from August, 1935, he had been actively recruited by Muralov, whom he had previously known to be still a Trotskyist. (236-7) On the strength of these and perhaps other accusations Muralov was arrested on April 17, 1936.[4] Thereafter Muralov was named as one of the Trotskyist leaders in the Kuzbass area by Shestov[5]

In his statement of December 19-20, 1936, Piatakov identified Muralov several times as one of the leading Trotskyists in the Kuzbass.

> 3/ To Shestov, whom I did not know personally but had heard that he was a reliable person, I told Trotsky's policies, although I knew that he already knew everything from I.N. Smirnov.

> To Shestov I entrusted the resurrection of the organization in the Kuzbass. I brought to Shestov's attention that there was one of Trotsky's loyal men – N.I. Muralov ... (LD 244)

---

[4] See the Russian Wikipedia page on Muralov at
https://ru.wikipedia.org/wiki/Муралов,_Николай_Иванович and the
biographical page at the online biographical dictionary at
http://www.hrono.ru/biograf/bio_m/muralov_ni.php
[5] Interrogations of Shestov of October 14, 1936 and October 16, 1936, PiLT2 329 and 339.

> I said that I did not have detailed information about the work of the Trotskyist center (Smirnov-Mrachkovskii) outside Moscow, but that in carrying out Trotsky's directive we had formed a center of the Trotskyist organization in the Ukraine, which was in contact with me personally. This center already had peripheral groups and was setting about preparing terrorist acts. I also reported that work on the creation of a Western Siberian center had begun, where Muralov led the active work ... (LD 248)

According to Piatakov, during his meeting with Trotsky in Norway in December, 1935, Trotsky spoke highly of Muralov:

> About Muralov Trotsky expressed his satisfaction, that he was one of the few who had never yielded his position and was actively working. (LD 270)

Muralov was one of the defendants in the Second Moscow Trial, the "Piatakov-Radek" trial, of January, 1937. At trial he testified that I.N. Smirnov had informed him in 1931 about Trotsky's turn to terror. (1937 Trial 216-7)

Conclusion

In the present chapter we have shown that the materials in PiLT2 can be employed as a check by which we can verify Piatakov's Statement to Ezhov of December 19-20, 1936. The PiLT2 materials do indeed confirm many of Piatakov's affirmations in his Statement.

This constitutes the best evidence we know of that confirms that Piatakov really did fly secretly to confer with Trotsky in December, 1935, as he testified during the second Moscow Trial of January, 1937.

Chapter 3. Defeatism, Terrorism, Assassination, Collaboration

On December 21, 1934 Trotskyist Rappoport-Dar'in testified that the leadership of the Trotskyist group supported Trotsky's "Clemenceau" position:

> Among the members of the leading center the question of the tactics of the Trotskyist organization in the event of war was also discussed. All members of the leading center stood on the position of the well-known slogan of Trotsky's about the Clemenceau tactic, i.e. of not stopping the struggle against the leadership of the Party in the event of war, but of sharpening the struggle and using the war to overthrow the Party leadership. (136)

Trotsky had used the example of Clemenceau to justify continuing to attack the Soviet leadership during wartime as Clemenceau had criticized the French government in wartime because of France's poor leadership in the conduct of the war.[1] Clemenceau had taken the helm of the French state in November 1917 – had become both Prime Minister and Minister of War -- in the face of defeatism and conducted the war against the enemy with renewed vigor. These underground Trotskyists wanted the ouster of the Party and government leadership and their replacement by Trotsky and other oppositionists.

---

[1] See Trotsky's essay of September, 1927 titled "The 'Clémenceau Thesis' and the Party Regime"
https://www.marxists.org/archive/trotsky/1927/09/clemenceau.htm
A draft of the Russian original is at https://www.you-books.com/book/Yu-G-Felshtinskij/Kommunisticheskaya-Oppozicziya-V-Sssr-19231927-Tom It was formerly at
http://web.mit.edu/fjk/www/Trotsky/sochineniia/1927/19270924.html but appears to be there no longer.

But Trotsky's analogy was flawed. For Clemenceau the primary goal was not at all to gain office for himself, but to win the war. In the case of Trotsky and his supporters, it was the other way around. For Trotsky and his followers, anticipated war was to be welcomed as an opportunity to get rid of the Stalin leadership and take power for Trotsky and the Opposition.

A number of oppositionists testified that they welcomed the defeat of the USSR in a war with capitalist states. On January 13, 1933, Illarion Konstantinovich Gassiev, a Trotskyist, said:

> In a conversation with Dzhoev I said that if in the near future
>
> 1) "The Soviet Union is in a war, then the organization should take a defeatist position and organize support within the country for the side that invades the Soviet Union." (31)

Trotsky argued that this "Clemenceau thesis" was not really defeatism since its goal was not the defeat of the USSR but the replacement of its leadership in order to win a war that appeared in 1927 to be on the horizon. Presumably the Stalin leadership would have proven itself unable to defeat one or more invaders.

Thus the Zinovievist Vinogradov, as quoted by Ezhov in his report of June 1935 to the Central Committee Plenum, had testified:

> We proceeded from the position that war with the imperialist states, a war that would come sooner or later, and the situation within the country which would give rise to the war, will create favorable conditions for broad demonstrations with the demand of returning to the leadership of Zinoviev, Kamenev, and others of the Zinovievist movement. (186)

Piatakov testified that, in November, 1931, after his meetings with Sedov in Berlin and his return to the USSR, he had received through Shestov a letter from Trotsky himself. Among Trotsky's other instructions was one about defeatism:

4/ We must take the coming war into account and **oc-cupy in relation to the war an unconditionally de-featist position**, and by means of preliminary negotia-tions with governments of capitalist powers (also mak-ing use of the contradictions between them) guarantee for ourselves favorable relations in case of our coming to power as a result of the war. (LD 247)

Piatakov said that he had visited Trotsky in Norway in December, 1935. In January, 1936, Radek received a letter from Trotsky and shared its contents with Piatakov. According to Piatakov Trotsky repeated his insistence on defeatism:

As regards the war, L. D. Trotsky spoke of this very ex-plicitly. From his point of view, war is inevitable in the near future. In this war the defeat of the "Stalin govern-ment" was inevitable. **He, Trotsky, considered it com-pletely essential to take a markedly defeatist posi-tion in this war.**

Defeat in war would mean the downfall of the Soviet government and for this very reason Trotsky insisted upon the creation of cells in the army, in the broadening of contacts among the command staff. He proceeded from the position that defeat in war would create a fa-vorable opportunity in the army as well for the return of himself, Trotsky, to power. He considers that the bloc's coming into power can certainly be hastened by the de-feat of the U.S.S.R. in war.

Trotsky pointed out in this regard that especially, count-ing upon defeat in war, it was necessarily in advance to reach agreements with the appropriate bourgeois gov-ernments (I do not recall whether precisely only the governments of German and Japan were mentioned in this regard). It seemed to him that he would be able to reach agreements at the same time with opposing groupings of bourgeois governments and maneuver upon their contradictions. Trotsky understood that we

must not rely in a naked and open way upon agreement
with Germany and Japan, and therefore he gave a plan of
playing upon contradictions. (LD 258-9)

We may doubt whether, as Trotsky claimed, Stalin and the Soviet
leadership had maliciously misconstrued his remarks about Clemenceau. After all, Clemenceau had *not* been a defeatist, but the opposite. He had assumed power to *replace* leadership that he
viewed as defeatist. For Clemenceau it was French victory, not his
own coming to power, that was primary.

But Trotsky's position was not the same as Clemenceau's had
been. Trotsky and the Trotskyists meant the "Clemenceau thesis"
as a means by which Trotsky and the Opposition could return to
power, rather primarily as a tactic to snatch victory from defeat in
wartime. On the contrary, Trotsky and the Trotskyists welcomed
Soviet defeat. But this meant that Trotsky's position was no different from the "Stalin" interpretation of it -- a form of collaboration
with an invader -- treason.

Plans for a Coup

There are two references in PiLT2 to plans by Soviet Trotskyists
for a *coup d'état* against the Soviet government. One is in the
statement by Vasilii Ivanovich Dzhoev of January 2, 1933, which he
made to the Secret-Political Section of the OGPU in disclosing his
knowledge of Trotskyist activities. Dzhoev summarized what his
friend Gassiev had told him in 1931, including the following:

> Kozhennikov also takes part in the activities of our orga-
> nization, therefore, and there is also corresponding work
> going on. We think that our seizure of power will be car-
> ried out **without resort to armed force** – there in the
> center they are isolating the leadership and in general
> the whole POLITBURO. (26)

Assuming Dzhoev was telling the truth, Trotsky's plans must have
evolved over time. Three years later, on March 9, 1936, Trotskyist

Aleksandr Gavrilovich Kolodin confessed about plans for an armed *coup d'état* against the Soviet regime:

> The members of our counterrevolutionary group also discussed the question of the preparation of **an armed uprising** against the Soviet government. (216)

This last reference to plans for a *coup d'état* echo Trotsky's plans as related by Piatakov. During their December, 1935, meeting in Norway Trotsky insisted that a *coup d'état* was the only way the Opposition could come to power in the USSR. By late 1935, Trotsky was insisting on the maximum use of violence.

> Trotsky also expressed the same extreme degree of dissatisfaction during my report about the terrorist acts that were under preparation. "These are all preparations, just preparations! You are not dealing with this question seriously enough. Remember that **without a whole series of terrorist acts**, which must be carried out as soon as possible, the Stalin government cannot be overthrown. For this is a question of a *coup d'état*. A mass uprising, he said, is one thing, for which, evidently, there is no basis now, and a *coup d'état* is something else."

> "This is the difference, I note, that many do not understand. They are unaware that the methods of a *coup d'état* differ fundamentally from the methods of organizing a mass uprising. I stand now precisely on the position of a *coup d'état*... (LD 263)

Trotsky continued:

> "... It is clear that if in the very near future we are not successful by one means or another in carrying out a *coup d'état*, then a prolonged period will set in, years of the monstrous existence of the Stalin state, supported by its economic successes, by new politically inexperienced young cadre, who will consider this regime natural, to be taken for granted ... That means the first and main thing

is the implacable struggle with Stalin and his state. In this struggle we must employ everything, the sharpest methods of preparation for a *coup d'état* and, in the first place, terror, diversions, and sabotage. On this basis we must educate our cadre, and not on the basis of rotten conciliation and compromise, the tendencies to which I discern in my supporters who live in the Stalin state." (LD 264, 266)

Trotsky's Collaboration with Britain and France: Sokol'nikov's confession

We have already seen that on December 12, 1936, Sokol'nikov confessed that on April 13, 1934, he had been approached by Japanese Ambassador Tamekichi Ota, who told him about Trotsky's agreement with the Japanese government.[2] Ota was not named at the Second Moscow (Trotskyist Center) trial of January, 1937. The corresponding passage in Sokol'nikov's trial testimony was disguised in such a way that the country in question could not be identified.

> Sokolnikov: I had a conversation with Kamenev in the beginning of 1934. During this conversation Kamenev informed me about the defeatist position taken by Trotsky and about his own defeatist views. Incidentally, one definite result of this conversation was that Kamenev warned me that someone might approach me with inquiries.
>
> Vyshinsky: Who might do this?
>
> Sokolnikov: The diplomatic representative of a certain country.

---

[2] The passage in which Ota is named was first published in *Izvestiia TsK KPSS* 9 (1989), p. 45. It was reprinted in *Reabilitatsia. Politicheskie protsessy 30-50 kh godov* (Moscow, 1991), 228-9.

Vyshinsky: Kamenev warned you about this?

Sokolnikov: Yes, Kamenev warned me about this.

Vyshinsky: Did Kamenev tell you what inquiries would be addressed to you?

Sokolnikov: Yes, he told me that I would be asked for confirmation of the fact that the negotiations which were being carried on by Trotsky abroad were not being carried on by him in his own name, but that behind Trotsky there really was an organization of which he was the representative.

Vyshinsky: You were to confirm this if inquiries in this sense were addressed to you?

Sokolnikov: Yes.

Vyshinsky: Such a question was addressed to you?

Sokolnikov: Yes, in the middle of April after one of my official talks with the representative of a certain country with whom I had frequent meetings in connection with my official duties. The conversation took place after the official talk was over, when the interpreters had withdrawn to the neighbouring room. While I was showing my visitor to the door he asked me whether I knew that Trotsky had addressed certain proposals to his government. I confirmed that this fact was known to me. He asked further whether these proposals were serious. I confirmed this too. He asked whether this was my own personal opinion. I said that this was not only my opinion but that of my friends as well. I understood this question of his as a confirmation of the fact that the government of that country had really received Trotsky's proposal and wanted to make sure that Trotsky's proposals were really known to the organization and that Trotsky's right to conduct these negotiations was not disputed. (1937 Trial 148-9)

Sokol'nikov also told Piatakov about Ambassador Ota's approach to him. Piatakov only mentions Ota's name in the briefest manner, in passing, in his December 19-20, 1936, statement to Ezhov.

> Also, Sokol'nikov told me that **he had a talk with the Japanese, with Ota, I think**, from which it was also clear that Trotsky was carrying on negotiations with representatives of the Japanese government. (LD 257)

As we have pointed out, Trotsky had informed Sokol'nikov about his, Trotsky's, agreement with Hess, second only to Hitler in the Nazi Party. We have no testimony that any official of the German government confirmed this. Here, however, we have testimony that a representative of the Japanese government confirmed Trotsky's collaboration with Japan.

There is no reason to think that Piatakov said this out of any force or compulsion. It is excellent evidence that Sokol'nikov really told him this.

This, in turn, constitutes strong evidence that Trotsky had not simply lied about having contacts with the Japanese (perhaps to impress his followers) but that Trotsky really had collaborated with the Japanese. In a future work we will publish and study Khristian Rakovsky's detailed account of his negotiation with Japanese officials on Trotsky's behalf.

Sokol'nikov's testimony here is also confirmed by a brief quotation from an earlier interrogation dated December 12, 1936, eight days earlier than this one, which is reproduced in Georgi Dimitrov's diary:

> Interrogation of Sokolnikov, 12 December 1936:

> Question: Thus, the investigation concludes that Trotsky abroad and the center of the bloc within the USSR entered into negotiations with the Hitlerite and Japanese governments with the following aims:

First, to provoke a war by Germany and Japan against the USSR;

Second, to promote the defeat of the USSR in that war and to take advantage of that defeat to achieve the transfer of power in the USSR to [their] government bloc;

Third, on behalf of the future bloc government to guarantee territorial and economic concessions to the Hitlerite and Japanese governments.

Do you confirm this?

Reply: Yes, I confirm it.

Question: Do you admit that this activity by the bloc is tantamount to outright treason against the motherland?

Reply: Yes, I admit it.[3]

However, the interrogation of Sokol'nikov of October 20, 1936 published in PiLT2 provides testimony that did not arise during the January 1937 trial.[4]

Sokol'nikov's testimony concerning discussions with the British Prime Minister through the intermediation of a journalist, Talbot, and a Member of Parliament, Boothby, is not alluded to in the trial. The two men concerned are no doubt:

* Stafford C. Talbot, former professor of Russian and editor of the journal *British-Russian Gazette and Trade Outlook*. Talbot was named as a clandestine contact for the "bloc" by Arkadii P. Rozengol'ts, a defendant at the Third Moscow Trial of March 1938:

---

[3] *The Diary of Georgi Dimitrov 1933-1949. Introduced and edited by Ivo Banac* (New Haven, CT: Yale University Press, 2003), 43.
[4] We have reproduced an English translation of this interrogation in the Appendix.

VYSHINSKY: So since 1923 you, accused Rosengoltz, began to supply espionage information to foreign states?

ROSENGOLTZ: That is right

VYSHINSKY: Proceed.

ROSENGOLTZ: I must also state, although I said it in my testimony during the preliminary investigation, that in 1926 I gave information to Farbman, an English journalist[5], who at the same time was a Trotskyite. This was information concerning the foreign policy of the U.S.S.R. After that, during 1932-35, I gave information about orders placed abroad to the editor of the "British-Russian Gazette," Talbot, who came to me on his behalf.

Now as regards wrecking activities. I want to state that in these wrecking activities our aim was to help mainly Germany, and partly Japan.

Since Talbot was also the "founder and first President of the Association of British Creditors of Russia"[6] he had a special interest in settling the Russian debt left over from Tsarist times. This is reflected in Sokol'nikov's description of his 1934 meeting with Talbot.

Then Talbot asked me whether I could tell him something about the possibility of recognizing the prerevolutionary debts. I told him that on this question the government of the bloc would also be ready to make significant concessions and to make proposals acceptable to the English government ... Summing up our talk Talbot said that he considered the question of the debts to be

---

[5] Probably Michael Farbman, a British journalist who covered Russia. See, for example, Farbman's interview with Lenin of October, 1922, printed in *Pravda* on November 10, 1922. Online at
https://www.marxists.org/archive/lenin/works/1922/oct/27.htm
[6] See "Debt Payment Plan Proposed to Soviet." *The New York Times* Dec. 8, 1927 p. 6

very important and I again reaffirmed to him the readiness of the government of the bloc to make serious concessions on this question. (326; see p. 190-1)

"Boothby" must be Robert Boothby, MP. He had been Parliamentary Private Secretary to Winston Churchill when Churchill was Chancellor of the Exchequer. Conservative Stanley Baldwin was British Prime Minister after June 7, 1935.

There is no reason that the NKVD would have compelled Sokol'nikov to testify falsely to this material, which was never used. Nor is there any evidence at all to suggest that Sokol'nikov's testimony here or elsewhere, or in fact that of any of the Moscow Trials defendants, was forced upon them. This is additional evidence that Sokol'nikov's testimony is genuine – that Sokol'nikov really had undertaken these talks, and that Trotsky really had been negotiating with the British.

This testimony is consistent with other evidence. Piatakov testified that at their meeting in Norway in December, 1935, Trotsky had told him that he had established contact not only with Germany (Hess) and "with the Japanese government" but also "with some conservative circles" in England.

> In France the contact was with the "Comité de Forges" and with banking circles. In England, with some conservative circles. (LD 268)

According to Piatakov Trotsky had stressed that it was essential to reach agreements with England and France as well, in order to balance them off against Germany and Japan, not to become too dependent on the latter.

> Trotsky further wrote that we must not limit ourselves only to the German and Japanese. We must secure benevolent relations with other governments too (like the English and French), especially from the perspective of the possibility of extremely strong pressure from the German and Japanese quarters... (LD 258)

> Of course, to reach agreements with Germany alone would be risky, since without a corresponding English and French counterweight Germany would put their feet on the table and it would be very tough for us. Therefore in his practical steps he, Trotsky, is carrying out simultaneous preparatory work in different directions. (LD 267)

Sokol'nikov's testimony about his negotiation with the British is consistent with what Piatakov testified about what Trotsky told him.

The countries that posed the most imminent military threat to the USSR were Germany and Japan. Agreements with England, as here, and France, were necessary in order to balance against agreements with Germany and Japan. Therefore, this interrogation of Sokol'nikov also offers additional indirect evidence of Trotsky's negotiations with Germany and Japan.

Sokol'nikov's testimony about the projected economic and political program of the bloc in power is also consistent with Piatakov's testimony in his statement to Ezhov. Piatakov wrote that both Kamenev and Trotsky had told him that "retreat" to capitalism would be necessary if agreements with powerful foreign powers were to be concluded, while such agreements were themselves essential either to help the bloc come to power or, if it came to power by its own efforts, to consolidate its power in the country. According to Piatakov, Kamenev told him in 1932:

> Yesterday's disagreements cannot be an obstacle to our agreement today, if today we have a common goal. And this common goal is:
>
> 1/ The overthrow of Stalin and the liquidation of the Soviet government;
>
> 2/ the rejection of the building of socialism in one country and, consequently, the appropriate change of economic policy. On these two points we reached agreement with the Rights very easily."

To my question what "change of economic policy" mean Kamenev, with his characteristic aplomb, answered: "Well, you know, we will concretize it when we are in power. Only one thing is clear: we will have to **retreat**, in order to weaken the internal situation and equalize the external."

"Yes, yes, Yuri Leonidovich, I know that you concern yourself little with questions of international politics. But inasmuch as you may possibly have to continue the business that we are now doing, it is necessary that we be informed."

"Keep in mind that, without the essential agreement with the government of the capitalist powers against the Stalin government, we will not come to power. It is essential for us to secure a favorable attitude towards us, and that means **we will have to make concessions to them**. But about that we must have already in advance had confidential talks with the governments of these states, and that is happening now. Radek and Sokol'nikov will inform you in more detail." (LD 248-9)

Trotsky had used similar language in his talk with Piatakov in Norway in December 1935:

"This means that **we must retreat**. This must be firmly understood. Retreat to capitalism. How far, on what a scale, it is hard to say now – it will only be possible to be more concrete after we come to power."

"You see, -- Trotsky continued – on this point **about a retreat** we have agreed with the Rights and my directive about the bloc with the Rights was not just tactically necessary, but correct in principle, all the more since **they have fully admitted the necessity of terrorist, diversionist, and sabotage means of struggle against Stalin**." (LD 269)

At the January, 1937, Moscow Trial, Piatakov, Sokol'nikov, and Karl Radek all testified about Trotsky's commitment to a "retreat" towards the restoration of capitalism.

> As for the **retreat**, Trotsky wrote that Radek and I were mistaken in thinking that the **retreat** would be inconsiderable -- we would have to **retreat** very far, and on this was based the bloc, not only with the Zinovievites, but also with the Rights. (1937 Trial 38-39)

> ... In this connection also it would be necessary, for considerations of home policy, to effect a fairly big **retreat**, in addition to concessions to foreigners. Radek quite justly mentioned this **retreat** in town and country, such as permitting capitalist trade and so forth. To put it simply, Trotsky explained that it would be a very serious **retreat**. This is exactly what he said: you and Radek are still under the sway of the old ideas of 1925-26 and you are unable to see that in essence our coming to power will mean that we will have to **retreat very far in the direction of capitalism.** (1937 Trial 65)

Karl Radek outlined how Trotsky's views changed between 1934 and 1935:

> VYSHINSKY: Three facts: the April letter of 1934, the December letter of 1935 and Pyatakov's meeting with Trotsky in December 1935. How was the question put in Trotsky's letter in 1934? War, working for defeat?

> RADEK: Yes.

> VYSHINSKY: A return to capitalism in substance?

> RADEK: No, a return to capitalism is not raised in the letter

> VYSHINSKY: No? What then?

> RADEK: A **retreat** which we then thought....

VYSHINSKY: To where?

RADEK: To the positions of the NEP, with industry strengthened in comparison with what it had been before 1928.

VYSHINSKY: A **retreat** towards strengthening what elements?

RADEK: A **retreat** which was to restore a part of the capitalist elements as well, but this **retreat**, if compared with the state of things in 1927 – there would be a possibility during this **retreat**, on the one hand, of admitting capitalist restoration, but at the same time of strengthening industry, thanks to the First Five-Year Plan, the state farms and part of the collective farms – that is to say, we would have an economic base on which in my opinion a proletarian government could have maintained itself.

VYSHINSKY: So a proletarian government could still have maintained itself? But the tendency was to go backward?

RADEK: The tendency was to go backward.

VYSHINSKY: In 1935 this stood out more clearly in comparison with 1934?

RADEK: In 1935 the question was raised **of going back to capitalism.**

VYSHINSKY: To what limits?

RADEK: What Trotsky proposed was without any limits. To such limits as the enemy might require. (1937 Trial, 122)

According to Sokol'nikov the Trotskyists understood that they had no choice; it was retreat or be crushed:

SOKOLNIKOV: ... We considered that fascism was the most organized form of capitalism, that it would triumph, would seize Europe and stifle us. It was therefore better to come to terms with it, it was better to consent to a compromise in the sense of **retreating from socialism to capitalism.** (1937 Trial, 151)

The hypothesis that Trotsky did advocate the "restoration of capitalism" as Radek, Piatakov, and others asserted, is also consistent with much other evidence we now possess.

Chapter 4. Piatakov's Statement to Ezhov

December 19-20

This lengthy statement was obtained from the FSB Archive in mid-2015. As of September, 2019, it is also available in an identical copy, retyped, from RGASPI.[1] We will study it carefully as it contains much information about Trotsky's conspiratorial activities.

Trotsky, then Khrushchev, then Gorbachev, and researchers under their direction, have claimed that the defendants' statements and confessions were false. But there has never been any evidence that the pretrial or trial statements of Piatakov or of any of the defendants at the three Moscow trials were lies – that the defendants were forced by torture or threats to mouth statements they and the prosecution knew were untrue.

In volume one of this study, *Trotsky's 'Amalgams'*, and again, in a revised version in *The Moscow Trials As Evidence*, we have verified that the Moscow Trials testimony is reliable by checking against independent evidence many of the assertions that the defendants made in their testimony. In this light of this verification, allegations that the defendants' statements and confessions were false are simply wrong. They should not be accepted and should never pass unchallenged. Such claims are not evidence. They are examples of the logical fallacy of "argument by authority."

It has been convenient to both ideological anticommunists and Trotskyists to "believe" – accept as true – the claim that the defendants were forced to repeat falsehoods concocted by the prosecution. For this reason we will begin our examination of Piatakov's statement with some considerations which ought to lead any ob-

---

[1] TsA FSB. R-33835. (Delo No. 3257 on the arrested Piatakov Iurii Leonidovich and others); RGASPI. f.17. op.171. d. 263. ll. 43-76. See the full text, in English translation, in the Appendix.

jective researcher to accept that this document represents what
Piatakov himself wished to say.

Gol'tsman and the "Hotel Bristol"

During the first Moscow Trial of August, 1936, defendant Eduard
Gol'tsman claimed that he had travelled by train from Berlin to
Copenhagen in November, 1932, and that he had met Leon Sedov,
Trotsky's son, in the lobby of the "Hotel Bristol," after which he
and Sedov had proceeded to visit Trotsky. A number of people, including Trotsky himself, pointed out almost immediately that
there was no "Hotel Bristol" in Copenhagen in 1932. This fact led
Trotsky, then the Dewey Commission, to conclude that Gol'tsman
had been lying.

In 2008 Swedish research Sven-Eric Holmström published "New
Evidence Concerning the 'Hotel Bristol' Question in the First Moscow Trial of 1936."[2] On the basis of meticulous research Holmström concluded that Gol'tsman must have mistaken the name of
the adjacent café "Bristol" for that of the hotel.

Holmström's conclusions have now received striking verification.
Documents from Gol'tsman's NKVD investigation file released in
2015 reveal that the NKVD checked up on this question before the
trial. The NKVD investigators determined that no hotel named
"Bristol" existed in Copenhagen in 1932, but that it was easy to
mistake the name of the café for that of the hotel.

On August 2, 1936 the Foreign Division of the Main Directorate for
State Security (GUGB) reported as follows to the Chief of the Secret
Political Division of the NKVD:

> According to the official references works / guides to the
> city of Copenhagen / telephone directories in the For-
> eign Division of the GUGB NKVD no hotel "Bristol" ex-
> isted either in 1932 or exists in 1936.

---

[2] At https://ojs.library.ubc.ca/index.php/clogic/article/view/191568/188679

However, in Copenhagen there is a small café "Bristol" above which is located the hotel "Grand Hotel Copenhagen." Since the "Grand Hotel" has a sign that is not very noticeable and the café "Bristol" has a sign in large gold letters on a black background many casual observers take the hotel "Grand Hotel" as the "Bristol."

The café "Bristol" and the hotel "Grand Hotel" are located very close to the Copenhagen train station and existed in 1932 as they do today.

Gol'tsman was asked whether he could have made this error and admitted that it was possible. Gol'tsman also accurately described the café's sign and said that it was right outside the hotel entrance and that the café and hotel lobby communicated with each other.

As SEDOV and I had arranged in advance in Berlin I went directly from the station to the hotel "Bristol."

This hotel is situated near the station, about a five-minute walk away. My meeting with SEDOV took place in the vestibule of the hotel, from which we went to the café situated on the first floor of this same hotel.

Now I remember precisely that at the entrance to the café there was a black sign on which in large gold letters it said "Bristol."

Question: Was this perhaps the name of the café, not of the hotel?

Answer: Perhaps, but I remember well the sign "Bristol" above the café, and this café is situated next to the vestibule of the hotel.[3]

---

[3] Gol'tsman file TsA FSB R-33833 Delo No. 3257. See the Appendix for the full text.

This is exactly what Holmström concluded on the basis of a careful study of the evidence he had gathered. It proves that Gol'tsman was not lying about the "Hotel Bristol." He had simply made an understandable error, one that, according to the Copenhagen-based NKVD men, "many casual observers" made.

For our present purposes, this set of documents proves that the NKVD did not "force" Gol'tsman to mouth phony confessions. Rather, the NKVD men did what investigators are supposed to do. They took Gol'tsman's testimony and tried to verify it. When they discovered the discrepancy in Gol'tsman's testimony, they asked him about it and recorded his comment.

In *Trotsky's 'Amalgams'* and in *The Moscow Trials As Evidence* we show that, whenever we can independently check statements made by defendants in the Moscow Trials, we find that the statements are genuine – that is, the defendants testified what they wanted to testify. The Gol'tsman – "Hotel Bristol" documents constitute yet more evidence of this.

There is a great deal of other evidence that corroborates the confessions and statements by Moscow Trials defendants. We will discuss some of it in this chapter; more such evidence is examined in other chapters. By contrast, we have no evidence at all that Moscow Trial defendants were compelled to make false statements.

Corroboration of Piatakov's Testimony

We possess other corroboration of the genuineness of Piatakov's testimony before and at trial. In 2002 the transcript of the December 7, 1936 *ochnaia stavka*, or face-to-face confrontation, between Piatakov and Nikolai Bukharin was published. There Piatakov named Bukharin as a participant in the Zinovievist-Trotskyist-Rightist network of conspiracies, as he also did in the statement of December 19-20, 1936, which we examine here.

Present at this *ochnaia stavka* were Kliment E. Voroshilov, People's Commissar for Defense; Sergo Ordzhonikidze, People's Commissar for Heavy Industry and Piatakov's immediate superior; Nikolai Ez-

hov, Commissar for Internal Affairs and, as such, head of the
NKVD; Stalin; and Bukharin himself. Bukharin insisted that
Piatakov was lying only in regard to his own, Bukharin's, guilt but
not otherwise. According to his wife, Anna Larina, Bukharin told
her about this *ochnaia stavka.* Decades later, Larina in turn related
in her memoir a version of what she remembered of what her husband had told her. From her account it is clear that Bukharin did
not convey to his wife that the rest of Piatakov's testimony was
false.

> Пятаков говорил, опустив голову, стараясь ладонью
> прикрыть глаза. В его тоне чувствовалось
> озлобление, озлобление, как считал Н.И., против тех,
> кто его слушал, не прерывая абсурдный спектакль,
> не останавливая неслыханный произвол.
>
> — Юрий Леонидович, объясните, — спросил
> Бухарин, — что вас заставляет оговаривать самого
> себя?
>
> Наступила пауза. В это время Серго Орджоникидзе,
> сосредоточенно и изумленно смотревший на
> Пятакова, потрясенный измученным видом и
> показаниями своего деятельного помощника,
> приложив ладонь к уху (Серго был глуховат),
> спросил:
>
> — Неужто ваши показания добровольны?
>
> — Мои показания добровольны, — ответил Пятаков.
>
> — Абсолютно добровольны? — еще с большим
> удивлением спросил Орджоникидзе, но на
> повторный вопрос ответа не последовало. Только
> лишь на процессе в своем последнем слове Пятаков
> сумел сказать: "Всякое наказание, какое вы
> вынесете, будет легче, чем самый факт признания",
> чем и дал понять, что его показания вынужденные.

Почему же в ту минуту, перед всеми членами Политбюро, Пятаков не решился сказать правду и рассказать, что с ним проделывали, чем довели его до такого состояния, что он едва держался на ногах? До конца этого постичь невозможно. Но, очевидно, Пятаков понимал, что после очной ставки ему придется вернуться не к себе домой и снова начнутся адовы муки в застенках НКВД. Возможно, медицинские средства парализовали его выдающуюся волю. [4]

Piatakov spoke, his head lowered, trying to cover his eyes with his palm. In his tone one could feel hostility, hostility, as N.I. [Bukharin] believed, against those who were listening to him without interrupting the absurd spectacle, not stopping the unheard-of caprice.

— Iurii Leonidovich, explain, — asked Bukharin, — what has compelled you to slander yourself?

A pause ensued. During this time Sergo Ordzhonikidze, who was looking at Piatakov with concentration and amazement, shaken by the haggard appearance and the confessions of his assistant, put his hand to his ear (Sergo was rather deaf) and asked:

— Are your confessions really voluntary?

— My confessions are voluntary, — answered Piatakov.

— Absolutely voluntary? — Ordzhonikidze asked with even greater astonishment, but no answer followed the repeated question. Only at the trial, in his last words, did Piatakov dare to say: "Any punishment you could inflict will be easier than the fact itself of admitting guilt," by which he made it clear that his confessions were made through compulsion.

---

[4] Anna Larina, *Nezabyvaemoe*. Moscow: APN, 1989, 328.

> But why, in that moment, in front of all the members of
> the Politburo, did Piatakov not dare to tell the truth and
> tell what happened to him were doing, what drove him
> to such a state that he could hardly stand? It is impossi-
> ble to comprehend this completely. But, obviously,
> Pyatakov knew that after the confrontation, he would
> not return to his home and the hellish torments would
> begin again in the dungeons of the NKVD. Perhaps medi-
> cation paralyzed his extraordinary will.

Larina was convinced that not just Piatakov, but all the defendants
at all the Moscow trials were innocent. But she had no *evidence* to
that effect. She *assumed* it, evidently because Piatakov accused her
husband Bukharin of involvement in the bloc of conspirators. Today we possess a great deal of evidence that Bukharin was indeed
one of the leaders of the bloc of oppositionists that included Zinovievists, Trotskyists, and Rights.

Piatakov testified about the activities of the bloc. He does not mention the participation of the Zinovievists, perhaps because it was
not relevant to his testimony against Bukharin, perhaps for some
other reason. We can be sure that Ordzhonikidze believed
Piatakov's testimony because we have the partial text of a talk he
gave to the heads of the chief directorates of the Commissariat of
Heavy Industry on February 5, 1937 in which he complains bit-
terly about Piatakov's deceitfulness.[5]

Piatakov's Statement of December 19-20 1936

This is the longest pretrial text of material from Piatakov's investigation file that we now possess. It is not an interrogation but a
statement, *zaiavlenie*. Further evidence that it was made voluntar-

---

[5] English translation in Getty & Naumov, 292-294. The Russian version of
Ordzhonikidze's speech was not available when Getty and Naumov wrote in the
late '90s. It was finally published in 2011 and is now online at
http://istmat.info/node/48634

ily comes from the beginning of what appears to have been the next interrogation of Piatakov, that of December 23, 1936.

> Question: You have submitted a statement in the name of the People's Commissar of Internal Affairs com. EZ-HOV, in which you outline your criminal activities in a more detailed and systematic manner and, in particular, tell about your personal meeting with Trotsky.
>
> May the investigation consider this statement of yours as an official investigative document?
>
> **Answer: Yes**, in writing this statement in the name of People's Commissar EZHOV I intended that it be included among the investigative materials.[6]

No objective student could conclude from this text, or from the evidence cited above, that Piatakov's testimony had been put into his mouth, or that he had been forced to lie according to a narrative composed by somebody else. Piatakov's testimony represented what he chose to say.

Confirmation of Piatakov's statement

Much of what Piatakov says in this Statement can be confirmed by other documents we now possess.

The Bloc of Trotskyists, Zinovievists, Rightists, and other Oppositionists

We know this bloc existed because evidence of it was discovered in 1980 in the Harvard Trotsky Archive by Pierre Broué. Piatakov's statements about it agree with what we know from the Trotsky Archive documents written by Trotsky and Sedov. Piatakov's Statement is yet more evidence that Broué was wrong in claiming, without any evidence, that the bloc was "ephemeral." Piatakov in-

---

[6] "Protokol doprosa Piatakova, Iuria Leonidovicha – ot 23 dekabria 1936 goda." LD 272.

sists that the bloc aimed at terror – political assassination – from the outset and continued this aim, along with that of sabotage, until its members were arrested.[7]

Confirmation of Trotsky's Policy of Terror

Piatakov's Statement confirms the claims made by Mark Zborowski, whom Sedov tried to recruit to kill Stalin and who expressed the view that the assassination of Stalin was all that was necessary for the Soviet government to collapse. We have studied Zborowski's reports in previous books.[8]

In his first confession statement, made on June 2, 1937, Nikolai Bukharin affirmed that Trotsky was "always urging assassination":

> RADEK informed me that TROTSKY was always urging the use of terror...[9]

Piatakov's testimony that Trotsky was urging sabotage. This confirms Bukharin's claim in his first confession:

> I remember yet another important conversation in which RADEK vaguely related that some kind of new directives on both internal and external politics had been received from Trotsky. I remember that I was angered by this way of generally treating any commands by Trotsky, to whomich the Trotskyites related as almost to the military commands of a unitary command center. RADEK hinted to me that this was a question of some sort of new negotiations of Trotsky's with Germany or

---

[7] We have studied this discovery, the "Sedov bloc letter," in Furr, Amalgams, and Moscow Trials.

[8] Furr, Amalgams, Chapters 3 and 13; Trotsky's Lies, Chapter 2; Moscow Trials, Chapter 3.

[9] Grover Furr and Vladimir L. Bobrov, "Nikolai Bukharin's First Statement of Confession in the Lubianka." *Cultural Logic* 2007, p. 37. At https://ojs.library.ubc.ca/index.php/clogic/article/view/191745

with England, but limited himself to this, having told me about Trotsky's directive concerning sabotage.

Trotsky and the Germans and Japanese

Piatakov's testimony about Trotsky's claim that he had made deals with Nazi Germany and Fascist Japan corroborates the substantial testimony from Soviet sources that we have studied elsewhere.[10] It is also confirmed by our analysis of Ivan Serov's report.[11] There we demonstrate that Rakovsky must have been telling the truth when, in his statement to the prosecution, he said that he had met with high-ranking Japanese officials and agreed to be a go-between for Trotsky.[12]

It is confirmed by Rakovsky in confession statements published in 2005 in a Bulgarian historical journal.[13] And it is also confirmed by the recently printed investigation materials in *Politbiuro i Lev Trotskii t. 2.* We examine those documents in the present volume.

Trotsky and the Trotskyist Conspiracy in the Army

Piatakov wrote that Trotsky put special emphasis on recruiting in the Red Army (LD 266) and considered Vitovt K. Putna and Vitalii M. Primakov as "a very valuable contact and it must be strengthened and developed in every way." (LD 270) Both men were co-defendants in the "Tukhachevsky Affair" trial of June 11, 1937 and were executed together with Tukhachevsky and the others. Both Putna and Primakov described their commitment to Trotsky and their activities on behalf of Trotsky's conspiracy. The sections of Marshal Semion Budyonny's letter to Marshal Klement Voroshilov that deal with Trotsky are examined in Chapter Nine of *Trotsky's 'Amalgams'*. We now have many of Tukhachevsky's own confessions. Moreover, we now possess the transcript of the trial of Tuk-

---

[10] Furr, *Leon Trotsky's Collaboration with Germany and Japan* (hereafter TC).
[11] See TC, Chapter Four.
[12] See the extensive discussion in TC Chapter 4.
[13] We will study these statements in a future book. Rakovsky was Bulgarian.

hachevsky and others of June 11, 1937, which was declassified in May, 2018.[14]

Trotsky and the United Front

In his journal of exile, *Biulleten' Oppozitsii* (Bulletin of the Opposition) No. 32 of December 1932 Trotsky seemed to be calling for a "united front" with the Social-Democrats. But Trotsky's attitude towards the "united front" was an equivocal one. Fel'shtinskii and Cherniavskii, Trotsky's sympathetic Russian biographers, conclude that he wanted a "united front" only with the rank-and-file, not with the S-D leaders, though he did not call them "social-fascists" like the Comintern was doing. (120) This is also the tenor of Trotsky's essay "In What Does the Error of the German Communist Party's Current Political Line Reside?"[15]

In other articles Trotsky was clearer about his call for a United Front with the Social-Democrats:

> I proposed to the German Communists to carry out the policy of a united front. The Communists ought to propose to the Social Democrats and to the trade unions led by them a program of cooperative, practical struggle against the attack of the fascists. The Social Democratic masses quite sincerely desire to wage such a struggle. If the leaders refuse, they will compromise themselves in the eyes of their own supporters. If the leaders agree, the masses, in practical action, will go beyond their leaders and support the Communists. ("Answers to Questions by

---

[14] As of this writing, December 29, 2018, these are
http://istmat.info/node/59108 and
http://lander.odessa.ua/doc/rgaspi_17.171.392_process_tuhachevskogo.pdf It is not yet available in text format, much less published in book form, and has not been translated.

[15] B.O. No. 27, March 1932. The English translation , "For a Workers' United Front Against Fascism," is misleading. Trotsky is very careful not to call for unity with the Social-Democratic Party itself – the leadership.

the New York Times," February 13, 1932. WLT 1932, p. 49)

Trotsky never advocated a "united front" in the formation of a government, as the Comintern did in France and Republican Spain.

According to Piatakov, Trotsky's view, as communicated through Radek, was hostile to the "united front":

> Besides this there were also directives about the Comintern. I did not remember them well and now recall them vaguely. I seem to remember that it was a question of a very "left" formulation against the united front in France. Unfortunately this part of Trotsky's directives did not stick in my memory. (LD 259)

Piatakov admits his memory was faulty on this point. But Piatakov also said that, of course, Trotsky could not publicly reveal his conspiracies with the capitalist powers. Trotsky had said that he, Piatakov, should not be troubled by the fact that

> much of what he was about to say must not only not be made public (and **therefore I should not be surprised that much of it will contradict what is said in his "Bulletins"), but also must not be made known to wider circles of his supporters in the USSR.** (LD 264; emphasis added)

We know from examination of the Trotsky Archive that Trotsky lied in his public writings when he thought it expedient to do so.[16] In fact Trotsky vigorously denied in public the very policies that he was pursing in private, such as his continued contact with "capitulators," his approval of the bloc with other Oppositionists, and the use of "terror" or violence and assassination.

Trotsky's policy of a conspiracy of assassination and sabotage against the Soviet Union in alliance with Germany, Japan, France

---

[16] For details see the discussion in Furr Amalgams and Furr, Trotsky's Lies.

and Great Britain, and of agreements to help the German General Staff to defeat the Red Army in wartime, was not compatible with a "united front" against Germany. No doubt this accounts for his seemingly "very 'left'" position against a United Front against Germany: the Germans naturally opposed it, so Trotsky did as well.

Soviet Economic Successes Necessitated Terror, Sabotage and Defeatism

This was the position of the Zinovievist assassins of Sergei Kirov. As we have shown[17], there is no basis at all to think that they were "forced" to say this by the NKVD. The Trotskyist and other arrestees whose statements and interrogations are published in PiLT2 also repeatedly refer to this.

Trotsky and the clandestine Oppositionists were relying upon the social stresses of collectivization and industrialization to somehow cause the Soviet government's collapse. When this did not occur they fell back upon force: plans for a *coup d'état* with attendant murders of Stalin and his highest associates, coupled with defeatism and sabotage in favor of the invader in the war with one or more capitalist states which they were sure would break out sooner rather than later.

The fact that no collapse occurred and that collectivization and rapid industrialization appeared to have been successful enough caused disruptions among the participants in the bloc of oppositionists. Evidently some of them were motivated more by fear that Stalin's policies were leading the USSR to ruin than either by the conviction that Trotsky's theory of "permanent revolution" was correct, or by hatred of Stalin himself. Piatakov, Radek, and Rakovsky were among those who were no friends of Stalin or his concept of how to build socialism in one country. But they were ultimately unwilling to unite with Nazi Germany and fascist Japan, bring about the defeat of the USSR in war, see the USSR split into smaller parts, and end up united with the fascist powers.

---

[17] See Furr, *The Murder of Sergei Kirov.*

Trotsky's Theory of "Permanent Revolution"

Trotsky himself stuck to his theory that it was impossible to build socialism in a single country. At first he believed that Soviet society would either collapse under the economic and social strain of simultaneous collectivization, famine, and industrialization, or would become ungovernable due to rebellions and the disaffection of the Army. This proved not to be so, as Sedov told Piatakov:

> Trotsky rules out any possibility at the present stage of any mass anti-Stalin movement. Stalin has succeeded in surviving the difficulties and we must frankly admit that we have missed the time. (LD 241) [18]

Trotsky concluded that the struggle against Stalin's project of socialism in one country should also be international. From that he drew the further conclusion that the Trotskyists and their Opposition allies would have to make arrangements with Germany and Japan, the capitalist states most likely to attack the USSR and, to counteract the Germans and Japanese, with Britain and France. First Smirnov, then Kamenev told Piatakov about this.

But neither Piatakov nor Radek were able to fully grasp the implications of this policy as Trotsky saw them. So they decided that Piatakov should meet with Trotsky. He asked Trotsky again at their meeting in Norway in December, 1935, and Trotsky expatiated upon his ideas in greater detail. (Smirnov, LD 238; Kamenev, LD 250; Radek, LD 259; Trotsky LD 267)

The main points of Trotsky's lecture to Piatakov are quoted in the transcript of the January 1937 Moscow Trial. [19] Sometimes Piatakov's statement provides the source of quotations in the trial transcript that are otherwise not identified. For example, Vyshinsky said the following:

---

[18] Also see the discussion of this passage in Chapter Two, above.

[19] The page numbers to this statement of Piatakov's as cited by Prosecutor Vyshinsky in the transcript of the January 1937 trial are the same as in the text we have obtained. They are included in the English translation.

Incidentally, in regard to this *Bulletin* of the Trotskyite opposition, Pyatakov told us that Trotsky had said to him: "Do not take everything we say in the *Bulletin* at its face value. Bear in mind that we cannot say in the *Bulletin* all that we say to you, and demand of you. Understand that sometimes, perhaps, in this Bulletin we shall say things which are the opposite of what we demand of you. (1937 Trial 508-509).

The parallel passage in Piatakov's Statement is as follows:

He mentioned once again the difference between the preparation of a *coup d'état* and a mass uprising and in this connection much of what he was about to say must not only not be made public (and therefore I should not be surprised that much of it will contradict what is said in his "Bulletins"), but also must not be made known to wider circles of his supporters in the USSR. (LD 264)

In *Trotsky's 'Amalgams'* and *Trotsky's Lies* we have established that Trotsky lied in his writings, including in his *Bulletin*, when he considered it expedient to do so. Piatakov's Statement, and his claim as quoted by Vyshinsky here, are consistent with that.

Ukrainian Independence

According to Piatakov, Trotsky said that the Germans demanded that a new government led by the Oppositionists should allow the Ukraine to separate from the U.S.S.R.:

3. In the event that the "nationalist forces" of the Ukraine should want to separate from the U.S.S.R. — not to oppose this. (LD 268)

Piatakov testified to this during the trial:

But in return the fascists are to receive the following compensation: a general favourable attitude towards German interests and towards the German government on all questions of international policy; certain territorial concessions would have to be made, and these territorial concessions have been defined—in particular, mention was made of territorial concessions in a veiled form which were called "not resisting Ukrainian national-bourgeois forces in the event of their self-determination."

Vyshinsky: What does that mean?

Pyatakov: It means in a veiled form what Radek spoke about here: should the Germans set up their Ukrainian government, ruling the Ukraine not through their German Governor-General but perhaps through a hetman—at any rate, should the Germans "self-determine" the Ukraine—the Trotskyite-Zinovievite bloc will not oppose it. Actually, this meant the beginning of the dismemberment of the Soviet Union. (1937 Trial 64)

In 1939, Trotsky published four articles in which he advocated independence for the Ukraine. The first, "The Ukrainian Question," is dated April 22, 1939, published first (in English) on May 9, 1939, and in the July, 1939, issue of the B.O.[20] "Independence of the Ukraine and Sectarian Muddleheads," is dated July 30, 1939, but apparently first published in mid-September, 1939, in English and in the B.O. issue of October, 1939.[21] "Democratic Feudalists and the Independence of the Ukraine," is dated August 5, 1939, but was first published on October 31, 1939, in English and also in the October issue of the B.O.[22] The last article, "Stalin — Temporary Holder of the Ukraine," is dated September 18, 1939, published on October 24, 1939, and not in the B.O.[23]

---

[20] WLT 1938-1939, p. 413, n. 296; http://web.mit.edu/fjk/www/FI/BO/BO-77.shtml
[21] WLT 1939-1940, p. 426 n. 48; http://web.mit.edu/fjk/www/FI/BO/BO-79.shtml
[22] WLT 1939-40, p. 429 n. 71; *ibid.*
[23] WLT 1939-40, p. 431 n. 88.

In the light of Piatakov's Statement and the 1937 Trial testimony Trotsky's articles in support of Ukrainian independence may be interpreted in two ways:

* Trotsky presents these articles as a Marxist-Leninist analysis of the national question from his own strongly anti-Stalin, anti-Soviet perspective.

* However that may be, the call to separate the Ukraine from the Soviet Union is consistent with what Piatakov and others describe as Trotsky's recognition of the necessity to permit Ukrainian nationalists forces friendly to Germany to secede from the U.S.S.R.

Which of these interpretations best fits the facts as we know them? They are not mutually compatible because of the complete lack of any left, working-class based Ukrainian nationalist movement. Trotsky's appeals to Ukrainian revolutionaries sound unrealistic if not deliberately misleading, for all the Ukrainian nationalist organizations were far-Right, pro-German and Nazi-like.

Any independence for the Ukraine would mean a pro-Nazi, intensely anticommunist and anti-working class state, a base for Hitler. Therefore it seems likely that these articles constituted a covert message to the Germans that, despite the setbacks suffered by his Soviet-based supporters, Trotsky remained ready to concede Ukraine to Germany in case of war.

"By Any Means"

According to Piatakov's account Trotsky emphasized that in the struggle to unseat Stalin "all means were good."

> In relation to this we must ruthlessly cast aside prejudices of any kind. (LD 241)

> 1/ The central task is not the resurrection of an organization for the sake of organization, but its resurrection for the purpose of liquidating Stalin and his closest supporters (in the letter it was said "'S' und Konsorten mit allen Mitteln aus dem Weg rauemen)..." (LD 246)

"Remember, in this struggle all means are good and every ally is useful...." (LD 270)

This concept was widely spread among Trotsky's firmest supporters in the Soviet Union. It is mentioned repeatedly in the interrogations and statements printed in PiLT2.

Sokol'nikov and the Japanese

One pre-trial interrogation by Sokol'nikov has been published in PiLT2. We have put its text in the "Appendix" section and will consider it in the present volume. Other pre-trial materials from Sokol'nikov have now been made available online.

In a section that has been published from another interrogation Sokol'nikov identifies the Japanese diplomat who contacted him about Japan's contacts with Trotsky as "Ota."

> ... to the file was associated a copy of notes of a talk between G. Ia. Sokol'nikov, who was at that time the vice-commissar of Foreign Affairs, with the Japanese ambassador Ota of April 13, 1935 on the question of the petroleum, fishing, and anthracite concessions on Sakhalin [Island]. At the preliminary investigation and at the trial G. Ia. Sokol'nikov confirmed the fact of this talk and stated that after the talk he supposedly had a short conversation with Ota on the subject of L.D. Trotsky's proposals to the Japanese government. The contents of the conversation, as it is reflected in the transcript of the interrogation of G. Ia. Sokol'nikov of December 12, 1936, was as follows:

> Sokol'nikov: . . . when Ota and the secretary of the embassy were about to leave, Ota stopped awhile. At that time both interpreters had already left my office. Taking advantage of this opportunity Ota, while I escorted him to the door, exchanged a few sentences with me.

> Question: Please reproduce your conversation with Ota word for word, as far as possible.

Answer: Ota asked me: "Are you aware that Mr. Trotsky has made certain proposals to my government?" I replied: "Yes, I have been informed of this." Ota asked: "How do you appraise these proposals?" I replied: "I think the proposals are quite serious." Then Ota asked: "Is this only your personal opinion?" I replied: "No, this is also the opinion of my friends." On this point our conversation ended.

Question: Did Ota return to the question of contact between the bloc and the Japanese government after that?

Answer: No. This conversation with Ota took place at the very end of my negotiations with him. Shortly after that I stopped working in the NKVD and did not meet with Ota again. (R-PP 228-229)

In another fragment of a pretrial interrogation quoted by Dimitrov in his diary Sokol'nikov confirms Trotsky's conspiracy with Germany and Japan. We have reproduced this passage in Chapter Two, above.

Piatakov Confirms Sokol'nikov's Claim

As we have already noted,[24] Piatakov's statement to Ezhov contains an important addition to the evidence of Trotsky's collaboration with the Japanese. Piatakov confirmed that Sokol'nikov had told him about this meeting

Also, Sokol'nikov told me that he had a talk with the Japanese, with Ota, I think, from which it was also clear that Trotsky was carrying on negotiations with representatives of the Japanese government. (LD 257)

Piatakov's confirmation here is very significant. Piatakov made it in passing, without any emphasis, in an almost offhand manner.

---

[24] See Chapter Two, above.

There is no indication that it was "forced" from him or "scripted" by the NKVD.

Therefore, there is no room for doubt that Ota approached Sokol'nikov. And that means that there can be no doubt Trotsky was conspiring with the Japanese. Elsewhere we discuss other evidence of Trotsky's contacts with the Japanese.[25]

Trotsky's Explanation of the Need for Sabotage

According to Piatakov, during his December 1935 meeting with Trotsky in Norway he informed Trotsky that the latter's directive to engage in the sabotage of the burgeoning Soviet economy had not met with a sympathetic response by Trotskyists within the Soviet Union and that he, Piatakov, and Radek did not really understand the reasons for it either. After heaping a mountain of abuse upon Piatakov Trotsky explained that the real reason for convincing his supporters to engage in economic sabotage was not to damage the economy:

> I understand very well – said Trotsky, for example – that small groups of Trotskyists cannot at this moment substantively change the course of economic development. But that is, in fact, not necessary. (LD 262)

He then explained that it was necessary to train Trotskyists to hate everything Stalin was doing no matter how positive it might appear, or those cadre would "degenerate" – be won over to the Stalin policy of industrializing the U.S.S.R.

> Unless we carry out this directive the degeneration of the Trotskyist cadre is inevitable, their assimilation by the Soviet government is inevitable, and that means our collapse together with the collapse of the Stalin state. (LD 263)

---

[25] See Furr, Trotsky's Collaboration, Chapter 4, and a later chapter in the present volume.

Between these two statements Trotsky evoked a comparison or parallel between what he, Trotsky, was advocating and the position of the Bolshevik Party during the late Tsarist period. Trotsky cited Petr Struve and Mikhail Tugan-Baranovskii, who were advocating the industrialization of Russia about the time that Lenin was concerned with the same questions, roughly 1895-1900. According to Piatakov, Trotsky said the following:

> You recall the attitude of Marxists towards the development of capitalism in Russia. We all considered that a progressive fact. But the positions of Struve and Tugan-Baranovskii, called to the service of capitalism, are one thing, while the positions of Lenin and the revolutionary part of social-democracy, which were organizing the future gravedigger of capitalism, are another. We must be the gravediggers of the Stalin state. (LD 262-263)

Trotsky said that, like the Bolsheviks of the Tsarist period, he too considered the industrialization being carried out by Stalin to be a positive thing:

> I will not deny that from the point of view of the country's development it is good that new factories are being built. (LD 263)

It is hard to understand why Trotsky used this comparison. Trotsky was trying to draw a parallel between his own aims and those of Lenin, whom both he and Piatakov admired. But Lenin and the Bolsheviks opposed terrorism and sabotage in the struggle against capitalism in Russia, while Trotsky was advocating both terrorism and sabotage. Trotsky's analogy appears not to support his policies but, on the contrary, to refute them.

Then Trotsky drew a conclusion completely at odds from that of the Bolsheviks:

> But the task of Trotskyists does not consist in building factories, but in organizing forces against Stalin and his regime, whose collapse is inevitable. For this, cadre are needed. These cadre will inevitably degenerate if all they

do is participate in positive work. That is the essence of
my directive, and you cannot seem to understand it at
all. (LD 263)

Evidently Piatakov did not understand how this example was supposed to help him convince the Trotskyist cadre to engage in sabotage and terror.

Not Mass Action and Revolution, but Conspiracy and *Coup d'état*

According to Piatakov Sedov, and then Trotsky, repeatedly
stressed that the opposition could not hope to organize mass action – that is, revolution – against the Soviet government. At one of
their 1931 meetings in Berlin Sedov spoke to Piatakov as follows:

After that Sedov went on to outline what he called "the
new methods of struggle."

Trotsky rules out any possibility at the present stage of
any mass anti-Stalin movement. Stalin has succeeded in
surviving the difficulties and we must frankly admit that
we have missed the time.

"If we waste time now we will definitively lose all our
cadre, and that will be the death of us.

For that reason now at the tip of the needle must be put

1) the terrorist struggle of tacitly conspiratorial groups
against the main leaders of the party and government 2)
active opposition against all the practical work of the
party and government and 3) the discrediting in every
possible way of Stalin's undertakings, especially on the
economic front. (LD 241)

At their December 1935 meeting in Norway Trotsky told Piatakov:

'...Remember that without a whole series of terrorist
acts, which must be carried out as soon as possible, the

Stalin government cannot be overthrown. For this is a question of a *coup d'état*. A mass uprising, he said, is one thing, for which, evidently, there is no basis now, and a *coup d'état* is something else."

"This is the difference, I note, that many do not understand. They are unaware that the methods of a *coup d'état* differ fundamentally from the methods of organizing a mass uprising. I stand now precisely on the position of a *coup d'état* and therefore, in the deciding of questions of tactics, I have rejected formulaic instructions, developed under other conditions, applied to other tasks." (LD 263)

He mentioned once again the difference between the preparation of a *coup d'état* and a mass uprising and in this connection much of what he was about to say must not only not be made public (and therefore I should not be surprised that much of it will contradict what is said in his "Bulletins"), but also must not be made known to wider circles of his supporters in the U.S.S.R. (LD 264)

Piatakov said that the Soviet masses had been won to the task of construction and so would be hostile to sabotage:

"The sharpest possible line of demarcation must be drawn between us and all those who are tied to Stalin and his state."

"However, we must do this not by means of public statements, propaganda, and explanations. Such statements at the present moment would not meet with sympathy from the masses. On the contrary, we would be compromised and destroyed before we could do anything at all. The organization cannot be built on this basis. That would mean to doom it in advance. For in fact the masses are under a psychosis of construction, which they falsely accept as the construction of socialism. To come out openly now against this construction means to doom our efforts." (LD 265)

Here Trotsky clarified the difference between Lenin's and the Bolsheviks' strategy during the Tsarist period, and Trotsky's strategy in the 1930s. The former relied on a mass revolution and the overthrow of capitalism. Trotsky, however, realized that he could not do that, since the masses were basically won to constructing socialism (or, as Trotsky said, what they believed was socialism) through industrialization.

Return to Capitalism

With no possibility of relying on the Soviet masses, the only means remaining to the bloc and to Trotsky were terror and sabotage.

Moreover, Trotsky realized that before seizing power the opposition would have to make agreements with the major capitalist countries so that, if they managed to overthrow the Soviet government, the capitalist countries would not simply throw them out and divide up the Soviet Union amongst themselves.

> "We cannot," Sedov transmitted Trotsky's views, "regard our struggle in an isolated manner. To keep our struggle in one country is just as absurd as Stalin's desire to build socialism in one country. Therefore we cannot swear off questions of relations between states and relations with capitalist states."
>
> - Sedov to Piatakov in 1931 (LD 242)
>
> 4/ We must take the coming war into account and occupy in relation to the war an unconditionally defeatist position, and by means of preliminary negotiations with governments of capitalist powers (also making use of the contradictions between them) guarantee for ourselves favorable relations in case of our coming to power as a result of the war.

- Trotsky's letter to Piatakov of November 1931 (LD 247)

"Keep in mind that, without the essential agreement with the government of the capitalist powers against the Stalin government, we will not come to power. It is essential for us to secure a favorable attitude towards us, and that means we will have to make concessions to them. But about that we must have already in advance had confidential talks with the governments of these states, and that is happening now.

- Kamenev to Piatakov, end of 1932 (LD 251)

"Military conflict with capitalist states is inevitable. I do not doubt that the result of such conflict will be unpleasant for the Stalin state. We must be prepared at this moment to take power into our hands." "Of course, -- emphasized Trotsky – we must understand that the seizure of power under these conditions means agreements with the corresponding capitalist states (for example with Germany, Japan, and others) on the basis of substantial concessions to them, including territorial concessions.

- Trotsky to Piatakov at their meeting in Norway in December 1935 (LD 267)

"This means, it will be necessary to retreat. This must be firmly understood. Retreat to capitalism. How far and to what degree, it is difficult to say now — this can be made concrete only after we come into power."

- Trotsky to Piatakov, Norway December 1935 (LD 269)

The capitalist powers that were capable of invading the Soviet Union, and therefore those with which Trotsky must make agreements, were clearly Germany, Japan, Britain, and France. Concerning Germany:

Trotsky said that in the struggle with Stalin we can in no way ignore relations between governments. Once we understand that Stalin's scheme of building socialism in one country is an empty and dangerous scheme, then we too in our struggle with Stalin must not slide to the position of "one country."

This struggle inevitably is interconnected with our relations with capitalist states. **It would be stupid to think that it is possible to assume power without securing a benevolent attitude of the most important capitalist governments, especially of the most aggressive ones, such as the present governments of Germany and Japan. It is completely essential even now to have contact and agreements with these governments. He, Trotsky, has taken the necessary steps in this regard.** He demanded from Radek and Sokol'nikov, who had the requisite possibilities, to put out feelers for the essential contact along these lines with the official representatives of these powers, and to support whatever he, Trotsky, was carrying out in practice.

In this connection, as I seem to remember, **Radek told me about some kind of conversations of his with Germans (I cannot recall the names of these Germans), from whom it was clear that Trotsky had made some arrangements with the German government.** (LD 257. Emphasis added.)

He, Trotsky, had secured a favorable attitude of the German fascist government in case the bloc came to power.

Of course this favorable attitude was not due to any special sympathy towards the bloc but to real interests.

At the basis of the agreement lies an appeal to the German government to help the bloc come to power. On his part Trotsky promised in the event of coming

to power to make very concrete concessions, stipulated in advance, to Germany. (LD 267)

Trotsky's Conspiracies with Germany, Japan, Britain, France

Specific concessions to Hitler's Germany were then enumerated (LD 267-268). Trotsky assured Piatakov:

> These principles of the agreement, as Trotsky related, were finally elaborated and adopted during Trotsky's meeting with Hitler's deputy — Hess. (LD 268)

During the Second Moscow Trial of January, 1937, Radek stated that he had learned about Trotsky's negotiations with Hess. (1937 Trial 132) It is not clear from this passage in the trial transcript whether Radek had heard about these negotiations only from Piatakov or whether Trotsky's letter that Radek said he had received in early January, 1937, had also mentioned them.

Sokol'nikov made it clear that he heard about Trotsky's negotiations with Hess from Piatakov:

> Vyshinsky: You spoke to Pyatakov after he had returned from abroad?
>
> Sokolnikov: Yes. That was in January 1936. Pyatakov told me that Trotsky had been negotiating with Hess. In these negotiations Hess was empowered to put forward **demands which concerned not only German interests but also the interests of another country**. Pyatakov told me that he had understood Trotsky to say that these were negotiations on a number of questions, and that agreement had been reached on them. (1937 Trial 152).

The "other country" was certainly Japan. Concerning Japan:

> ... Sokol'nikov told me that he had a talk with the Japanese, with Ota, I think, from which it was also clear that

> Trotsky was carrying on negotiations with representatives of the Japanese government. (LD 257)

> In just the same manner he had fully established contact with the Japanese government. (LD 268)

Tamekichi Ota was Japanese Ambassador to the USSR between 1932 and 1936. Unlike the previous case, where Hess and his putative agreement with Trotsky was mentioned during the trial, Ota's name never came up during the trial.

Sokol'nikov's claim that Ota had contacted him concerning Trotsky's agreement with the Japanese government was made public only in 1989.[26] Therefore Piatakov had heard about Ota from Sokol'nikov before the latter's arrest on July 26, 1936 (Piatakov himself was arrested on September 12, 1936).

There is no basis to think that Sokol'nikov would have lied to Piatakov about Ota's words to him. *Therefore this passage presents good additional evidence that Trotsky really had conspired with the Japanese.*

Concerning Britain and France:

> Of course, to reach agreements with Germany alone would be risky, since without a corresponding English and French counterweight Germany would put feet on the table and it would be very tough for us. Therefore in his practical steps he, Trotsky, is carrying out simultaneous preparatory work in different directions. (LD 267)

> Furthermore Trotsky informed me that at the same time he had succeeded in establishing businesslike contacts with leading persons of Great Britain and France.... Trotsky also mentioned that the latest negotiations with the Germans were conducted in the presence of the English and the French.

---

[26] See Izv TsK KPSS 9 (1989) p. 45; reprinted in R-PP 228-9.

> In France the contact was with the "Comité de Forges"[27]
> and with banking circles. In England, with some conser-
> vative circles. (LD 268)[28]

Given Trotsky's premises and his goals, his logic here, as described
by Piatakov, appears sound. Once he had ruled out the possibility
of a mass uprising or revolution against the Soviet government,
there remained only assassination (*terror*) and a *coup d'état.* War
with powerful capitalist states would result either in social disor-
der following a *coup* or through military action by the capitalist
states themselves.

If no *coup* took place, then defeatism in war would remain as a tactic. Under any of these circumstances prior agreements with the
major capitalist countries were all necessary either for seizing
power (with the help of the invading capitalist powers) or for retaining it (if a *coup* were successful).

This outline of Trotsky's plan for wartime is confirmed by a number of other sources including Marshal Tukhachevsky's confession
statement, Marshal Budyonny's report to Marshal Voroshilov
about the trial of the "Tukhachevsky Affair" defendants, the transcript of the trial of Tukhachevsky and his co-defendants, and Ezhov's interrogation of April 26, 1939. We have discussed
Budyonny's report and Tukhachevsky's confession in *Trotsky's
'Amalgams'* and *Trotsky's Lies*[29].

In his interrogation Ezhov said:

> Koestring touched on the NKVD. He said: "In the general
> plan of the tasks we face, the People's Commissar for In-

---

[27] On the Comité des Forges see the article at
https://en.wikipedia.org/wiki/Comité_des_forges and at the corresponding
French Wikipedia page.
[28] A longer passage from this same quotation is in Chapter Two, above.
[29] Furr, Amalgams, Chapter 9; TL Chapter 9. An English translation of Budyonny's
letter to Voroshilov is at
https://msuweb.montclair.edu/~furrg/research/budiennyiltr.html

ternal Affairs must play a determining role. Therefore for the success of the coup d'état and our seizure of power you must create in the NKVD a broad organization of those who agree with you, and it must be united with the military men." Koestring declared that these organizations, in the army and in the NKVD, must be prepared in such a way as to guarantee united actions at the outbreak of war towards the goal of seizing power.[30]

Persons Incriminated by Piatakov

In addition to the well-known Moscow Trials defendants Piatakov named a number of persons (all men) whom he said were mentioned to him by Trotsky in the course of their talk in Norway in December 1935.

> I just add that among the individual persons mentioned in the course of this talk by Trotsky were: Radek, Sokol'nikov, Serebriakov, Muralov, Beloborodov, Rakovsky, Budu Mdivani, V.M. Smirnov, Sapronov, Bukharin, Rykov, Tomsky, Uglanov, Preobrazhensky, Putna, Primakov, Krestinsky. (LD 270)

Of these a number had not yet been arrested by the date of Piatakov's Statement. Rakovsky was arrested on January 27, 1937; Bukharin and Rykov on February 27, 1937. Evgeniy A. Preobrazhensky was arrested on December 20, 1936. This was possibly a direct result of Piatakov's naming him. But the investigation had to have additional testimony against him, so perhaps the date is just a coincidence. Nikolai N. Krestinsky was not arrested until May 29, 1937. In December 1936 Timofei V. Sapronov had been confined in the Verkhneuralsk political isolator on a previous charge. He was

---

[30] Transcript of the Interrogation of the Prisoner (lit. 'Arrested Person') Ezhov Nikolai Ivanovich of April 26 1939." Lubianka 1939-1946, 62. At https://msuweb.montclair.edu/~furrg/research/ezhov042639eng.html The Russian text is online at https://msuweb.montclair.edu/~furrg/research/ezhovru.html (Text encoding Cyrillic – Windows).

not rearrested in connection with the Trotsky conspiracy until August 10, 1937.

Piatakov's Motive

It should be noted that in his Statement Piatakov does not praise Stalin or his policies. Nor did he do so at trial, even in his final statement, or in his post-sentence appeal. Nowhere did Piatakov claim that he now agreed that socialism in one country was possible, or that under Stalin the Soviet Union had followed the correct path to socialism and that now, at last, he realized that.

Neither Radek nor Sokol'nikov, of whom we have only their trial testimony, said that they now realized that Stalin's course was the correct one. All of them claimed that they regretted following Trotsky onto the path of terror and sabotage. All were in accord that the greatest crime was abetting Trotsky's alliance with the fascists.

The same is true of Rakovsky, and we have more evidence about him. We have some of his pretrial testimony. We also possess some documentary evidence about his post-trial imprisonment, information that we do not have about Radek and Sokol'nikov (Piatakov was executed on February 1, 1937.[31]) It is evident that Rakovsky remained hostile to the Soviet government and continued to protest against it while in prison.[32] We will also devote a separate chapter to them in a future book.

This failure to claim that Stalin's policy was correct is not consistent with any hypothesis that these men were forced to make false confession, or that they were trying to say what would be most pleasing to their captors in return for some kind of leniency for them, their families, etc. Other defendants, like Kamenev, did praise Stalin. Shestov, who asked to be executed, in his final words to the court praised Stalin "who holds and carries the banner of

---

[31] http://lists.memo.ru/d27/f408.htm#n86
[32] We discuss these issues in TC, Chapter Four..

Marx, Engels and Lenin in his strong, firm hands." (1937 Trial 562) But most of the defendants did not.

Moreover, we know that some of them did not confess all that they could. Radek, for example, praised Marshal Mikhail Tukhachevsky (1937 Trial). Yet he must have been aware that Tukhachevsky was part of the bloc of conspiracies against the Soviet state and was in contact with Trotsky. Radek named Vitovt Putna, who had previous been exposed by others. But he said nothing about Vitaly Primakov. We know that Piatakov, trying to convince the Politburo of his innocence, had offered to shoot the defendants at the 1936 Moscow Trial with his own hand including, if guilty, his own wife.[33]

Bukharin and Iagoda, at least, knew about Ezhov's participation in the network of conspiracies. Neither one exposed him, at a time when doing so could have stopped the huge mass murders of the "Ezhovshchina" and saved perhaps hundreds of thousands of lives.

Conclusion

Piatakov's statement offers an account of the Trotskyist conspiracy, including important facts about Trotsky's personal leadership that has not been available before.

* As we have shown here, it simply cannot have been "scripted" by the NKVD or prosecution. It represents what Piatakov chose to say.

* It confirms Piatakov's and Radek's accounts in their testimony at the second Moscow Trial of January 1937.

* It confirms that Piatakov did indeed make a secret visit to Trotsky in Norway in December 1935.

* It confirms Trotsky's collaboration with both Germany and Japan.

[33] "Extract from J.V. Stalin's presentation (Dec. 1936 CC Plenum)." *Voprosy Istorii* 1, 1995, 9-11. In English translation at
https://msuweb.montclair.edu/~furrg/research/stalinonoppsvi11995.html
Online, in Russian, at http://www.memo.ru/history/1937/VI9501.htm#_VPID_9

Chapter 5. Trotsky in the Transcript of the Tukhachevsky Affair Trial of June 11, 1937

In May and June, 1937, eight high ranking military commanders of the Soviet Union were arrested. The most famous among them was Mikhail Nikolaevich Tukhachevsky, one of the five marshals of the Soviet Union. The case is often called the "Tukhachevsky Affair" after him. The others were Iona E. Iakir, Ieronim P. Uborevich, Avgust I. Kork, Robert P. Eideman, Boris M. Fel'dman, Vitalii M. Primakov, and Vitovt K. Putna.

All of these officers confessed very quickly to various charges amounting to treason. They were put on trial on June 11, 1937, sentenced to death, and executed immediately.

On February 25, 1956, Nikita Khrushchev delivered his infamous "Secret Speech"[1] to the XX Party Congress of the Communist Party of the Soviet Union. In it he accused Joseph Stalin and, secondarily, Lavrentii Beria, of serious crimes, principally of the frame-up and execution of leading Party members. Khrushchev specifically stated that the Party leaders whom he named in his Speech and who had been executed during the 1930s had in fact been innocent, falsely framed on Stalin's orders.

Later in 1956 Khrushchev convened a high-level commission, the "Molotov Commission," to study this issue. Balanced between former long-time associates of Stalin and supporters of Khrushchev, the Molotov Commission did not agree to "rehabilitate"[2] – declare

---

[1] In Russian: "Zakrytyi Doklad," or "Closed Report," in that guests at the XX Party Conference were not invited to hear Khrushchev read it.
[2] "Rehabilitation" meant the declaration that a person had been improperly convicted (and, usually, executed). Rehabilitations were rarely, if ever, based on evidence. See the quotation from the fervently anticommunist scholar Marc Junge, in the Introduction.

innocent – most of the defendants in the three public Moscow Trials of 1936, 1937, and 1938.

The commission members did agree to declare innocent Marshal Mikhail Tukhachevsky and the seven other military commanders tried and executed with him.

> Комиссия также считает, что обвинения, выдвинутые против Тухачевского, Якира и других осужденных по делу «Военно-фашистского заговора» в июне 1937 года, являются необоснованными и должны быть с них сняты.[3]

The commission also considers that the charges against Tukhachevsky, Iakir and other convicts in the case of the "Military Fascist Conspiracy" in June 1937 are unfounded and should be removed from them.

This appears to have been a compromise. Khrushchev's men wanted the rehabilitation of all the accused, while the former Stalin associates probably wanted no rehabilitations at all.[4]

At the XXII Party Congress in October, 1961, where Khrushchev's people attacked Stalin with even more venom (and also attacked his principal supporters Molotov, Malenkov, Kaganovich, and even Voroshilov). Afterwards, from 1962 until he was deposed in October, 1964, Khrushchev authorized a large number of books and

---

[3] "Zapiska Komissii TSK KPSS pod Predsedatel'stvom V. M. Molotova v TSK KPSS o Predstavlenii Vyvodov po Rassmotrennym Materialam." ("Note of the Commission of the CPSU Central Committee under the Chairmanship of V. M. Molotov to the CPSU Central Committee on the Presentation of Conclusions on the Materials Considered") December 10, 1956. RKEB 2, 207.

[4] We know that Ivan Serov, Khrushchev's man as Chair of the KGB, withheld documents from the Commission. See Furr, *The Murder of Sergei Kirov*, pp. 128 ff. Even Matthew Lenoe, whose work on the Kirov murder is incompetent and dishonest in many respects, recognizes that Serov – meaning, of course, Khrushchev too – deliberately deceived the Molotov Commission. On May 21, 1974, Molotov told Feliks Chuev that Tukhachevsky had indeed been a loathesome and very dangerous traitor. *Sto sorok besed s Molotovym*. Moscow: "Terra",1991, 30.

articles praising the Tukhachevsky Affair defendants and a great many others who had been executed during the late 1930s.

Under Brezhnev, Andropov, and Chernenko, few rehabilitations took place, virtually all of these unpublicized. A year or so after Mikhail Gorbachev became First Secretary of the CPSU (March, 1985) he began to sponsor a flood of "rehabilitations" and also a large number of books and articles concerning the Tukhachevsky Affair defendants.

Since Khrushchev the innocence of Tukhachevsky and his co-defendants, along with a great many other military, Party, and other figures executed during the 1930s, has been taken for granted.[5] However, neither under Khrushchev nor under Gorbachev, nor since then, has any *evidence* been discovered that might support the contention that the Tukhachevsky defendants were innocent.

A great many documents from former Soviet archives have been published since the end of the USSR in 1991. These documents permit us to see that many – even, quite possibly, all – of the Khrushchev-era and Gorbachev-era accusations against Stalin are lies. A large amount of primary source evidence has been published that points to the guilt of Tukhachevsky and his co-defendants. But the central documents – the investigation files, including interrogations and confessions of Tukhachevsky et al., and especially the transcript of the trial of June 11, 1937, remained top-secret, inaccessible to all researchers.

The Tukhachevsky File Is Declassified

In 2017 Tukhachevsky's investigative file was quietly made available to researchers, in that it is available to be studied at the FSB Archive in Moscow. In May, 2018, the transcript of the Tuk-

---

[5] To give a recent example: in his 2017 book *Stalin. Waiting for Hitler, 1929-1941,* Stephen Kotkin simply claims: "in this case there was no military conspiracy." (377) For a critical study of Kotkin's dishonest and incompetent book, see Furr, SW.

hachevsky trial was published, again without any announcement, on one Ukrainian and one Russian internet site.[6]

A study of Tukhachevsky's investigative file and the trial transcript will be sufficient to prove to any objective student that Tukhachevsky and the commanders convicted and executed with him were guilty beyond doubt. They all confessed their guilt and gave detailed, and interestingly differentiated, confessions.

Trotsky in the Tukhachevsky Trial Transcript

Our specific interest in this article is the trial transcript and the additional evidence it contains that Leon Trotsky did indeed collaborate and conspire with the Germans and Japanese against the Soviet government. I have discussed much important evidence of Trotsky's collaboration with the fascists in my 2017 book *Leon Trotsky's Collaboration with Germany and Japan: Trotsky's Conspiracies of the 1930s, Volume Two*. Since that book was published, much additional evidence of Trotsky's Nazi and Japanese collaboration has come to light. Other chapters in the present study examine some of this extensive evidence.

Numbers in parentheses in this chapter are to the pages of the 172-page Russian-language transcript of the trial of Tukhachevsky et al. of June 11, 1937. I have translated into English only those passages from the transcript that concern Trotsky specifically.

A translation of the whole transcript is beyond the scope of this specific study. I do not think it would add much to the discussion of Trotsky's fascist collaboration. Objective students will understand that the testimony of the accused in this trial, coupled with the vast amount of evidence from other sources that confirms it, cannot have been faked in any way by "Stalin," i.e. the Soviet government.

---

[6] For links see the footnote in Chapter Four.

Denial of the Evidence

In the case of Tukhachevsky, and in the case of Leon Trotsky, there is a great deal of outright denial. Some people, primarily anticommunists and Trotskyists, will insist that all this evidence *must* have been faked and "planted" by the Soviet government, on the grounds that "Stalin was evil, so he must have been falsely accusing these people and Trotsky too," and/or "Trotsky was a true, principled revolutionary who would never have done the terrible things the defendants accuse him of." Such persons are not interested in the truth and will not be more convinced by a translation of the complete transcript than by the selections I provide here.

Indeed, *no* conceivable evidence would convince them. To such persons, evidence is irrelevant; all that counts is "faith" and "political correctness." This is the "argument from incredulity," a well-known and flagrant logical fallacy which, however, is ubiquitous among anticommunists, including well-known scholars, and among Trotskyists. It is common because it is *essential* to the retention of what I call the "Anti-Stalin Paradigm" – a false historical framework that can only be maintained through denial, prevarication, and fallacious reasoning.

Thematic Approach

The analysis below focuses on the most important themes concerning Trotsky's activities that are to be found in the Tukhachevsky Affair trial transcript. I have chosen to study the trial transcript here rather than the Tukhachevsky investigation file in part because of its inherent interest.

An additional and important consideration is the nature of the circumstances in which these defendants gave their testimony. These men knew that this trial was their last chance to assert that they had been falsely accused, "framed," tortured or threatened into making false confessions. If they had really been innocent, they surely would have made this known in some way at this trial.

It is futile to claim that persons accused of capital crimes and who, moreover, have confessed their guilt during interrogations, would restate their guilt in the strongest terms at trial and in their last words to the court – and yet be innocent victims of a frame-up. This is, of course, what the proponents of what I have called the Anti-Stalin Paradigm, anticommunists and Trotskyists, will in fact claim.

But they will do so in defiance of all reason and logic. Confessions of guilt may, under certain circumstances, be wrung by force or threat from innocent persons. But confessions of guilt themselves can never be evidence of innocence.

A claim of innocence is not conclusive evidence of innocence, since we expect that, in most cases, both the innocent and the guilty will profess their innocent. But these defendants did not claim that they were innocent. On the contrary: they admitted their guilt in the firmest and most convincing terms. Under these circumstances, their confessions at trial must be considered to be the strongest possible evidence of their guilt.

Defeatism and Fear of Defeat

We have a great deal of evidence from other sources that Trotsky was pushing for the defeat of the USSR in war against Germany, Poland, Japan, or a combination of these powers. Trotsky's advocacy of defeat and defeatism is mentioned by at least five of the defendants.

Iakir:

> Tukhachevsky first, more or less definitively, told me the current weakness of our abilities, the unity of the **fascist** activities of **Germany** and **Japan** with Poland, were leading to a situation when we needed to destroy the existing order, and he told me then and there that he had contact with **Trotsky** and with the **German General Staff**. In either my first talk with Tukhachevsky or the second, but in one of those talks Tukhachevsky, without

going into details, told me that **Trotsky** had set forth the essential assignment of strengthening the work of the counterrevolutionary and anti-Soviet elements in the army, and that he, Tukhachevsky, took upon himself the assignment of organizing and uniting these anti-Soviet and counterrevolutionary elements. Further, Tukhachevsky laid out for me **Trotsky's** directive, agreed upon with the **German General Staff** and detailed to some extent by himself personally. (11)

Tukhachevsky:

In accordance with **Trotsky's** instructions that it was necessary to establish contact with the **German General Staff**, in London in 1936 I had a talk with General Rundstedt of the **German General Staff**. He told me that he knew I was leading a conspiracy and that he had instructions to talk with me. I said that the conspiracy indeed existed and that it was led by me. **I asked Rundstedt where the main forces of the German army would attack, and I referred to Trotsky's directive that we should organize defeat where the German army would be in action.** (47)

Kork:

... the Red Army would suffer such losses that would permit the Right-**Trotskyists** to come to power and take power out of the hands of the Stalin government. (86)

Fel'dman:

I must return to **Trotsky's** directives. Later, when from **Trotsky's** first directives, about which Mikhail Nikolaevich [Tukhachevsky] informed me, he went on to discuss the preparation for the defeat of the Red Army, he said to me that he was doing this according to a new directive from **Trotsky**, adding that all means are good in the struggle to achieve our aims, in the struggle against Soviet power. (142)

When contact with Trotsky had been set up through Putna, who had been transferred to London, there began talks about defeatism ... (146)

Trotsky's Collaboration with the German General Staff

Iakir:

> Tukhachevsky laid out for me **Trotsky's** directive, agreed upon with the **German General Staff** and detailed to some extent by himself personally. (7)

Fel'dman:

> When contact with **Trotsky** had been set up through Putna, who had been transferred to London, there began talks about defeatism, and methods of terror and espionage appeared – all this in order to overthrow Soviet power and guarantee **Trotsky's** coming to power. **Trotsky** did not have real forces numbering in the thousands besides those that you see here and **therefore whatever Trotsky dictated to us, the German General Staff was dictating.** That's the way I see it and that's the way we should put it. (146)

Uborevich:

> The trial has freed me from the nightmares of conspiracy and the diabolical directives of Tukhachevsky, -- that is to say, of **Trotsky**, and the **German General Staff**. (155)

Putna:

> Many people know that I was a different person, and'for me now there is no other solace except that I was once a different person. And now, in a very short time, in my own internal feelings, I have returned to my former self. I believe that in a sick organism, one that is decaying, struck down as though by poisonous gases, in an organ-

ism rotted by **Trotsky**, who led me into service to the **German General Staff** ... (163)

Trotsky and the "Palace Coup" or *Coup d'État*

Iakir:

> ... **Trotsky's** directive ... came down to the following. The first point of the program laid out by **Trotsky** was **a coup d'état**, prepared by the "Muscovites," the participants in the counterrevolutionary anti-Soviet Right-**Trotskyist** organization, who had succeeded in feeling out and entering into contact with a number of Kremlin-based Chekists and with the immediate military guard of the Kremlin in the person of the chief of the Kremlin military school Egorov. (7)

Fel'dman:

> There were talks, as I have explained, about **a palace coup**. When contact with **Trotsky** had been set up through Putna, who had been transferred to London, there began talks about defeatism, and methods of terror and espionage appeared – all this in order to overthrow Soviet power and guarantee **Trotsky's** coming to power. (146)

IUrii Piatakov, Trotsky's Representative in the USSR

Iakir:

> The next assignment Tukhachevsky told me about was that he would maintain direct relations with **Trotsky** and with the **German General Staff**. With the first, through **Piatakov**, and with the second through Putna. (11-12)

> In particular, Tukhachevsky told me twice that he had received information from **Piatakov** and spoke about

his talks with the Rights, with Enukidze, and about one talk with Bukharin. (13)

Tukhachevsky:

> I mentioned Primakov. He told me that he was in contact with **Piatakov**, who was the leader of the **Trotskyist** center in Moscow. After that I got into personal contact with Piatakov.

> Ul'rikh: Personal contact?

> Tukhachevsky: Yes. Then in 1934-35 **Piatakov** told me of the plan of determined aggression by the **German** army, which would be linked with the loss by the USSR of Ukraine and the Primor'ye. He confirmed **Trotsky's** directive of 1934 that was set forth in a letter from **Sedov** and in oral form by Putna. **Trotsky** then gave me the assignment of activating the work as much as possible. Finally Putna arranged a meeting for me with **Sedov** in 1936. (46)

> Bliukher: Through whom, and how, were the talks concerning concessions to German fascism of the Ukraine and of Primor'ye to Japan?

> Tukhachevsky: It was **Piatakov** who told me, so really it was **Trotsky**, through Piatakov, but it was **Piatakov** who personally told me this. (66)

Primakov:

> In 1936 I spoke with Fel'dman, and, when I arrived in Leningrad, with Gar'kavy, and then retained my Trotskyist contact with **Piatakov**, with whom I met in the spring.

> Chairman: Did you systematically maintain contact with the leadership of the military center and the parallel Trotskyist center?

Primakov: Basically I maintained contact with **Piatakov.** (129)

[I asked] Tukhachevsky several times about his contacts with civilian counterrevolutionary organizations. Only in 1933 or the beginning of 1934 did he tell me that he was in contact with **Piatakov.**

Contact with **Piatakov** helped carry out sabotage in the area of artillery armament from the viewpoint of lowering our orders. (138)

Break Ties, Cut Off All Contract with Other Trotskyists

Iakir:

Despite the fact that Tukhachevsky repeatedly spoke to me about the necessity of the very greatest secrecy (**Trotsky** was repeatedly telling him this, saying that **the military conspiracy and its participants must not in any case be connected with other ways and lines** [of the conspiracy]), contact took place all the same. (13)

Tukhachevsky:

I regard my entry into the organization as of 1932. ... By the way, **I always and at every occasion have spoken out against Trotsky during discussions, just as I have against the Rights.** (37)

Primakov:

In 1934 I received the directive from **Piatakov** to break ties with the Dreitser group and with the old Trotskyists .... (125)

Tukhachevsky added that **Trotsky**'s directive stated that the work of the military organization must be led extremely independently, not by any means to be in contact with the anti-Soviet groupings that exist in our country among civilian organizations. (137)

Unity of the Rights and Trotskyists

Uborevich:

> ... [Tukhachevsky] began by showing the inevitability of our defeat in war against Japan, Germany, and Poland, and our internal difficulty. He began to tell me that he was heading an organization, that **he had contact with the Rights and Trotskyists**. (73)

Kork:

> In 1931, when I began my talk with Tukhachevsky, he explained the situation like this: we must unquestionably go with Rykov. It was not expedient at that time to defend **Trotsky** since he had lost authority in the country [the USSR]. But soon thereafter, in 1932, **Trotsky** was mentioned more and more often. And then in 1933, when the **fascist** coup took place in **Germany**, among those leaders under whose flag we were supposed to go were **Rykov, Bukharin, and Trotsky**. Later Tukhachevsky began to state, not by hinting but openly, that in the end the political group that would come out on top was hard to predict, whether **Rykov** or **Trotsky**, ... (92)

> ... I was shot through with doubts and gave in to the vile slander of the Rights and the even viler activities of the Trotskyists, **when the Rights and Trotskyists fused into one whole** and plotted the most criminal acts that can come into a person's head. (157)

Primakov:

> Tukhachevsky also said that there was also contact with the Rights. To my doubtful question – how with the Rights? From where? I knew that **Trotsky** was leading the conspiracy. Tukhachevsky answered that now **the**

separation between the Rights and Trotskyists has been wiped away, and since this is useful for our general business, why not have contact with the Rights also? (138)

Trotsky's Collaboration with the Japanese

Iakir:

> ... in one of the letters of **Trotsky** to Tukhachevsky **Trotsky had pressed us to develop work in the Far East with the goal of contact with the Japanese** for carrying out joint activity of the Germans. (27)

Fel'dman:

> Speaking of **Trotskyist cadres in the Far Eastern Region**, there were many of them, but I did not know any members of the conspiracy. (147)

Tukhachevsky:

> ... the road of the group, that put me on the road of foul Right opportunism and of three-times cursed **Trotskyism, that led to contact with German fascism and the Japanese general staff** ... (154)

Romm the Contact between Trotsky and Tukhachevsky

Tukhachevsky:

> ... when in 1932 **Romm** brought me **Trotsky's** proposal to gather together the **Trotskyist** cadres, I agreed. (37)

> Then in 1932 **Romm was sent from Trotsky**. This was approximately in August or September.

> Chairman: What did he say to you?

Tukhachevsky: **Romm gave me, in Trotsky's name**, the assignment of organizing and bringing together the Trotskyist cadre in the army. (37)

Trotsky Relied on Hitler's Coming to Power

Tukhachevsky:

> Later, in 1933-34 ... **Romm** gave me **an instruction of Trotsky's that we should evaluate Hitler's coming to power as a favorable factor** and we needed to take every measure to strengthen fascist power in Germany.
>
> I should add that already in 1932 **Romm** had told me that **Trotsky was counting on Hitler's coming to power and was sure that Hitler would support him, Trotsky,** thanks to which we could count upon the overthrow of Soviet power. Then in 1933-34 **Romm confirmed to me that fascism supported Trotsky** ... (37-38)

Primakov:

> When in 1933-34 Hitler came to power, we were given an official directive to stress our coolness towards the Germans at banquets. Tukhachevsky told me that **on Trotsky's directive, it was essential to let the Germans know that his attitude towards the Reichswehr remained just as good as earlier.** (138)

Trotsky's Son Leon Sedov

Tukhachevsky:

> [Piatakov] confirmed Trotsky's directive of 1934 that was set forth in a letter from Sedov and in oral form by Putna. **Trotsky** then gave me the assignment of activating the work as much as possible. Finally Putna arranged a meeting for me with Sedov in 1936. (46)

Putna:

> After the first discussions with generals Adam and Schleifer, **when I reported to Sedov** what I had achieved, I received a second **directive from Trotsky via Sedov** that this first success was not enough ... (109)

> On my way to London I met with **Sedov** ...Through **Sedov** I received parallel instructions from **Trotsky**, which came down to this: I should resurrect my German contacts ... (112)

> Ul'rikh: Did you organize a meeting with **Sedov**?

> Putna: Yes, at the request of Tukhachevsky I organized a meeting with **Sedov**. (115)

I.N. Smirnov, Leader of the Trotskyist Conspirators in the USSR

Putna:

> ... I stated that in 1931 in Berlin Ivan Nikitich **Smirnov**, in a talk with me in the embassy building, told me that **in order to show the Germans serious decisiveness of the Trotskyists towards collaborating with them**, we needed negotiations with them. (108)

> Question: From whom did you have the authority to conduct **talks with the German command**?

> Putna: From the Trotskyist organization.

> Ul'rikh: In the person of whom?

> Putna: I received it as a directive from **Trotsky,** through **Sedov** and Smirnov. (109)

Trotsky Agreed to Give Ukraine to Germany, the Primor'e[7] to Japan

Tukhachevsky:

> I mentioned Primakov. He told me that he was in contact with **Piatakov, who was the leader of the Trotskyist center in Moscow**. After that I got into personal contact with **Piatakov.**

> Ul'rikh: Personal contact?

> Tukhachevsky: Yes. Then in 1934-35 **Piatakov** told me of the plan of determined aggression by the German army, which would be linked with the loss by the USSR of Ukraine and the Primor'ye. (46)

> Bliukher: Through whom, and how, were the talks concerning concessions to German fascism of the Ukraine and of Primor'ye to Japan?

> Tukhachevsky: It was Piatakov who told me, so really it was **Trotsky, through Piatakov**, but it was Piatakov who personally told me this. (66)

Putna:

> After the first discussions with generals Adam and Schleifer, when I reported to Sedov what I had achieved, I received **a second directive from Trotsky via Sedov** ... Along with this it was proposed that I specify **what we promised generally in the way of compensation.**

> Chairman: Who is "we"?

---

[7] "Primor'e" refers to the Amur-Sakhalin region with its large petroleum deposits.

Putna: The Trotskyist organization. **The Trotskyist organization promises, first, territorial compensation** ...

Chairman: What did you promise in exchange for help?

Putna: The territory of the Ukraine. (109)

Trotsky and the German General Staff

Tukhachevsky:

> **In accordance with Trotsky's instructions that it was necessary to establish contact with the German General Staff,** in London in 1936 I had a talk with General Rundstedt of the German General Staff. [See under subhead "Defeatism & Fear of Defeat", above.]

Kork:

> Ul'rikh: You confessed that during 6-7 years you carried out sabotage, counterrevolutionary work. One thing I don't understand is: Who was the boss? **You mentioned the Trotskyist center, the center of the Rights, you have mentioned German circles. But who in fact was the boss,** who gave the basic directives up to the present time: Rykov, Trotsky, or German military circles?
>
> Kork: Under the circumstances that have been created most recently, **the boss is the German General Staff.**
>
> Ul'rikh: That means that your main boss was the German General Staff?
>
> Kork: **Yes.**
>
> Ul'rikh: The German General Staff – that is a concise answer. (101

Putna:

At Trotsky's direction I conducted such negotiations with generals Schleifer and Adam, who had established contact with us through Hoffmeister. (108-109)

Ul'rikh: With whom personally of the representatives of the German command did you carry on negotiations?

Putna: With major Hoffmeister, General Schleicher, and General Adam. (111)

In 1935, when I returned to London from the USSR, **Tukhachevsky** informed me about the successes in the Kiev and Belorussian military districts concerning the strengthening of aviation and of tank formations and **gave me instructions to pass this information however I could to the German General Staff**. On my way to London **I met with Sedov** ...

Ul'rikh: I did not understand – did you carry out your instructions and then return?

Putna: No, before carrying out my instructions. **Sedov gave me similar instructions from Trotsky**.

Ul'rikh: You had instructions to pass information. Did you meet **Sedov** and give information to him?

Putna: I tried to pass them **to the German General Staff.** (112)

Tukhachevsky:

I wish to draw a conclusion for myself from this vile work that has been done. I wish to draw the conclusion that under the conditions of the victory of socialism in our country every grouping becomes an anti-Soviet group and **every anti-Soviet groups becomes one with the vilest Trotskyism**, with the vilest current of the Rights. And since there is no base for these forces within our country, then whether they wish it or not, these groups slide further, **into contact with fascism, into contact with the German General Staff.** (153)

Trotsky Advocated the Restoration of Capitalism

Tukhachevsky:

> ... since there is no base for these forces within our country, then whether they wish it or not, these groups slide further, into contact with fascism, into contact with the German General Staff. This is the downfall of this counterrevolutionary work that was in its essence directed towards **the re-establishment of capitalism in our country.** (153)

Primakov:

> ... whom did **the fascist flag of Trotsky** join together? It joined together all the counterrevolutionary elements that we had. All of them, from the rags of the old officers' groups, to the Trotskyist group, with its vile terrorist directives, with its practice of struggle against the Party, though the remains of the Zinovievists, everything that was counterrevolutionary in the Red Army – all were gathered into one place, under one flag, **under the fascist flag in the hands of Trotsky.**

> What means did this conspiracy choose that are unequaled in history? All means, from the blackest betrayal, from treason, from the preparation of the defeat of one's own country through sabotage, through espionage, through terror, directed against the brain and heart of our country. These are the means that the conspiracy chose. **For what goal? For the restoration of capitalism.** (165)

Uborevich:

Chairman: For whose benefit was all this done, for what state, for which classes did you carry out your anti-Soviet struggle?

Uborevich: For the purpose of **restoring capitalism.** (77)

Trotsky Urged Sabotage and Terror

Primakov:

> Contact with **Piatakov** helped carry out **sabotage** in the area of artillery armament from the viewpoint of lowering our orders. (138)

> What means did this conspiracy choose that are unequaled in history? All means, from the blackest betrayal, from treason, **from the preparation of the defeat of one's own country through sabotage, through espionage, through terror**, directed against the brain and heart of our country. (165)

Fel'dman:

> When contact with **Trotsky** had been set up through Putna, who had been transferred to London, there began talks about defeatism, and **methods of terror and espionage** appeared – all this in order to overthrow Soviet power and guarantee **Trotsky's** coming to power. (146)

> Tukhachevsky told me in 1936 that in carrying out **Trotsky's directive about having recourse to terror**, and in particular in relation to Voroshilov, he gave such a directive to Primakov in 1936. (142)

Tukhachevsky:

> Then in 1933-34 **Romm** confirmed to me that fascism supported **Trotsky**, and therefore the latter demanded the activation of our work, especially in the area of or-

ganizing sabotage and terrorist activity in the army. (46)

Putna:

> Ul'rikh: How, then, did the Germans consider that the **Trotskyist** organization ought to show its strengths? In what way?

> Putna: This we thought would be **activities of a sabotage and terrorist nature.** (142)

Trotsky Plotted an Armed Uprising within the USSR

Primakov:

> Chairman [Ul'rikh]: Specifically, do you confirm your confessions about the preparation of a terrorist act by Trotskyist activists?

> Primakov: I did not give any such confessions. I confessed about **the preparation of an armed uprising**. (123)

> Primakov: **I had the following basic instruction: Until 1934 I worked for the most part, as an organizer, in gathering Trotskyist cadre.** In 1934 I received the instruction from **Piatakov** to break off ties with the group of Dreitser and old Trotskyists, who were assigned to prepare terrorist acts, and I myself was to prepare, in the military district where I worked, **to foment an armed uprising that would be called forth either by a terrorist act or by military action.** This was the assignment I was given. The military Trotskyist organizational center considered this assignment to be very important and its importance was stressed to me. I was told to break any personal acquaintance with old Trotskyists, with whom I was in contact. (125-126)

Primakov: I was instructed to seize Leningrad for the Trotskyists.

Ul'rikh: But if Germany had made war on the USSR, **for whom would you have seized Leningrad?**

Primakov: **For Germany**. (132)

Fel'dman:

> I remember that we talked in more detail on the eve of the trip to Germany (Tukhachevsky was the head of the delegation). **We spoke about overthrowing Soviet power by means of an armed uprising** and if this was not successful in peacetime, then to hope for problems at the front that might lead to armed demonstrations inside the country. Our method of work would be **supporting Trotskyist cadres**, support for those commanders who had earlier belonged to the Trotskyist or Zinovievist opposition, from among whom it would be easier to recruit people; ... (136)

Trotsky, An Agent of Fascism

Tukhachevsky:

> ... in 1933-34 **Romm** confirmed to me that **fascism supported Trotsky** ... (46)

Putna:

> Ul'rikh: How did he [German captain Salzman] repay you for this information?
>
> Putna: He did not repay me. I asked him, as an intermediary, to help me establish contact and to speak with Ribbentrop, because **I had an assignment from Trotsky to establish contact with the Germans.** (114)

Fel'dman:

In this way, summing up, I must say that everything we did were actions that served the interests of **the fascists and their agent Trotsky**, whose will we were carrying out ...

Trotsky did not have real forces numbering in the thousands besides those that you see here and therefore **whatever Trotsky dictated to us, the German General Staff was dictating.** That's the way I see it and that's the way we should put it. (146)

Iakir:

I have already said that I had a long, good, honorable life before that moment when I fell into the abyss, fell into the hands of the enemy, fell into the hands of the vilest of vile enemies that progressive humanity has, into the hands of **that murderer, that agent of German fascism, Trotsky.** (152)

Eideman:

I can now say without hesitation that I accept this harsh verdict so that with the last bit, the last minutes of my life, the last hours of my life to cover with curses **that vile enemy of the people, Trotsky, agent of German fascism, because of whom I too became an agent of German fascism**. (161)

Primakov:

All of them, from the rags of the old officers' groups, to the Trotskyist group, with its vile terrorist directives, with its practice of struggle against the Party, though the remains of the Zinovievists, **everything that was counterrevolutionary in the Red Army – all were gathered into one place, under one flag, under the fascist flag in the hands of Trotsky.** (165)

> The second group to which I belong is the Trotskyist
> group. ...the most cursed group in the conspiracy be-
> cause it has travelled the most vile path, has the most
> vile school and has as **its leader Trotsky, who de-
> manded the fascist banner.** (167)

Conclusion

The testimony of the Tukhachevsky Affair defendants is consistent
with a great deal of other evidence which we now possess that
Leon Trotsky did indeed conspire with Hitler's Germany and fascist Japan to encompass his return to power in the USSR through
assassination – the common Russian term is "terror" – sabotage, a
coup d'état against the Stalin leadership, and/or the organized defeat of the Red Army in a war against invading fascist powers coupled with an armed insurrection, evidently in Leningrad.

This testimony is consistent with the evidence we have collected
and studied in the books *Leon Trotsky's Collaboration with Germany and Japan* (2017), *Trotsky's "Amalgams"*, and *Trotsky's Lies.*

It is also consistent with the testimony of the defendants in the
three Moscow Trials. In *Trotsky's 'Amalgams'* and *The Moscow Trials As Evidence* we have shown that many of the fact-claims made
by defendants in their testimony at the Moscow Trials can be
checked against other evidence. We also showed that in a few
cases Moscow Trials defendants testified falsely, but in order to
conceal crimes they had committed that the prosecution did not
discover. Thus we concluded that the Moscow Trials testimony, far
from having been "fabricated" by the prosecution, is valid evidence.

Trotsky denied the accusations that he had collaborated with fascist German and Japanese leaders. But Trotsky would have denied
the accusations whether he were guilty of them or not. So his denials mean nothing – they are not evidence.

In addition, we know that Trotsky lied. Unquestionably, he did so
in order to conceal his conspiracies. Trotsky denied that a "bloc" of

Rights and Trotskyists existed. Yet in 1980 Pierre Broué, the most famous Trotskyist historian of his day, discovered documents in the Harvard Trotsky Archive that prove that such a bloc existed and that Trotsky had approved it. Trotsky swore that he had cut off all ties to those who "capitulated" to Stalin, yet American historian Arch Getty discovered evidence in the same archive that Trotsky did in fact contact some of these men. Getty also discovered that the Harvard Trotsky Archive had been "purged," undoubtedly of incriminating materials. We refer the interested reader to our detailed study of these matters in Trotsky's 'Amalgams' and Trotsky's Lies.

We have good non-Soviet evidence that military conspiracies did threaten the Soviet leadership. American researcher Alvin D. Coox revealed that NKVD General Genrikh S. Liushkov, who defected to the Japanese in June, 1938, privately told his Japanese military handlers that there was indeed a conspiracy among the military leaders in the Soviet Far Eastern Army.[8] Such a conspiracy is alluded to in the Tukhachevsky trial transcripts and in Tukhachevsky's own confessions.

We have the Arao document, and the confession of Nikolai Ustrialov, both of which implicate Tukhachevsky in conspiracy with the Japanese.[9] Ustrialov's confession ties the Soviet-based Trotskyists to this collaboration as well. All these matters are thoroughly examined in Trotsky's 'Amalgams' and The Moscow Trials as Evidence. We have the large amount of testimony in PiLT2 that we explore in other chapters of the present book.

We know that in early 1937 Hitler's regime was expecting a military coup against the Stalin government. On page seventeen of his

---

[8] For a fuller discussion, see Furr, The Murder of Sergei Kirov, Chapter 17. See also Trotsky's 'Amalgams' Chapter 7, and The Moscow Trials as Evidence, Chapter 7.
[9] For the Arao Document see Furr, Moscow Trials,, Chapter 10; Furr, Amalgams, Chapter 10; Stalin. Waiting For ... the Truth, Chapter 9. For Ustrialov's confession, see Furr, Amalgams, Chapter 11, and Furr, Trotsky's Lies, Chapter 11.

book *Mission to Moscow* (1941) Joseph E. Davies noted that he was warned of such an event by a German official in 1937.[10]

We have the Mastny-Benes note of February, 1937, from the Czech national archives, in which Czech diplomat Mastny informs the Czech president that a German diplomat had told him that Hitler was no longer interested in an agreement with Czechoslovakia, since he expected a military coup in the USSR shortly.[11] We know that, in 1944, Heinrich Himmler asked Russian defector General Andrei Vlasov why Tukhachevsky's conspiracy had failed.[12]

We have a great deal of evidence that Tukhachevsky and the others were guilty. We have evidence that Trotsky was indeed conspiring with Germany and Japan. And in the trial transcript, we have the testimony that Tukhachevsky and the other military men were collaborating with Trotsky and with Germany and Japan.

There is no plausible scenario that could account for all this evidence except that Trotsky, along with the Soviet military commanders, was indeed collaborating with Hitler's government and the Japanese militarists.

---

[10] Quoted in *Stalin. Waiting* ..., 153-4.
[11] See Furr, Amalgams, Chapter 7, and Moscow Trials, Chapter 7.
[12] See the quotations by Himmler, Vlasov, and Goebbels in Grover Furr, "New Light On Old Stories About Marshal Tukhachevskii : Some Documents Reconsidered." *Russian History/Histoire Russe* 13, nos. 2-3 (Summer-Fall, 1986), 303. This article can be retrieved in facsimile at https://msuweb.montclair.edu/~furrg/tukhpdf.pdf and in html format at https://msuweb.montclair.edu/~furrg/tukh.html

Conclusion

President Putin's Remarks about the Start of World War II

On December 20, 2019, Russian President Vladimir Putin gave a talk to representatives of the Commonwealth of Independent States (CIS). In that talk he refuted the often-repeated falsehood that the Soviet Union shared with Hitler's Germany the responsibility for starting World War II.[1]

Putin cited more than thirty primary source documents. None of them are secret. All of them have long been known to specialists in the history of this period. These documents show that it was Poland and the Western imperialist countries that made the war inevitable by catering to Hitler and by rejecting all the Soviet Union's honest attempts to build collective security against Hitler.

Responses from Polish and Western sources were quick in coming.[2] In *The Atlantic*, anticommunist commentator Anne Applebaum called it "Putin's Big Lie."[3] But what Putin said is not a lie: it is the truth. *None* of these responses confronted, or even mentioned, the primary source evidence that Putin cited. The reason is clear: the documents do indeed prove the guilt of the governments of Poland, the U.K., France, and even the USA, in mollifying Hitler and refusing collective security.

---

[1] The Russian text of Putin's talk is at https://rg.ru/2019/12/20/stenogramma-vystupleniia-vladimira-putina-na-neformalnom-sammite-sng.html The English version is at http://en.kremlin.ru/events/president/transcripts/62376

[2] The response of the Polish Ministry of Foreign Affairs: https://www.gov.pl/web/dyplomacja/stanowisko-msz-rp-wobec-falszywych-narracji-historycznych-prezentowanych-przez-federacje-rosyjska The English translation: https://www.gov.pl/web/diplomacy/statement-of-polish-mfa-on-false-narratives-presented-by-the-russian-federation

[3] At https://www.theatlantic.com/ideas/archive/2020/01/putin-blames-poland-world-war-ii/604426/

Instead of dealing forthrightly with the evidence the Polish and Western responses called his remarks "Stalinist propaganda." This is true — Putin's remarks echoed the position of the Soviet government of the late 1930s and the post-war period.

In the dishonest world of anticommunist propaganda, to term a statement "Stalinist" means that *it does not need to be refuted.* Any statement called "Stalinist" is *assumed* to be false, even when it is true.

Anyone who reads the text of Putin's remarks would notice this trick. But few people will do so. Many more will read the dishonest attacks by the Polish government and anticommunist writers.

The Academic History of the Stalin Period is Dishonest

The mass media do not deal with research. They must publish too quickly. Writers for the mass media rely upon legitimated authorities such as academic experts. Writers of popular and semi-popular works, and authors of textbooks for use in schools and colleges, rely on academic historians too.

The media and the public assume that academic authorities base what they write and say upon evidence. But in the field of Soviet history of the Stalin period, this assumption is not valid. Certain fundamental falsehoods about Soviet history of this period cannot be questioned, regardless of the evidence. To question, much less refute, them is forbidden. Evidence that contradicts this taboo is ignored, while false evidence is invented. This is how the Anti-Stalin Paradigm works.

The conclusions to be drawn from the primary source evidence are as firmly established as they are unacceptable – unacceptable to "mainstream" anticommunist scholarship and to Trotskyists, and thereby, unacceptable in public discourse. Briefly, the conclusions are as follows:

* The defendants in the three Moscow Trials of August, 1936, January, 1937, and March, 1938, were provably guilty of at least those crimes to which they admitted guilt.

* The "Tukhachevsky Affair" commanders arrested in May, 1937, tried and executed in June, 1937, did indeed conspire to join forces with Nazi Germany to seize control over the USSR.

* Leon Trotsky was indeed provably guilty of plotting to murder Sergei Kirov, Stalin, and other Soviet leaders; of conspiring with the German General Staff and the Nazi leadership to overthrow the Soviet government and Party leadership, either by a *coup d'état* or by aiding a German and/or Japanese invasion; and of conspiring with German agents, Russian fascists, Ukrainian nationalists, plus his own followers, to sabotage various economic enterprises in the USSR in order to weaken Soviet defense.

These are the same charges that were leveled by the Stalin government against Trotsky during the 1930s. They are the same as those that were summarized very well in the famous book by Michael Sayers and Albert E. Kahn, *The Great Conspiracy. The Secret War Against Soviet Russia*, first published in 1946, translated into dozens of languages and republished until Khrushchev's "Secret Speech."

We need to follow the logic of these facts, now thoroughly established through primary source evidence, in order to draw out their full implications.

What If Trotsky Had Succeeded?

Counterfactual history, also sometimes referred to as virtual history, is a form of historiography that attempts to answer "what if" questions known as counterfactuals. Black and MacRaild provide this definition: "It is, at the very root, the idea of conjecturing on what did not happen, or what might have happened, in order to understand what did happen." (Wikipedia)[4]

The Wikipedia entry continues:

> One goal is to estimate the relative importance of a specific event, incident or person.

Below I briefly outline two aspects of counterfactual history. They help to clarify the issues at stake in any objective, truthful study of Soviet history of the Stalin period.

* What would the world have looked like if Trotsky's conspiracies had in fact succeeded?

* What would world history look like if historians recognized the truth and rewrote their histories accordingly?

If Trotsky's Conspiracies Had Succeeded

Trotsky's goal was to take control of the Soviet Union. This goal dictated the nature of his conspiracies, including his cooperation with the fascist powers.

If Trotsky and his allies, the fascist powers, had overthrown the Stalin and the Soviet leadership, and seized control over the Soviet Union, there would have been many drastic changes. We will cite only this one: Hitler, Mussolini, and the Japanese fascist militarists, the Axis powers, would have been immeasurably stronger.

* Hitler and, in the East, the Japanese would have had the immense natural and human resources of the USSR to use in their wars against the Western imperialist powers, especially the U.K., France, and the United States.

---

[4] At https://en.wikipedia.org/wiki/Counterfactual_history (accessed January 25, 2020)

* The Western imperialist powers might well have chosen to compromise with Hitler and the Japanese, rather than risk an all-out war against a very much stronger fascist enemy. After all, Britain and France were far more eager to go to war against the USSR in early 1940, in alliance with pro-German Finland, than they were to send their armies against Hitler.

Either scenario would have left fascism secure and in control of a great part of the world. Much, if not most, of the world would resemble Francisco Franco's Spain – a murderous, viciously exploitative police state, maintained by fascist terror against everyone who opposed fascist aims.

The antiracist and anti-imperialist struggles for national liberation from imperialism would have been dealt a tremendous blow. The consequences for the fates of hundreds of millions of the non-white people in the world can hardly be overestimated.

Hitler's stated goal in "General Plan East" was to murder most of the Slavic peoples – tens of millions -- and keep the rest for cheap labor. The Nazis and their fascist allies like the Vichy French and Ukrainian nationalists killed almost half the world's Jews. Had Hitler prevailed, that number would have been 90 per cent or more.

All around the world, the labor movement would have suffered much more intense repression. In a world much of which was directly ruled by fascists, while the rulers of the rest of the world temporized and collaborated with the fascists, the standard of living of working people would have fallen drastically, while their mortality would have skyrocketed.

Human progress would have suffered an enormous setback in every area of life. A great many persons alive today would never have been born at all. Most other people would be suffering far more exploitation and oppression.

Trotsky, his supporters, and his co-conspirators like Tukhachevsky, Bukharin and Rykov, now at the mercy of their "allies" the German, Japanese, British, and French ruling classes, would never have been successful in retaining power in a weakened, shrunken USSR. Tukhachevsky saw himself as the eventual "Napoleon." At the Third Moscow Trial of March, 1938, Bukharin admitted that he and his fellow conspirators had no reason to believe that Hitler would remain faithful to any deal they made with him.

If Historians Recognized that Trotsky and the Moscow Trials Defendants Were Guilty

The Soviet Union was able to defeat the fascist invasion *because* the chain of conspiracies, with Trotsky at the center and with the fascists providing the military might, while the Western imperialists facilitated both, was smashed by the Soviet government. The Soviet Union – "Stalin" – saved the world from fascism not just once, by defeating the Nazi juggernaut, but *twice*: the first time, by smashing the Trotskyist-Nazi-fascist-capitalist conspiracies to turn the Soviet Union into Hitler's ally. Understanding of this fact was widespread after World War II, when *The Great Conspiracy* became a worldwide best-seller. But the authors were forced to withdraw the book from publication after Khrushchev gave his "Secret Speech."

The Effects of Khrushchev's Lies

The force that overthrew this understanding of history did not come from anticommunist historians, but from within. Nikita Khrushchev's infamous "Secret Speech" to the XX Congress of the Communist Party of the Soviet Union began the process of denying the truth about the anti-Soviet conspiracies and Trotsky's role in them.[5] Khrushchev accelerated his attack on the truth at the XXII Party Congress in 1961.

The lies of Khrushchev and his historical propagandists were avidly taken up by anticommunist historians around the world. Millions of communists, workers, students, and other anti-capitalist

---

[5] For the evidence that Khrushchev's "Secret Speech" was virtually nothing but lies see Furr, *Khrushchev Lied*.

forces and *potential* pro-communist activists also believed Khrushchev. They would never have believed any overtly capitalist propaganda, no matter how "scholarly" it appeared. But they accepted the word of Khrushchev, leader of the Soviet Communist Party and the world communist movement.

Inspired by Khrushchev's slander of Stalin, anticommunist propagandists got to work. But their lies would never have been so widely accepted if Khrushchev had not loosed an army of pseudoscholars, phony historians, to add false details to his attack on Stalin.

Within a few years Khrushchev's propagandists had accused Stalin of dozens of crimes and atrocities. Some, such as the "Katyn Massacre," were real atrocities that had been committed by others – in the case of Katyn, by the German invaders and their Ukrainian nationalist allies. Others, like the great famine of 1932-33, were natural events that were falsely blamed on "Stalin's" – the Soviet government's – policies.

None of these accusations were supported by primary source evidence. In 1962 Petr Pospelov, one of Khrushchev's top officials, told a convention of historians that they would *not* be permitted to go to the Party archives to search for evidence, but had to rely on the statements of top Party officials.[6] Today, with the partial opening of former Soviet archives, we know why Pospelov did this. No evidence for the accusations against Stalin exists! On the contrary: all the evidence shows that Khrushchev and his men were lying.

Within a decade of Khrushchev's speech the Moscow Trials defendants were widely believed to have been innocent. Many people started to consider Trotsky a lone, courageous voice for true communism against the monster Stalin. This remains the historical orthodoxy to this day.

---

[6] See Politbiuro member Petr Pospelov's remarks to Party historians *in Vsesoiuznoe soveshchanie o merakh uluchshenia podgotovki nauchno-pedagogichesikh kadrov po istoricheskim naukam. 18-21 dekabria 1962 g.* M: Izdatel'stvo "Nauka", 1964, 298, quoted in English translation in Furr, Collaboration, 8.

Leon Trotsky's Guilt

Though he never admitted it, Khrushchev copied some of his flagrant lies about Stalin from Trotsky's writing. Anticommunist
writers chose to believe Trotsky's lies, just as they chose to believe
the lies of Khrushchevites.

In 1956, Trotskyism was a tiny movement with little influence.
Khrushchev's "Secret Speech" and subsequent avalanche of lies
about Stalin changed that. To some people Trotsky now appeared
to be the "prophet" that British historian and Trotsky admirer
Isaac Deutscher had called him. Anticommunist writers now accepted -- believed -- Trotsky's version of events, just as they "believed" the lies of Khrushchev and his men. For anticommunists
and Trotskyists, this torrent of filth that the "communist" leaders
were pouring over their own heritage was too good not to make
full use of.

Trotskyist groups soared in membership, as they claimed to be the
"good" communists. But they paid a price. Trotskyism became
parasitical on overtly anticommunist scholarship. Trotskyists con-
structed a "cult of personality" around their hero. For them, Trotsky's writings became the source of all political wisdom.

Today, with the flood of primary source documents coming out of
former Soviet archives, we have the evidence to prove that Trotsky
lied, flagrantly and frequently. As this and my previous books have
demonstrated, we also have the evidence to prove that Trotsky
was involved in serious conspiracies of sabotage, assassination,
and fascist collaboration.

The Trotskyist movement had wedded itself to the professional
anticommunist "scholars" more firmly than ever. Trotskyist writers cite these scholars frequently, in defense of their own or Trotsky's assertions. It is clearer than ever that Trotskyism functions
as the "left wing" of conventional, pro-capitalist anticommunism.

Regardless of the evidence, Trotskyists -- at least the leadership of Trotskyist groups -- are never going to admit the truth. In this too they resemble the professional anticommunist "scholars."

Not a "Political Line" But the Truth

Anticommunists and Trotskyists will reject the research in this book, but not because of any fault in that research. They will reject it because they cannot honestly confront the evidence, and the conclusions that follow from it. They are not interested in the truth. Rather, they are promoting a political "line" – the Anti-Stalin Paradigm.

People who push a political "line" instead of the truth tend to assume that everyone is acting in the same dishonest manner and is promoting *their* political "line." So they will call this book "pro-Stalin," "Stalinist," etc., as though I too am pushing some political "line."

But they are wrong. I am not promoting any political line or position. I am interested in the truth. I strive for objectivity as much as any scientist. I try hard to question my own biases and prejudices (everybody has them) and to give an especially generous reading to any evidence that tends to cast doubt on those prejudices or that tends to disprove the hypotheses I have chosen to test in my research.

For many years I have been diligently searching for evidence of crimes that Stalin committed. I have searched for them in the only legitimate way – by identifying, locating, obtaining, and studying primary source evidence, and then by drawing logical conclusions from that evidence. Likewise, I have given Trotsky every benefit of the doubt in my research.

No one asks what Sherlock Holmes' politics are. We just want him to solve the mystery! In the same way, my own political proclivities are irrelevant. Nevertheless, the results of my research in this book, as in my other works, will be rejected by those who are un-

able or unwilling to consider the possibility that their own preconceived ideas are mistaken.

To all other readers – the vast majority – I submit this research,
and the conclusions based upon it. I welcome your comments and
especially your criticisms. My email address is easy to find on the
Internet.

Grover Furr
February, 2020

Appendix: Documents

Sokol'nikov Transcript of Interrogation of October 20 1936

Transcript of Interrogation of Sokol'nikov Grigorii Iakovlevich, of October 20, 1936

Sokol'nikov G.Ia., born 1888, born in city of Romny (former Poltava oblast'), until arrest the Vice-Commissar of the Forest Industry, former Candidate Member of the CC VKP(b) and former member of the VKP(b) since 1905.

Question: In the transcript of your interrogation of October 4, 1936 you stated that you established contact with Baldwin. Through the English journalist Talbot you told him about the existence and plans of the bloc and asked Baldwin to give support to the government of the bloc after its coming to power.

Did you inform Talbot of the composition of the government that the bloc intended to form after its accession to power?

Answer: When I met with Talbot in 1934 he asked me to tell him the composition of the government planned by the bloc. I answered him that the bloc had not yet determined the full composition of the government as we considered this premature.

However, as concerns the basic group of persons who would enter the government, there was complete unanimity.

In this basic group would be included: Rykov, Kamenev, Zinoviev, Bukharin, Piatakov and I – Sokol'nikov.

Talbot asked what distribution of functions was planned for the members of the government group. I answered that no final and firm distribution of functions could be determined at the present moment, but for all of us it was without question that Rykov would be proposed as Chairman of the Council of People's Commissars

(Sovnarkom), Kamenev –Chairman of the Council of Labor and De-
fense, and possibly also People's Commissar of Foreign Affairs,
Piatakov – People's Commissar of Heavy Industry, I – Sokol'nikov –
People's Commissar of Finance.

To Talbot's question about who was planned as head of the Party
leadership I answered that by general agreement of all the groups
in the bloc Trotsky would be at the head of the Party leadership.
Here I cautioned Talbot that it was possible that Trotsky would
not be put at the head of the Party leadership immediately after
the coup since he was politically compromised in the eyes of the
broad masses. However, as soon as the situation had become
strong enough, Trotsky would be at the head of the Party leadership.

Question: Did you tell Talbot how the bloc intended to effect the
coup and seize power in the USSR?

Answer: Talbot himself asked me this question. I understood that
he wanted to clarify the extent to which the bloc was a real power.

I explained to Talbot that the bloc represented a serious political
factor since it was the result of a political agreement between the
Trotskyists, the Zinovievists, and the Rights, and thus it united all
the oppositional forces. Thanks to this unity the bloc had very
broad contacts in the country.

To Talbot's question about what plan for seizing power the bloc
had, I told him that I could not tell him these kinds of details. However, I told Talbot that the bloc was relying on the forces of its
supporters in the country, on the one hand, and on the other hand
was counting on the possibility of disorganization and weakness of
the Party leadership.

I did not consider it possible to inform Talbot about the bloc's
plans more concretely.

Question: What did you tell Talbot about the program of activity of the government of the bloc?

Answer: In my previous confession I have already said that I informed Talbot about the bloc's program, consisting in the rejection of the current policy of industrialization and collectivization. I explained that this meant permitting capitalist elements in the country's economy alongside the socialist elements. I stressed to Talbot that since the current government has completely liquidated the capitalist elements in the country, the government of the bloc would be forced to carry out its measures gradually at first, developing its program more broadly as it becomes stronger in the country.

/ 326 /

I told Talbot that it was essential to warn Baldwin about this so that during this first period there should be no misunderstanding abroad of the program of the bloc and, as a result of this, a hostile attitude towards the government of the bloc.

Question: What concretely did you tell Talbot about the further relations between the government of the bloc and the English government?

Answer: Talbot asked me how the coming to power in the USSR of the government of the bloc would affect Anglo-Soviet relations. I answered that the foreign policy of the bloc would unquestionably permit the removal of the friction that now exists between the English and Soviet governments by means of important concessions that would go far to meet the demands of conservative English circles in the areas of economic and political relations.

I said that large orders would be given to English industry, that together with this the government of the bloc would agree to grant broad concessions to English capital in the USSR. I brought to Talbot's attention the positive attitude of Trotsky, Kamenev, and Rykov to the broad development of concessions in the USSR – these have long been well known. Then Talbot asked me whether I could tell him something about the possibility of recognizing the prerevolutionary debts. I told him that on this question the government of the bloc would also be ready to make significant concessions and to make proposals acceptable to the English government.

I also told him that on the question of the Comintern the government of the bloc would be ready to give all the necessary guarantees that it would completely refuse any help to the Comintern.

Summing up our talk Talbot said that he considered the question of the debts to be very important and I again reaffirmed to him the readiness of the government of the bloc to make serious concessions on this question.

On this point my talk with Talbot of the end of the summer of 1934 ended.

Question: Did you return again to these questions during your meeting with Talbot in the summer of 1935?

Answer: As I have already confessed in the transcript of my previous interrogation, when I met with Talbot in 1935 our talk consisted, in the main, of his giving me Baldwin's answer. Talbot told me that through Boothby, a Conservative Member of Parliament who was very close to Baldwin, he had transmitted to Baldwin Talbot's talk with me in all its details. Both Boothby and Baldwin had expressed great interest in Talbot's report. Through Boothby Baldwin tasked Talbot to inform me that he would guarantee friendly relations with the government of the bloc from the side of the governing conservative circles and expressed satisfaction with the course of internal and external policies that would be carried out by the government of the bloc.

At that same time Talbot told me that Baldwin considered it quite possible to guarantee the government of the bloc a loan and credits from England under the condition that the government of the bloc carried out the political and economic program that had been indicated.

As I have already confessed, Talbot and I agreed to maintain contact during Talbot's trips to the USSR. But after this talk Talbot did not contact me anymore.

Question: You say that you did not meet with Talbot any more. Did you try to contact him?

Answer: I made no attempt to contact Talbot since I expected that Talbot would come to the USSR in the spring or summer of 1936. He had expressed such a proposal during our talks.

Written down accurately from my words, read through by me. (Signed: Sokol'nikov)

Interrogator: Ass't Chief of the EKO* of the GUGB** of the NKVD of the USSR Major of State Security (Signed: Chertok)

RGASPI, F. 17. Op. 171. D. 246. L. 151-158. Copy. Typewritten.

Handwritten note on the first page: Distribute to the members of the CC VKP(b) J. Stalin

* Economic Division ** Main Directorate of State Security

Note: Talbot is probably Stafford Talbot, former editor of the British-Russian Gazette and Trade Outlook. Boothby is probably Robert Boothby, later Baron Boothby. Baldwin is Stanley Baldwin, British Prime Minister.

Piatakov Statement to Ezhov December 19-20 1936

РГАСПИ. ф.17. оп.171. д.263. лл. 43-76. (Russian State Archive of Socio-Political History, fond 17, opis 171, delo 263, pages 43-76. This archive is in Moscow). Page numbers here marked // //

ЦА ФСБ. Р-33835. Дело № 3257 по обвинению Пятакова Юрия Леонидовича и других. (Central Archive of the Federal Security Service. R-33835 (Case No. 3257 concerning the accusation against Piatakov, Iurii Leonidovich and others. This archive is also in Moscow).

Том 1, Лист дела (далее —ЛД) 237 (Volume 1, list of the file (= LD) 237)

//43//

To the People's Commissar of Internal Affairs of the U.S.S.R.

Com. N.I. Ezhov

My previous confessions in the course of interrogations about our criminal counter-revolutionary activity were fragmentary and incomplete. It is hard to pile all the filth upon oneself at one time.

I have considered the entire course of my own and my co-participants' struggle against the party and the soviet state and I have decided that I must finally and as completely as possible tell the whole truth about our treasonous work which can only be called betrayal of our country. I was one of the leaders of that base and detestable work that we actively carried out during the last 4-5 years against the party and the working class.

I have only one wish now – to tell everything I know as fully as possible.

Therefore please permit me to return in this statement to a few substantive incidents in our counter-revolutionary activity that I touched upon earlier, so that I may tell about them more systematically and specifically.

1/ Resumption of contact with Trotsky and renewal of my criminal work

My active Trotskyist work began again in 1931.

LD 238

I have already confessed about my frame of mind before 1931 and will not return to this.

In 1931 I happened to be in Berlin for purposes of my work. At that same time I.N. Smirnov also arrived in Berlin for work during that summer. I.N. Smirnov visited me at my room in Berlin and told me that he had a meeting with Trotsky's son L. Sedov and that Sedov had communicated to him a series of very serious directives of Trotsky's. //44//

Sedov briefly informed me about "Trotsky's new orders," as he put it. In particular he told me that Trotsky thinks that the main task is the overthrow of Stalin and his closest associates by any means possible, and also the active opposition to all practical undertakings of the government, especially in the economic sphere.

Trotsky considers that the reconstruction on this basis of the Trotskyist-Zinovievist organization in the U.S.S.R. and the unification in one form or another of all force that can help to overthrow the "Stalinist regime" is the most essential task.

At the same time I.N. Smirnov uttered a phrase whose meaning became clear to me only much later: "Lev Davidovich believes that one of the basic causes of our previous defeat is that in our struggle we remained within the limits of the state alone and did not seek help from outside it."

The renewed struggle will inevitably post international questions and we will decide these questions in the manner that is favorable to us."

LD 239

Thus Smirnov informed me that Sedov had been assigned by Trotsky to meet and talk with me and that he would bring the two of us together if I did not object. Smirnov himself urged me to meet with Sedov.

I agreed. Smirnov said that Sedov would first contact me by telephone. Soon after that Sedov did in fact phone me. Our phone conversation was quite short; we agreed on a meeting place. That same day I went to the "Café am Zoo" (where we had agreed to meet) and there I found Sedov, whom I had known very well before.

Sedov immediately told me that he was speaking to me not on his own //45// account but on behalf of his father L.D. Trotsky. When Trotsky found out that I was in Berlin he had given him the most strict instruction to meet with me at any cost and give me his, Trotsky's, instructions.

Sedov proceeded to expound what he had been instructed to say. Of course I cannot repeat word for word what he said, but I give the essence precisely.

"The struggle against Stalin is being renewed with new force. It must be understood that Trotsky had not abandoned this struggle for an instant. A temporary lull had been unavoidable, caused by Trotsky's geographical movements. Now the period of lull had ended. Contacts are being renewed. Within the country a new center was being formed, with which he, Trotsky, was already in contact. A bloc with the Zinovievists was being considered."

"Trotsky considers it essential to form a unified organization, regardless of his concerns about Zinoviev and Kamenev, who will undoubtedly attempt to

LD 240

occupy the leading role in this bloc. This danger of course cannot be excluded if Trotsky's supporters play only an observer's role instead of the active work that the present situation demands."

"Trotsky knows that the Rights – Bukharin, Tomsky, and Rykov, had also not laid down their weapons, and have only been silent. They have cadre, contacts, whole groups, sometimes very militant ones. It is not a problem that we had sharp disagreements only recently. These disagreements are nothing in comparison with our common anti-Stalin policy. Indeed it was on the eve of the bloc with Zinoviev-Kamenev that we had very sharp battles with the "Leningradists," with whom soon afterwards we //46// went shoulder to shoulder against Stalin."

"As far as he, Trotsky, was aware, there were also other elements who were dissatisfied with the Soviet government. We must draw them to us. We must understand that a very sharp struggle is beginning, not a discussion and not an exchange over principles, but a struggle for power. Therefore we must mobilize directly or indirectly all those forces that can collaborate in resolving the basic, the root task of the day – the task of overthrowing Stalin whatever it takes and at no matter what cost."

"We must discard old prejudices. Today's policy is: "Everything that is against Stalin is for us and must be mobilized.""

Trotsky demands and is convinced that I, Piatakov, will not decline active participation in this struggle."

"He knows your tendency to bury yourself in the practical business of the moment. This is completely impermissible now. This intolerable passivity must end

LD 241

– you understand that it is not I, but Lev Davidovich, who demands it."

I answered that I understood Trotsky's demand and was ready to carry out his directive."

Sedov expressed his great happiness and declared with feeling:

"Lev Davidovich has always had confidence in you. He has not doubted for a second that, if we act decisively and do not hesitate at extraordinary methods of struggle, then our success is assured."

After that Sedov went on to outline what he called "the new methods of struggle."

Trotsky rules out any possibility at the present stage of any mass //47// anti-Stalin movement. Stalin has succeeded in surviving the difficulties and we must frankly admit that we have missed the time.

"If we waste time now we will definitively lose all our cadre, and that will be the death of us.

For that reason now at the cornerstone [of our work – GF] should be laid the following:

1) the terrorist struggle of tacitly conspiratorial groups against the main leaders of the party and government; 2) active opposition against all the practical work of the party and government; and 3) the discrediting in every possible way of Stalin's undertakings, especially on the economic front.

In relation to this we must ruthlessly cast aside prejudices of any kind. At the same time it is most essential to establish contacts in the army as broadly as possible.

Just as Smirnov had done, Sedov again mentioned briefly one fundamental position of Trotsky's.

LD 242

"We cannot," Sedov transmitted Trotsky's views, "regard our struggle in an isolated manner. To keep our struggle in one country is just as absurd as Stalin's desire to build socialism in one country. Therefore we cannot swear off questions of relations between states and relations with capitalist states."

To fear these questions means to issue a certificate of one's own poverty."

At that time Sedov did not go into more detail about this question. It is possible that Trotsky specially instructed Sedov to only mention this but not to go into any details.

I charged Sedov to give to Trotsky my request to concretize his directives "about opposing practical work" and "discrediting all of Stalin's initiatives." I informed Sedov //48// that there were several Trotskyists in Berlin and that in case I departed Sedov could transmit these essential explanations of Trotsky's through one of them. And I named them (besides I.N. Smirnov): Loginov, Shestov, Bitker, Moskalev.

We agreed not to meet any more since meetings with me were a very risky affair. Sedov agreed.

With this my first talk with Sedov ended.

About my meeting with Sedov and the directives of Trotsky that he gave me I told at various times the Trotskyists who were then in Berlin: Loginov, Shestov, and Bitker. Separately, as I have already confessed, I had a substantive discussion about this question with Smirnov.

LD 243

We both agreed then that upon his arrival in Moscow he would introduce all these directives of Trotsky's officially through the Trotskyist center.

And concerning me Smirnov then expressed the opinion that it was not worthwhile to draw me into the center which the Trotskyist-Zinovievist bloc would create.

"For we must have reserves," said Smirnov. Re-establish your contacts and guard them. They will come in handy. Later we shall see what we shall do with them."

At that time the question of a "reserve" and "parallel" center had not yet been raised and the idea about it had only begun to be formed in a foggy way.

Here I would like to lay out more fully my talks with Bitker, Loginov, and Shestov.

1/ To Bitker I told everything in detail. //49//

I had to consolidate Bitker behind me, since he in the past had been a person very close to Trotsky, was closely tied to me personally, and in the future could undoubtedly play an important role in the Trotskyist organization.

Bitker agreed fully with Trotsky's policies and he and I arranged to discuss the practical implementation of Trotsky's directives in Moscow.

2/ With Loginov, whom I had known very well for a long time, besides outlining Trotsky's policies (during which I did not say anything about the "international" affairs) I agreed with him about concrete steps to resurrect a Trotskyist organization in the Ukraine.

LD 244

First of all we outlined a center consisting of himself, Loginov, N. Golubenko, IA. Lifshits, and IU. Kotsiubinskii. Then we outlined the way of resurrecting the organization. We agreed that Trotsky's policies would be the basis and about these policies Loginov would tell Golubenko, Lifshits and Kotsiubinskii, that they would begin to make contacts, but that there was no need to tell all of them about Trotsky's policies. We would have to test people for a long time and only after that, having been fully tested, so that there would not be any surprises, make the corresponding Trotskyists aware of Trotsky's real views.

3/ To Shestov, whom I did not know personally but had heard that he was a reliable person, I told Trotsky's policies, although I knew that he already knew everything from I.N. Smirnov.

To Shestov I entrusted the resurrection of the organization in the Kuzbass. I brought to Shestov's attention that was one of Trotsky's loyal men – N.I. Muralov – was there, that Vladimir Kossior was also there somewhere, and that he should, while observing the necessary caution, see who of the Trotskyists in Siberia could //50// be drawn into the organization. I told Shestov that the basic thrust of his work in the Kuzbass was sabotage, and that for this work he would have to attract not only Trotskyists but also persons of anti-Soviet orientation from the engineering and technical personnel.

Moreover I told Shestov that it was possible that Sedov would assign him to transmit something to me, and that in that case he should pass it all to me without delay.

Shestov promised to do this.

LD 245

Also in 1931 about 3 weeks after my first meeting with Sedov I.N. Smirnov told me that, despite the fact that we had agreed not to meet, Sedov wanted me to meet with him again and that he, Sedov, would await me the following day at the same place and time.

The next day I went to the same café. This time our talk was brief. Sedov immediately raised the question of money. At first he said, "You understand, Yuri Leonidovich, that for this work we need money. Can you get money?" I answered that I had no possibility at that time. Then Sedov said that he had such possibilities but that it would be hard to do it without my help. He wanted me to give as many orders as possible to the firms "Demag" and "Borsig" and not to fuss over prices; he himself would arrange with the firms about these conditions. "Obviously you will have to pay too much, but the money will go for our work, since we have some kind of agreement with representatives of these firms." I did this.

How Sedov conducted these operations with the firms I do not know.

In conclusion, Sedov informed me that he had told Trotsky about our first talk, and while he did so alerted //51// Trotsky to my hesitation on the question of sabotage. "I am expecting a letter from my father. If I receive it before your departure I will immediately give it personally to you or, if more convenient for you, through one of the Trotskyists you named to me earlier."

I asked Sedov if an answer from Lev Davidovich came, to transmit it to me through Shestov.

I think that is everything about my meetings in Berlin in 1931.

LD 246

In the fall of 1931 I finished my duties in Berlin and returned to Moscow.

After my return to the U.S.S.R. I think in November, 1931, Shestov came to me at Vesenkha.[7] He was returning from Berlin to the Kuzbass and had a letter from Sedov for me. How he had brought this letter I did not ask him. The letter was in a sealed envelope and on the envelope were only my initials: "IU. L."

Shestov handed me the letter and said he had met with Sedov and was going to the Kuzbass. When I had unsealed the letter I was very surprised: I had expected a note from Sedov but it turned out to be a letter from Trotsky himself. The letter was written in German and marked "L.T." I know Trotsky'[s handwriting well and even without this mark I would have known that he had personally written it. The letter was not in code (Trotsky and I had no code).

In this letter Trotsky expressed his satisfaction that I had "discerned his insistence" -- Dass Sie meinen Forderungen nachgefolgt haben[8] – and formulated his position.

---

[7] The Supreme Soviet of the National Economy,
[8] That you have followed my demands.

Trotsky wrote:

1/ The central task is not the resurrection of an organization //52// for the sake of organization, but its resurrection for the purpose of liquidating Stalin and his closest supporters (in the letter it was said "'S' und Konsorten mit allen Mitteln aus dem Weg rauemen)[9]...

2/ Positive collaboration with the regime is impermissible. It is essential to struggle against the regime, stopping at nothing, to discredit in every way measures undertaken

LD 247

by Stalin, and that means also to ruin the measures he has undertaken (in the first place along economic lines);

3/ We must unconditionally strengthen the bloc with the Zinovievists, who fully shared his, Trotsky's, policy. We must establish contact with the Rights, and feel out and unify all anti-Stalin elements both inside and outside the party;

4/ We must take the coming war into account and occupy in relation to the war an unconditionally defeatist position, and by means of preliminary negotiations with governments of capitalist powers (also making use of the contradictions between them) guarantee for ourselves favorable relations in case of our coming to power as a result of the war.

About these directives of Trotsky's at various times I told Loginov, Kotsiubinskii, Golubenko, Drobnis, Norkin, Rataichak, Iulin, Bitker, and Boguslavskii.

I will tell about that separately.

In the middle of 1932 I was again in Berlin. This time Sedov, having found out through the firm "Demag" that I was in Berlin, contacted me himself, on his own initiative, and asked for a meeting,

---

[9] To get 'S' and his men out of the way by any means.

for the reason that it was very necessary. We arranged by telephone to meet "at the same place" – that is, in the "Café am Zoo."

Sedov asked me whether I had received Trotsky's letter through //53// Shestov. I answered that I had, but that this letter was unsatisfactory. Although Trotsky stated the questions very concretely, he had said nothing substantive about perspectives and goals. I asked him to pass this on to Trotsky and say that his supporters in the U.S.S.R. insistently demand an answer to the question about

LD 248

the perspectives and goals of the struggle. This was especially important because of the unusual nature of the means of struggle that Trotsky was setting into motion.

Sedov promised to pass this on to Trotsky and, for his part, asked to give him information about the situation of the Trotskyist organization in the U.S.S.R.

I told him that Trotsky's directives were being put into effect, that in Moscow negotiations were taking place about the creation of a united Trotskyist-Zinovievist center and that terrorist groups were being formed.

"I know about that," said Sedov. I regularly receive news about the work in Moscow. I need to know what is being done in other centers of the U.S.S.R."

I said that I did not have detailed information about the work of the Trotskyist center (Smirnov-Mrachkovskii) outside Moscow, but that in carrying out Trotsky's directive we had formed a center of the Trotskyist organization in the Ukraine, which was in contact with me personally. This center already had peripheral groups and was setting about preparing terrorist acts. I also reported that work on the creation of a Western Siberian center had begun, where Muralov led the active work, and that Boguslavskii and Shestov led work there too. However, I proposed to strengthen this center and planned to transfer there, under one pretext or another, Drobnis, whom Trotsky knows very well and who is a very energetic, implacable Trotskyist. //54//

Sedov reported that Trotsky was expressing the greatest degree of dissatisfaction because the work was going sluggishly and was not developing with the necessary speed. "We are losing time. And

LD 249

this is extremely harmful. It is necessary to force the development of the work. It is especially necessary to force the preparation of terrorist acts and actively develop measures of diversion, including acts of sabotage." "For you know Lev Davidovich – said Sedov – he is burning with impatience and is consistently demanding activity, especially in the direction of terror."

Besides this, in this same conversation I raised the question of one of Trotsky's articles, about which I confessed on December 13.

The Formation of the Counter-Revolutionary Trotskyist "Reserve" Center

At the end of 1932, after my last meeting with Sedov, I had a conversation with Kamenev.

On his own initiative Kamenev came to me at the Commissariat on some work-related pretext.

I understood that this arrival of Kamenev was the establishment of contact with me according to Trotsky's directive, although Kamenev did not mention this and did not make reference to I.N. Smirnov. But from the nature of our conversation it was clear that Kamenev knew about everything.

Kamenev informed me that the center had been formed and it consisted of him, Kamenev, Zinoviev, Mrachkovskii, and I.N. Smirnov. Trotsky's directives about terror and sabotage were the basis of the creation of the bloc.

The center had decided not to bring into its membership me, Sokol'nikov, Radek, and Serebriakov. They had discussed this question and decided to hold us "in reserve." //55//

LD 250

In the event the center failed we would be required to lead the work ahead. He said that the question had already been discussed with Sokol'nikov, Radek, and Serebriakov, and decided positively.

Kamenev further told me that the center had established contact with the Rights (Bukharin, Rykov, Tomsky). "It would be good, -- said Kamenev, -- if you now had the necessary contact with Bukharin, with whom you have good relations."

Wishing to be clear about how far Kamenev would accept Trotsky's directives, I put the question to Kamenev: "How does the center conceive of the contact with the Rights? After all, only recently we had very sharp disagreements with them."

Kamenev answered me: "IU. L., when will you finally grow out of your schoolboy years and become a politician? Yesterday's disagreements cannot be an obstacle to our agreement today, if today we have a common goal. And this common goal is:

1/ the overthrow of Stalin and the liquidation of the Soviet government;

2/ the rejection of the building of socialism in one country and, consequently, the appropriate change of economic policy. On these two points we reached agreement with the Rights very easily."

To my question what "change of economic policy" mean Kamenev, with his characteristic aplomb, answered: "Well, you know, we will concretize it when we are in power. Only one thing is clear: we will have to retreat, in order to weaken the internal situation and equalize the external."

"Yes, yes, Yuri Leonidovich, I know that you concern yourself little with questions of international politics. But inasmuch as you may possibly have to continue the business

LD 251

that we are now doing, it is necessary that we be informed."
//56//

"Keep in mind that, without the essential agreement with the governments of the capitalist powers against the Stalin government, we will not come to power. It is essential for us to secure a favorable attitude towards us, and that means we will have to make concessions to them. But about that we must have already in advance had confidential talks with the governments of these states, and that is happening now. Radek and Sokol'nikov will inform you in more detail."

In this way the "reserve center" was formed, which we later transformed into the "parallel" center, about which I will say more.

Somewhat later (as far as I recall it was at the beginning of 1933) I also met with Radek. At that time I explained that Radek knew about the decision of the Trotskyist-Zinovievist center concerning the creation of the "reserve center" consisting of me, Piatakov, Radek, Sokol'nikov, and Serebriakov.

At that time Radek told me that Mrachkovskii was dissatisfied with the great overrepresentation of Zinovievists in the center and posed the question of supplementing the center – it was a question of me, Radek and Serebriakov on one side, and Sokol'nikov on the other. He, Radek, also thought that we had to correct this matter in some way.

We, that is Radek and I, discussed this question and arrived at a different conclusion. Inasmuch as the decision about the "reserve center" had been taken, it was not worthwhile to disturb it. If we were to insist on a revision of the decision and on supplementing the center with us, that naturally would elicit reactions from the Zinovievists' side, and in the underground there might arise dangerous divisions and unnecessary arguments.

LD 252

Therefore thoughts of entering the center were set aside. All the more since from considerations of conspiracy a "reserve center" was expedient in case of the failure of the basic center. //57// And since in the "reserve center" the predominant influence was with the Trotskyists, the thought arose of turning this "reserve center" into a "parallel center."

We decided to consult Trotsky on these questions. Radek took it upon himself to communicate our question to Trotsky and did this, as far as I know, through Romm.

Trotsky responded.

According to Radek Trotsky's answer came down to this: we should not under any circumstances create a conflict with the Zinovievists, that the bloc with them was an extraordinarily important event in the whole struggle against Stalin, and that this bloc must be maintained at all costs.

However, Trotsky considered our proposal to be expedient and proposed that the "reserve center" should immediately set to work.

In this way the vague idea about a parallel organization, expressed in 1931 by I.N. Smirnov, received its formulation in 1933 and was sanctioned by Trotsky.

Of course until the arrest of the Trotskyist-Zinovievist center the activity of the parallel center came down, in the main, to organization and preparation measures: to be more precise, to the creation of Trotskyist organizations where that was possible.

LD 253

In connection with this, and also for reasons of caution, the parallel center did not meet even once in its full membership.

Proceeding from these guidelines sanctioned by Trotsky I had, as I confessed earlier, a meeting with Serebriakov in Gagry at the end of 1933. During this meeting I established that Serebriakov knew about the "reserve //58// center" and its membership, and that he fully shared the thought of turning the "reserve center" into a parallel center. I informed Serebriakov in detail about Trotsky's policies, about which he was already partly aware. Serebriakov said that his contacts remained and he, in accordance with the common decision, would undertake to activate them.

About that time I also established a series of firm organizational contacts. Radek and Sokol'nikov had a series of contacts. In this manner by the beginning of 1934 there had been set up not only a parallel center but a parallel organization.

Of course this organization in its concrete forms was built on a basis of personal ties. In this way for example Radek's or Serebriakov's contacts were not transmitted to me, as I did not transmit my contacts to Radek or Serebriakov. We did this by mutual agreement.

In this way also contact between members of the "parallel center" was maintained by means of personal and very rare social get-togethers between them, and not by means of joint meetings. All the more, since the basic principal policies were given by Trotsky. It need not be said that all Trotsky's directives, whether or not any of us had large or small disagreements with one or another directive, were accepted by all of us to be carried out.

LD 254

During the first period after the arrest of the basic center we out of caution undertook no activity. From the beginning of 1935 we, that is the "parallel" center, began to work more actively, carrying out the decision of the basic center that had been taken by them in 1932 concerning the formation of the "reserve center."

Here I mean not that peripheral activity that we undertook earlier as I have already confessed, but //59// activity of the center itself. In this respect the substantive moments were:

1/ meetings of members of the center amongst themselves; 2/ attempts to convene a meeting of the center; 3/ Trotsky's directives.

During the first period of time we supposed it possible to limit ourselves to arranging a system of separate meetings of members of the center among themselves. Thus, I met during 1935 twice with Sokol'nikov, two or three times with Radek, also with Serebriakov. Moreover, I met with Tomsky who formally, though he was not a member of the center, but in essence it turned out that the center was put together with participation of the Rights. I knew that Sokol'nikov was in contact with Radek and also met with Tomsky. It appears that there were meetings between Radek and Serebriakov (and with Bukharin, of the Rights).

The thought arose of convening a meeting of the center together with Tomsky in order to work out a common line of tactical actions.

This meeting, as I have already confessed, did not take place.

In view of this the sole and basic leading material were those directives that came from Trotsky.

It was these directives that were, I repeat, the only leading materials, because the center did not have any worked-out positions of its own.

LD 255

About Trotsky's directives of 1931-1932 I have already testified.

After that, right up until my personal meeting with Trotsky in December 1935, his directions (except for those that went to the basic Trotskyist-Zinovievist center) came through Radek. About these directives Radek told me in 1934, 1935 and the beginning of 1936. //60//

Trotsky's directives to the "parallel" center.

The line of contact with Trotsky was in Radek's hands. He would send written information to Trotsky and personally received directives from him. True, in December 1935 I had a personal meeting with Trotsky, but I will tell about that below.

It is hard for me to remember during which conversations with Radek the latter informed me about the corresponding directives of Trotsky's. I remember the essence of these directives, but I cannot precisely separate the reporting about these directives according to the separate conversations with Radek.

Concerning terror there were, strictly speaking, no further directives. There were only demands for the quickest carrying-out of directives given earlier. Trotsky expressed impatience about slowness and insufficient activity.

Further, there were repeated orders concerning the necessity of the active carrying-out of sabotage. Trotsky explained that it was necessary to educate people in implacable hatred towards everything that Stalin initiated. Since concerning this question both Radek and I had hesitations, and since in our talks with Trotskyists we often met with doubts and even more,

LD 256

with disapproval, then we decided to question Trotsky especially on the specific question.

Radek sent such a question and at the beginning of 1936 the answer was received.

In this answer Trotsky stated the question very sharply: he who does not understand that practical opposition (as far as I can recall the word "sabotage" was not mentioned, but in essence, of course, the subject was precisely sabotage) to all //61// Stalin's undertakings is the essential and basic component of the whole struggle with Stalin in these new conditions, he does not understand the first thing about his, Trotsky's, politics.

He pointed out that this was not only a question of the quantity of the harm we caused, but of the education of cadre and of preparing them for a more serious clash, at the appropriate moment, with the "regime of Stalin."

On this question – wrote Trotsky – there must be no wavering. This is especially important in view of the fact that, as he was aware, the practical work of construction distracted, attracted, and drew many people to itself. This shows that people often do not see farther than their own nose, do not see tomorrow, live only by the interests of today, are under the pressures of today's situation. He, Trotsky, draws our attention to the fact that he views practical opposition to Stalin's undertakings not as one of the less important methods of struggle, which one could simply reject, but as the most essential component part of the whole struggle against the "Stalin regime."

On this question there must be neither wavering nor doubts.

Before this there were directives on the question of the impending war and of relations between states.

LD 257

These directives showed that those fragmentary instructions that had been transmitted to me in 1931 by Smirnov and Sedov and about which Kamenev spoke to me in 1932 had much greater meaning than I realized at that time.

Trotsky said that in the struggle with Stalin we can in no way ignore relations between governments. Once we understand that Stalin's scheme of building socialism in one //62// country is an empty and dangerous scheme, then we too in our struggle with Stalin must not slide to the position of "one country."

This struggle inevitably is interconnected with our relations with capitalist states. It would be stupid to think that it is possible to assume power without securing a benevolent attitude of the most important capitalist governments, especially of the most aggressive ones, such as the present governments of Germany and Japan. It is completely essential even now to have contact and agreements with these governments. He, Trotsky, has taken the necessary steps in this regard. He demanded from Radek and Sokol'nikov, who had the requisite possibilities, to put out feelers for the essential contact along these lines with the official representatives of these powers, and to support whatever he, Trotsky, was carrying out in practice.

In this connection, as I seem to remember, Radek told me about some kind of conversations of his with Germans (I cannot recall the names of these Germans), from whom it was clear that Trotsky had made some arrangements with the German government.

Also, Sokol'nikov told me that he had a talk with the Japanese, with Ota, I think, from which it was also clear that Trotsky was carrying on negotiations with representatives of the Japanese government.

LD 258

Trotsky further wrote that we must not limit ourselves only to the German and Japanese. We must secure benevolent relations with other governments too (like the English and French), especially from the perspective of the possibility of extremely strong pressure from the German and Japanese quarters. //63// Of course we must take into account that in relation to this we must make concessions, both territorial and of an economic nature.

As regards the war, L. D. Trotsky spoke of this very explicitly. From his point of view, war is inevitable in the near future. In this war the defeat of the "Stalin government" was inevitable. He, Trotsky, considered it completely essential to take a markedly defeatist position in this war.

Defeat in war would mean the downfall of the Soviet government and for this very reason Trotsky insisted upon the creation of cells in the army, in the broadening of contacts among the command staff. He proceeded from the position that defeat in war would create a favorable opportunity in the army as well for the return of himself, Trotsky, to power. He considers that the bloc's coming into power can certainly be hastened by the defeat of the U.S.S.R. in war.

Trotsky pointed out in this regard that especially, counting upon defeat in war, it was necessarily in advance to reach agreements with the appropriate bourgeois governments (I do not recall whether precisely only the governments of German and Japan were mentioned in this regard). It seemed to him that he would be able to reach agreements at the same time with opposing groupings of bourgeois governments and maneuver upon their contradictions. Trotsky understood that we must not rely in a naked and open

LD 259

way upon agreement with Germany and Japan, and therefore he gave a plan of playing upon contradictions.

If we add up all these directives it becomes completely obvious that this could be nothing else than yielding to the mercy of the victor, that is complete capitulation before advancing fascism in the supposition that these plans of Trotsky would be realized, of course. //64//

Besides this there were also directives about the Comintern. I did not remember them well and now recall them vaguely. I seem to remember that it was a question of a very "left" formulation against the united front in France. Unfortunately this part of Trotsky's directives did not stick in my memory.

All the directives about relations between governments were received from Trotsky during the period 1934-1935. I have expounded them as they have remained in my memory from Radek's words.

I just say that these directives of Trotsky's produced in me a feeling of oppression. I felt the desire to meet with Trotsky and to clarify his views more precisely. I did not allow myself to think that he might be mistaken and believed that there was something that I was failing to take into account. And during my meetings with Radek both he and I expressed ourselves in the same sense, that it was completely essential to see Trotsky and that I had to find some opportunity or other for this.

As I recall, Radek especially emphasized the strange position that Trotsky took on international questions and said that it was necessary to somehow discuss these questions with Trotsky. What's more, we both considered it impossible to take the responsibility upon ourselves and said that perhaps we should discuss these questions in meetings with the more prominent and trusted Trotskyists.

LD 260

In any case, we both considered a meeting with Trotsky by one of us to be completely essential.

That is why, as soon as the chance presented itself I, despite all its risks, willingly took advantage of it in order to meet with Trotsky and have a discussion with him.

Concerning my Personal Meeting with Trotsky

The situation was like this:

In December 1935 I had to urgently go //65// to Berlin on business.

There in our embassy I met with Dm. Bukhartsev, about whom I had known earlier from Radek that he, Bukhartsev, was in contact with Trotsky.

I assumed that Bukhartsev would help me to have a meeting with Trotsky.

However, from my conversation with Bukhartsev it became apparent that he had known earlier about my forthcoming arrival in Berlin (this was known at the embassy) and had informed Trotsky about it. The latter requested a personal meeting with me.

Thus although by agreement with Radek I myself had intended to meet with Trotsky, the latter, after Bukhartsev's communication about my arrival, anticipated my concrete steps in that direction and organized this meeting himself.

A few days after my talk with Bukhartsev an emissary from Trotsky arrived, with whom the same Bukhartsev put me in touch

LD 261

(I don't know the name of this emissary. If I am not mistaken his name is either Gustav or Heinrich), with a short note from Trotsky. In it there were just a few words that I could trust this person completely and the address on it was "Yu. L."

The note was not signed, but I know Trotsky's handwriting well enough.

This emissary took on himself all the technical problems in sending me to Norway and I did not involve myself in his activities.

On the following day early in the morning I took off with him in an airplane. With him he had an extra passport on which I traveled. We arrived at an airport near Oslo. From there we went by car to a place with houses, where I met with Trotsky in a private //66// apartment. The meeting lasted no more than two hours, and then together with this Heinrich (or Gustav) I returned to the airport and from there on the same day and in the same airplane I flew back to Berlin.

The talk with Trotsky began with my information about the situation in the U.S.S.R. and in the Trotskyist organization. Already in this part [of our talk] I had to listen to a whole series of indignant retorts about "cowardice," "conciliation," "failure to understand the essence of the questions," etc. They were caused by the fact that in my information I strove to tell Trotsky objectively what was happening in reality, because it seemed to me that insufficient and incomplete information had led him to certain incorrect deductions. However, as our further conversation showed, it was not a question of insufficient information.

Especially sharp replies were elicited by those parts of my information in which I expounded the undeniable, sizeable successes of the U.S.S.R. in the matter of industrial construction and collective agriculture. We must not fail to take

LD 262

these facts into account, I said. We must not dismiss them, but accept them as the facts we should begin with. "You are exaggerating," "bureaucratic distractions," "you have always suffered from the inclination towards 'positive work' independently of the regime." "You are turning away from politics," etc. With these replies Trotsky would constantly interrupt my communication of information.

Further, I told him that his directive about sabotage and diversion had for the most part not met with sympathy in Trotskyist circles and that I in particular, like Radek, did not understand it well enough, although for understandable reasons – inasmuch as the directive came from Trotsky – we were following it. Here Trotsky exploded in a whole torrent of the most vicious and scalding remarks. //67// He said that we were not able to tear ourselves from Stalin's umbilical cord, we were looking at things in a near-sighted manner, we were stuck by the psychosis of construction and could not see further than our own noses. We needed to remember that the question was not whether this or that factory would or would not be built, whether this or that collective farm would come to be, etc., but it was a question of the indoctrination of cadre of Trotskyists, even a small number of them, in hatred towards everything that was now being done in the U.S.S.R.

"I understand very well – said Trotsky, for example – that small groups of Trotskyists cannot at this moment substantively change the course of economic development. But that is, in fact, not necessary.

You recall the attitude of Marxists towards the development of capitalism in Russia. We all considered that a progressive fact. But the positions of Struve and Tugan-Baranovskii, called to the service of capitalism, are one thing, while the positions of Lenin and the revolutionary part of social-democracy, which were organizing the future gravedigger of capitalism,

LD 263

are another. We must be the gravediggers of the Stalin state.

I will not deny that from the point of view of the country's development it is good that new factories are being built. But the task of Trotskyists does not consist in building factories, but in organizing forces against Stalin and his regime, whose collapse is inevitable. For this, cadre are needed. These cadre will inevitably degenerate if all they do is participate in positive work. That is the essence of my directive, and you cannot seem to understand it at all.

Unless we carry out this directive the degeneration of the Trotskyist cadre is inevitable, their assimilation by the Stalin //68// regime is inevitable, and that means our collapse together with the collapse of the Stalin state."

Trotsky also expressed the same extreme degree of dissatisfaction during my report about the terrorist acts that were under preparation. "These are all preparations, just preparations! You are not dealing with this question seriously enough. Remember that without a whole series of terrorist acts, which must be carried out as soon as possible, the Stalin government cannot be overthrown. For this is a question of a *coup d'état*. A mass uprising, he said, is one thing, for which, evidently, there is no basis now, and a *coup d'état* is something else."

"This is the difference, I note, that many do not understand. They are unaware that the methods of a *coup d'état* differ fundamentally from the methods of organizing a mass uprising. I stand now precisely on the position of a *coup d'état* and therefore, in the deciding of questions of tactics, I have rejected formulaic instructions, developed under other conditions, applied to other tasks. And you there in the U.S.S.R. are often thrown off balance, find yourselves in thrall

LD 264

to a formula, a scheme, ideas, that were developed to apply to other conditions."

After I finished my report I asked Trotsky how he assessed the situation and how he imagined future developments. "Is it possible that you do not understand? Strange, strange! It appears that I have given enough instructions. I don't see any basis to change anything at all in my policies. Your information only confirms that I am right. And if it is necessary to draw my conclusions, then there is only one: we must sharpen the struggle even more, broaden it even more, we must literally stop at //69// nothing to overthrow Stalin, overthrow this regime. It is clear that if in the very near future we are not successful by one means or another in carrying out a *coup d'état*, then a prolonged period will set in, years of the monstrous existence of the Stalin state, supported by its economic successes, by new politically inexperienced young cadre, who will consider this regime natural, to be taken for granted."

I insisted on the necessity of a short exposition by him, Trotsky, of his views. Trotsky thought a bit and warned that 1) he could not, in such a short time (I had very little time at my disposal) fully set forth all of his ideas and 2) that not everything that he was going to say should be reported to his followers in the U.S.S.R. He mentioned once again the difference between the preparation of a *coup d'état* and a mass uprising and in this connection much of what he was about to say must not only not be made public (and therefore I should not be surprised that much of it will contradict what is said in his "Bulletins"), but also must not be made known to wider circles of his supporters in the U.S.S.R.

LD 265

From the rest of the exposition of our talk it is evident that, apparently, even to me, Trotsky did not state all the fundamental deductions he had made in proceeding from the viewpoint of the so-called "*coup d'état*."

"The root of the question comes down to the fact – said Trotsky – that socialism in one country cannot be built. All the efforts of the Stalin state (by the way, Trotsky avoids saying "U.S.S.R.," "Soviet Union," "the Soviet state," and says "the Stalin state") are doomed to collapse. This collapse is inevitable //70// unless we maneuver in time. The downfall of the Stalin state, if it occurs naturally, under the pressure of the unbearable economic burden of industri-

alization and collectivization, on the one hand, and military clash
with a capitalism that is once again growing in strength, on the
other hand, will inevitably bury us too, if we allow ourselves to
become identified, even in the smallest way, with this state. The
sharpest possible line of demarcation must be drawn between us
and all those who are tied to Stalin and his state."

"However, we must do this not by means of public statements,
propaganda, and explanations. Such statements at the present
moment would not meet with sympathy from the masses. On the
contrary, we would be compromised and destroyed before we
could do anything at all. The organization cannot be built on this
basis. That would mean to doom it in advance. For in fact the
masses are under a psychosis of construction, which they falsely
accept as the construction of socialism. To come out openly now
against this construction means to doom our efforts."

LD 266

"We must look to tomorrow. The line of demarcation must be
drawn, therefore, in secret struggle against the Soviet government,
so that at the appropriate time we can – when it is necessary – step
forward openly and say that we are not this Stalin state, we have
been waging struggle against it with all means available to us, including terror, diversion, and sabotage."

"In this – Trotsky returned several times to this theme – is the essence of my policy. That is why I have always and consistently, in
the sharpest possible manner, rejected any positive //71// participation by my supporters in the U.S.S.R. in practical work, that is
why I have always expressed dissatisfaction when it has been reported to me that you, nevertheless, continue to collaborate with
the Stalin government. That is absolutely intolerable."

"That means the first and main thing is the implacable struggle
with Stalin and his state. In this struggle we must employ everything, the sharpest methods of preparation for a *coup d'état* and, in
the first place, terror, diversions, and sabotage. On this basis we
must educate our cadre, and not on the basis of rotten conciliation

and compromise, the tendencies to which I discern in my supporters who live in the Stalin state."

"It is especially important, stressed Trotsky, to have contacts in the Red Army. Military conflict with capitalist states is inevitable. I do not doubt that the result of such conflict

LD 267

will be unpleasant for the Stalin state. We must be prepared at this moment to take power into our hands." Of course, -- emphasized Trotsky – we must understand that the seizure of power under these conditions means agreements with the corresponding capitalist states (for example with Germany, Japan, and others) on the basis of substantial concessions to them, including territorial concessions.

Of course, to reach agreements with Germany alone would be risky, since without a corresponding English and French //72// counterweight Germany would put feet on the table and it would be very tough for us. Therefore in his practical steps he, Trotsky, is carrying out simultaneous preparatory work in different directions.

Concerning Germany, there matters are essentially settled:

He, Trotsky, had secured a favorable attitude of the German fascist government in case the bloc came to power.

Of course this favorable attitude was not due to any special sympathy towards the bloc but to real interests.

At the basis of the agreement lies an appeal to the German government to help the bloc come to power. On his part Trotsky promised in the event of coming to power to make very concrete concessions, stipulated in advance, to Germany.

According to Trotsky (I will not undertake to confess that he told me everything) he was obliged to make the following concessions:

1. To guarantee a generally favorable attitude towards the German government and the necessary collaboration with it in the most important questions of an international character.

LD 268

2. To agree to territorial concessions.

3. In the event that the "nationalist forces" of the Ukraine should want to separate from the U.S.S.R. — not to oppose this.

4. To permit German industrialists, in the form of concessions (or some other forms), to exploit enterprises in the U.S.S.R. which are essential as complements to German economy (iron ore, manganese, oil, gold, timber, etc., were meant). //73//

5. To create in the U.S.S.R. favorable conditions for the activities of German private enterprises.

In return the Germans would not object to the admission under certain conditions of concessions of English and French enterprises.

6. In time of war to develop extensive sabotage activities in enterprises of the war industry and at the front. These diversive activities are to be carried on under Trotsky's instructions, agreed upon with the German General Staff.

These principles of the agreement, as Trotsky related, were finally elaborated and adopted during Trotsky's meeting with Hitler's deputy — Hess

Furthermore Trotsky informed me that at the same time he had succeeded in establishing businesslike contacts with leading persons of Great Britain and France.

In just the same manner he had fully established contact with the Japanese government.

Trotsky also mentioned that the latest negotiations with the Germans were conducted in the presence of the English and the French.

In France the contact was with the "Comité de Forges" and with banking circles. In England, with some conservative circles.

"If, -- said Trotsky, diversionist, sabotage, and terrorist activity attains such a scale that the Stalin leadership is disorganized before the military clash, so much the better, we will come to power and adjust our policy so that,

LD 269

utilizing our agreements with the capitalist states, we will severely reduce the economic stress within the country.

"This means, it will be necessary to retreat. This must be firmly understood. Retreat to capitalism. How far and to what degree, it is difficult to say now — this can be made concrete only after we come into power."

"You see, -- Trotsky continued – on this point about a retreat we have agreed with the Rights and my directive about the bloc with the Rights //74// was not just tactically necessary, but correct in principle, all the more since they have fully admitted the necessity of terrorist, diversionist, and sabotage means of struggle against Stalin."

"And I am aware that some of you have started to discuss the question of how far this unity might go."

"Let this be 'contact' at first – for we started in 1926 with contact with the Zinovievists and came to a unified organization (although with fractional subdivisions) – I think that in the future our unity will be closer. For me it is completely obvious that in the future government not only my supporters and the Zinovievists but the Rights will have to take a most active role."

In conclusion, Trotsky once against showered those of us who are working in the "Stalin state" with a hail of reproaches for insufficient activity, empty talk, absence of concrete terrorist acts, etc. He stressed that the arrests of Zinoviev, Kamenev, et al. not only must not weaken the work, but on the contrary must – as he said – "increase your energy a hundredfold."

LD 270

"Remember, in this struggle all means are good and every ally is useful. Here we must not sand on ceremony and live by old memories."

I just add that among the individual persons mentioned in the course of this talk by Trotsky were: Radek, Sokol'nikov, Serebriakov, Muralov, Beloborodov, Rakovsky, Budu Mdivani, V.M. Smirnov, Sapronov, Bukharin, Rykov, Tomsky, Uglanov, Preobrazhensky, Putna, Primakov, Krestinsky. //75//

Concerning these persons there were the following conversations. About the first three there is nothing to say. About Muralov Trotsky expressed his satisfaction, that he was one of the few who had never yielded his position and was actively working. With Beloborodov Trotsky firmly insisted we maintain close contact. About Rakovsky and Preobrazhensky he said that it was essential that we talk with them and spur them on to work.

About B. Mdivani he said that he knew he was developing the work in the Transcaucasus.

Concerning V. Smirnov and Sapronov Trotsky spoke with the highest degree of praise and expressed the thought that it was essential to arrange an escape for them, "because they are firm and determined people."

About Putna and Primakov Trotsky said that this was a very valuable contact and it must be strengthened and developed in every way.

Trotsky asked me to explain to what extent we could rely on Krestinsky.

With Bukharin, Rykov, and Tomsky he demanded that we not weaken our close organizational ties and regretted that Uglanov was not in Moscow because he was "distinguished by practicality and great organizational talents."

LD 271

With this my meeting with Trotsky ended.

Upon my arrival in Moscow I soon met with Radek and told him in detail about my talk with Trotsky. This was in January, 1936. About that time Radek received an answer from Trotsky that had evidently been written before my meeting with Trotsky. //76//

X X

X

I have tried to write down everything that I remember about the shameful and criminal activity of the Trotskyist parallel center. It is possible that not everything that I have laid out here is sufficiently clear.

Needless to say, if any questions occur to you concerning this declaration, I will give all the necessary explanations to the investigation.

Piatakov

19-20 December 1936

Concerning the accusation against Gol'tsman E.S. Vol. 1

[ЦА ФСБ Р.-33833 Дело № 3257
по обвинению Гольцман Э.С. Т. 1]

L.D. 116

Copy
31 July 1936

To: Chief, INO (=Foreign Division), GUGB (=Main Directorate of State Security)

Commissar of State Security, 2nd rank

TO COM. SLUTSKY

I urgently request that you report to me whether in Copenhagen in 1932 and today in 1936 there has existed/exists a hotel "Bristol."

I also request that you report to me at what distance from the train station the hotel "Bristol" is located.

Chief of the Secret Political Division of the GUGB

Commissar of State Security, 2nd rank

(G. MOLCHANOV)

_____

L.D. 16a

TOP SECRET

To the Chief of the Secret Political Division of the NKVD
Commissar of State Security 2nd rank com. Molchanov

In answer to your request of 31 July of this year I report:

According to the official references works / guides to the city of Copenhagen / telephone directories in the Foreign Division of the GUGB NKVD no hotel "Bristol" existed either in 1932 or exists in 1936.

However, in Copenhagen there is a small café "Bristol" above which is located the hotel "Grand Hotel Copenhagen." Since the "Grand Hotel" has a sign that is not very noticeable and the café "Bristol" has a sign in large gold letters on a black background many casual observers take the hotel "Grand Hotel" as the "Bristol."

The café "Bristol" and the hotel "Grand Hotel" are located very close to the Copenhagen train station and existed in 1932 as they do today.

Yesterday we received a telegram from Copenhagen that confirms the accuracy of the above report.

Chief of the 3rd Section of the foreign Division of the GUGB
Major of State Security / Sili /
<signature>

2 August 1936

No. 250728

_____

L.D. 117

Transcript of Interrogation
GOL'TSMAN Edward Solomonovich

of 1 August 1936

GOL'TSMAN, E.S., born 1882, place of
birth Krasnovitsy / Poland /, former member
of the VKP(b) since 1903, expelled in 1936
in connection with his arrest in the present
case.

Question: In interrogations of July 5 and 25 of this year you confessed that your meeting with L. SEDOV in Copenhagen in 1932 took place in the hotel "Bristol." Do you recall precisely the name of the hotel in which you met with L. SEDOV in Copenhagen?

Answer: If my memory does not deceive me the name of the hotel in Copenhagen where I met with L. SEDOV in 1932 was "Bristol."

Question: Describe the circumstances in which your meeting with L. SEDOV took place.

Answer: As I confessed earlier, I left Berlin from the Stettin station by an evening train that has a direct connection to Copenhagen. The train arrives in Copenhagen at 8 or 9 a.m.

As SEDOV and I had arranged in advance in Berlin I went directly from the station to the hotel "Bristol."

This hotel is situated near the station, about a five-minute walk away. My meeting with SEDOV took place in the vestibule of the hotel, from which we went to the café situated on the first floor of this same hotel.

Now I remember precisely that at the entrance to the café there was a black sign on which in large gold letters it said "Bristol."

Question: Was this perhaps the name of the café, not of the hotel?

Answer: Perhaps, but I remember well the sign "Bristol" above the café, and this café is situated next to the vestibule of the hotel. I seem to recall also that on the other side of the café in a location on the first floor of the hotel there was a newspaper kiosk.

Question: How soon did you go to TROTSKY?

Answer: SEDOV and I spent about an hour in the café, had breakfast, and then called a taxi and went to TROTSKY. I do not remember the address of the building where I met with TROTSKY.

Written down accurately from my words, read through by me. GOL'TSMAN

> Chief of the first section of the Secret-Political
> Division of the GUGB
> Major of State Security: <signature> / SHTEIN /

Interrogators:

> Assistant Chief of the 7th section of the Secret Political
> Division of the GUGB
> Captain of State Security: <signature>

/ KOGAN /

Passages about Trotsky in the Transcript of the Tukhachevsky Trial

Source:

Стенограмма судебного заседания Специального Судебного Присутствия Верховного Суда СССР от 11 июня 1937 года по делу Тухачевского М,Н., Якира И.Э.. и др.

РГАСПИ Ф. 17, Оп. 171, Д.392 Л.1-172

http://istmat.info/node/59108

Transcript of the judicial hearing of the Special Judicial Session of the Supreme Court of the USSR in the case of M.N. Tukhachevsky, M.N., Iakir, I.E., etc.

RGASPI fond 17, opis 171, delo 392, listy 1 – 172.

* * * * *

Iakir:

7

In this way I approached the moment when after a very serious illness of the liver in 1934, Tukhachevsky first, more or less definitively, told me the current weakness of our abilities, the unity of the **fascist** activities of **Germany** and **Japan** with Poland, were leading to a situation when we needed to destroy the existing order, and he told me then and there that he had contact with **Trotsky** and with the **German General Staff**. In either my first talk with Tukhachevsky or the second, but in one of those talks Tukhachevsky, without going into details, told me that **Trotsky** had set forth the essential assignment of strengthening the work of the counterrevolutionary and anti-Soviet elements in the army, and that he, Tukhachevsky, took upon himself the assignment of organizing and uniting these anti-Soviet and counterrevolutionary elements. Further, Tukhachevsky laid out for me **Trotsky's** directive, agreed upon with the **German General Staff** and detailed to some extent by himself personally. [It is not clear to whom or what this pronoun refers: to Tukhachevsky, to **Trotsky**, or to the **German General Staff**.] This directive came down to the following. The first point of the program laid out by **Trotsky** was a coup d'état, prepared by the "Muscovites," the participants in the counterrevolutionary anti-Soviet Right-**Trotskyist** organization, who had succeeded in feeling out and entering into contact with a number of Kremlin-based Chekists and with the immediate military guard of the Kremlin in the person of the chief of the Kremlin military school Egorov.

11

Iakir:

I had information and knew that Lifshits and his organization, and also Appoga and the military men he was in contact with, had worked out a plan for a whole series of traffic jams at intersecting and major stations that would cause delays for the troops when they were being concentrated at the border …

This assignment was given to us, and the people of Lifshits's **Trotskyist** organization, and of Appoga's military contacts, were prepared for it.

The next assignment Tukhachevsky told me about was that he would maintain direct relations with **Trotsky** and with the **German General Staff**. With the first, through Piatakov, and with the

12

second through Putna.

. . .

At our next talk Tukhachevsky told me that he had received from **Trotsky** a series of clarifications to his directive and his [**Trotsky's**] agreement with the measures planned by our anti-Soviet organization.

13.

Iakir:

Despite the fact that Tukhachevsky repeatedly spoke to me about the necessity of the very greatest secrecy (**Trotsky** was repeatedly telling him this, saying that the military conspiracy and its participants must not in any case be connected with other ways and lines [of the conspiracy]), contact took place all the same. True, it was episodic, rather unspecified, for the most part, about mutual information. In particular, Tukhachevsky told me twice that he had received information from Piatakov and spoke about his talks with the Rights, with Enukidze, and about one talk with Bukharin.

27.

Iakir:

I have told you about Tukhachevsky's directives about how [conspiratorial] work should be developed in the Far East. **I said that during our talks about this we considered it essential to develop work in the Far East because in one of the letters of Trotsky to Tukhachevsky Trotsky had pressed us to develop work in the Far East with the goal of contact with the Japanese for carrying out joint activity of the Germans. This is very important.**

31

Dybenko: Did you know that Gamarnik had been a **Trotskyist** since 1921?

Iakir: I knew that Gamarnik had been a **Trotskyist** since 1921.

37.

Tukhachevsky

I regard my entry into the organization as of 1932. ... By the way, I always and at every occasion have spoken out against **Trotsky** during discussions, just as I have against the Rights.

...

Finally, when in 1932 Romm brought me **Trotsky's** proposal to gather together the **Trotskyist** cadres, I agreed. Therefore I consider the beginning of the organization of our military conspiracy to be 1932.

45

Tukhachevsky

Then in 1932 Romm was sent from **Trotsky**. This was approximately in August or September.

Chairman: What did he say to you?

Tukhachevsky: Romm gave me, in **Trotsky's** name, the assignment of organizing and bringing together the **Trotskyist** cadre in the army. Since I had already begun to do this, I agreed. I thought that it would be possible to attract a significant number of military commanders and to carry out **Trotsky's** directive. Later, in 1933-34 (I am not certain

46

of the exact date) Romm gave me an instruction of **Trotsky's** that we should evaluate **Hitler's** coming to power as a favorable factor and we needed to take every measure to strengthen **fascist** power in **Germany**.

I should add that already in 1932 Romm had told me that **Trotsky** was counting on **Hitler's** coming to power and was sure that **Hitler** would support him, **Trotsky**, thanks to which we could count upon the overthrow of Soviet power. Then in 1933-34 Romm confirmed to me that **fascism** supported **Trotsky**, and therefore the latter demanded the activation of our work, especially in the area of organizing sabotage and terrorist activity in the army.

...

I mentioned Primakov. He told me that he was in contact with Piatakov, who was the leader of the **Trotskyist** center in Moscow. After that I got into personal contact with Piatakov.

Ul'rikh: Personal contact?

Tukhachevsky: Yes. Then in 1935-36 Piatakov told me of the plan of determined aggression by the **German** army, which would be linked with the loss by the USSR of Ukraine and the Primor'ye. He confirmed **Trotsky's** directive of 1935 that was set forth in a letter from **Sedov** and in oral form by Putna. **Trotsky** then gave me the assignment of activating the work as much as possible. Finally Putna arranged a meeting for me with **Sedov** in 1936.

47

In accordance with **Trotsky's** instructions that it was necessary to establish contact with the **German General Staff**, in London in 1936 I had a talk with General Rundstedt of the **German General Staff**. He told me that he knew I was leading a conspiracy and that he had instructions to talk with me. I said that the conspiracy indeed existed and that it was led by me. **I asked Rundstedt where the main forces of the German army would attack, and I referred to Trotsky's directive that we should organize defeat where the German army would be in action.** I also asked Rundstedt when we could expect this intervention. He said that he did not know where the main **German** forces would be, but he knew that we should organize defeat in the Ukraine. Concerning the beginning of the intervention Rundstedt told me that this was a question that was difficult to answer. It had been proposed to begin war in 1937, but the difficulties of forming the Reichswehr were too great to begin a **German** intervention in 1937. In the development of this assignment of **Trotsky's** and Rundstedt's after the war games in April 1936 an important discussion about planning the defeat took place between Iakir, Uborevich, and me.

66

Blyukher: Through whom, and how, were the talks concerning concessions to German fascism of the Ukraine and of Primor'ye to Japan?

Tukhachevsky: It was Piatakov who told me, so really it was Trotsky, through Piatakov, but it was Piatakov who personally told me this.

70

Dybenko: According to Kork's testimony it is obvious that the **Trotskyist** organization and the traitor Rykov were the ancillary organs in order to bring out the dictatorship of Tukhachevsky.

Tukhachevsky: No, I think the real relationship of forces was that our organization, our center, coordinated its activities with the organization of Rights and **Trotskyists**.

73

Uborevich: At the beginning of 1934 I did not have anti-Soviet ideas and, not knowing that Tukhachevsky was leading that kind of work, I spoke up against his harmful [sabotage] plan to organize brigades instead of infantry divisions in the army. I remember well that in March 1935 he, in essence, set before me his whole plan of political and military activities, his first variant. Then he began by showing the inevitability of our defeat in war against **Japan, Germany**, and Poland, and our internal difficulty. He began to tell me that he was heading an organization, that he had contact with the Rights and **Trotskyists**.

77

Chairman: For whose benefit was all this done, for what state, for which classes did you carry out your anti-Soviet struggle?

Uborevich: **For the purpose of restoring capitalism.**

81

Kork:

I personally was drawn into the counterrevolutionary Right-**Trotskyist** military organization in June, 1931. Enukidze recruited me to this organization. From Enukidze I received the assignment of contacting Tukhachevsky, Gorbachev, and Egorov…

86

Kork:

… the Red Army would suffer such losses that would permit the Right-**Trotskyists** to come to power and take power out of the hands of the Stalin government.

92

Kork:

In 1931, when I began my talk with Tukhachevsky, he explained the situation like this: we must unquestionably go with Rykov. It was not expedient at that time to defend **Trotsky** since he had lost authority in the country [the USSR]. But soon thereafter, in 1932, **Trotsky** was mentioned more and more often. And then in 1933, when the **fascist** coup took place in **Germany**, among those leaders under whose flag we were supposed to go were Rykov, Bukharin, and **Trotsky**. Later Tukhachevsky began to state, not by hinting but openly, that in the end the political group that would come out on top was hard to predict, whether Rykov or **Trotsky**, and that we military men must consider ourselves not as playthings in the hands of the politicians, but must have the strong hand of the military man, and he began to lead the talks in the direction of Bonapartism.

101

Ul'rikh: You confessed that during 6-7 years you carried out sabotage, counterrevolutionary work. One thing I don't understand is: Who was the boss? You mentioned the **Trotskyist** center, the center of the Rights, you have mentioned **German** circles. But who in fact was the boss, who gave the basic directives up to the present time: Rykov, **Trotsky**, or **German** military circles?

Kork: Under the circumstances that have been created most recently, the boss is the **German General Staff**.

Ul'rikh: That means that your main boss was the **German General Staff**?

Kork: Yes.

Ul'rikh: The **German General Staff** – that is a concise answer.

108

Putna:

... I stated that in 1931 in Berlin Ivan Nikitich Smirnov, in a talk with me in the embassy building, told me that in order to show the Germans serious decisiveness of the Trotskyists towards collaborating with them, we needed negotiations with them.

At Trotsky's direction I conducted such negotiations with generals Schleifer and Adam, who had established contact with us

109

through Hoffmeister. After the first discussions with generals Adam and Schleifer, when I reported to Sedov what I had achieved, I received a second directive from Trotsky via Sedov that this first success was not enough, that it was necessary to agree with Adam and Schleifer more precisely about the extent to which Germany itself would take steps against the Soviet Union. In addition it was essential to clarify what help Germany could render to the Trotskyist organization in the way of obtaining weapons, supplies, and technical means essential for arming Trotskyist cadres who were not in the army. Along with this it was proposed that I specify what we promised generally in the way of compensation.

Chairman: Who is "we"?

Putna: The Trotskyists organization. The Trotskyist organization promises, first, territorial compensation.

Chairman: In the name of what institution, country, or state?

Putna: In the name of the **Trotskyist** organization.

Chairman: Did they really have such great influence [lit. great weight]?

Putna: Judging from Schleifer and Adam, they did not believe in any great power of this organization. The organization itself wanted to describe its specific weight as rather significant, and therefore I received this instruction, which I carried out.

Chairman: What did you promise in exchange for help?

Putna: The territory of the Ukraine.

Chairman: Perhaps something else as well?

Punta: I was not authorized to promise anything else.

Ul'rikh: You were authorized to promise the **German General Staff** only the Ukraine?

Putna: At that time there were no talks about the Far East.

Question: From whom did you have the authority to conduct talks with the German command?

Putna: From the Trotskyist organization.

Ul'rikh: In the person of whom?

Putna: I received it as a directive from Trotsky, through Sedov and Smirnov.

111

Ul'rikh: You promised at first to give information, and then the Ukraine? Advance by the Ukraine – do I understand correctly? You said that you had promised to give the **Germans** the Ukraine. Were the **Germans** satisfied with this?

Putna: The **Germans** were not satisfied. They did not specify their promises, saying that this was premature and that the **Trotskyist** organization must demonstrate its strengths and possibilities through its activity inside the country.

Ul'rikh: How, then, did the **Germans** consider that the **Trotskyist** organization ought to show its strengths? In what way?

Putna: This we thought would be activities of a sabotage and terrorist nature.

Ul'rikh: With whom personally of the representatives of the **German** command did you carry on negotiations?

Putna: With major Hoffmeister, General Schleicher, and General Adam.

112

Ul'rikh: On behalf of whom did you carry on these diplomatic negotiations with the Germans?

Putna: On behalf of Trotsky.

112

Ul'rikh: With whom were you in contact directly from the leadership of the military **Trotskyist** organization?

Putna: With Tukhachevsky.

Ul'rikh: What assignments did you receive in 1935 and 1936?

Putna: In 1935, when I returned to London from the USSR, Tukhachevsky informed me about the successes in the Kiev and Belorussian military districts concerning the strengthening of aviation and of tank formations and gave me instructions to pass this information however I could to the **German General Staff**. On my way to London I met with **Sedov** ...

Ul'rikh: I did not understand – did you carry out your instructions and then return?

Putna: No, before carrying out my instructions. **Sedov** gave me similar instructions from **Trotsky**.

Ul'rikh: You had instructions to pass information. Did you meet **Sedov** and give information to him?

Putna: I tried to pass them to the **German General Staff**. I did not give anything to **Sedov**. Through **Sedov** I received parallel instructions from **Trotsky**, which came down to this: I should resurrect my **German** contacts and pay less attention to making contact with England and America, that I did not have to bother with these matters, that there were persons who were negotiating with England ...

114

Ul'rikh: How did he [German captain Salzman] repay you for this information?

Putna: He did not repay me. I asked him, as an intermediary, to help me establish contact and to speak with Ribbentrop, because I had an assignment from Trotsky to establish contact with the Germans.

115

Ul'rikh: Did you organize a meeting with Sedov?

Putna: Yes, at the request of Tukhachevsky I organized a meeting with Sedov.

120

Bliukher: With what **Trotskyists** in the regional center were you in contact? Were you a member of the regional center?

Putna: I knew that Mrachkovskii worked in the regional center. I knew that he was also in the general **Trotskyist** center, but I never had the occasion to meet with him.

123

Chairman: Accused Primakov, do you confirm the confessions that you gave to the organs of the NKVD in May and June of this year? Do you confirm your **Trotskyist** anti-Soviet work?

Primakov: Yes.

Chairman: Specifically, do you confirm your confessions about the preparation of a terrorist act by Trotskyist activists?

Primakov: I did not give any such confessions. I confessed about the preparation of an armed uprising.

125

Chairman: Did you hear Tukhachevsky's confessions?

Primakov: Nothing was proposed to me except to organize an armed uprising.

Chairman: We are interested in what assignments you had from the Trotskyist military organization in relation to the organization of this uprising in Leningrad and in connection with this assignment of preparing a terrorist act.

Primakov: I had the following basic instruction: Until 1934 I worked for the most part, as an organizer, in gathering Trotskyist cadre. In 1934 I received the instruction from Piatakov to break off ties with the group of Dreitser and old Trotskyists, who were assigned to prepare terrorist acts, **and I myself was to prepare, in the military district where I worked, to foment an armed uprising that would be called forth either by a terrorist act or by military action. This was the assignment I was given. The military Trotskyist organizational center considered this assignment to be very important and its importance was stressed to me. I was told to break any personal acquaintance**

126

with old Trotskyists, with whom I was in contact. This is the reason that I moved away from Dreitser's group, this is why I worked at the assignment that had been given me.

129

Primakov

In 1935 and 1936 I met with Tukhachevsky. In 1936 Kork arrived in Leningrad. We met. In 1936 I spoke with Fel'dman, and, when I arrived in Leningrad, with Gar'kavy, and then retained my **Trotskyist** contact with Piatakov, with whom I met in the spring.

Chairman: Did you systematically maintain contact with the leadership of the military center and the parallel **Trotskyist** center?

Primakov: Basically I maintained contact with Piatakov.

131

Ul'rikh: With whom did you propose to fight in Leningrad?

Primakov: This was a traitorous armed uprising against the motherland and the government.

131

Ul'rikh: [Repeats the question] With whom did you propose to fight in Leningrad?

Primakov: I proposed to fight against those infantry units that remained loyal to the government, against the OGPU forces and against the OGPU itself, against the militia [police], against all forces that remained loyal to the government.

Ul'rikh: On whose behalf were you preparing to fight? Who was your boss?

Primakov: For **Trotsky** and the **Trotskyist** center.

Ul'rikh: Who was your boss, the **Germans**?

Primakov: I did not know about the **Germans** until the trial.

Ul'rikh: How did you propose

132

to act in the event **Germany** declared war on the USSR?

Primakov: I was instructed to seize Leningrad for the **Trotskyists**.

Ul'rikh: But if **Germany** had made war on the USSR, for whom would you have seized Leningrad?

Primakov: For **Germany**.

135

Fel'dman: I was recruited to the center of the conspiratorial military **Trotskyist** organization in the summer of 1932 by Tukhachevsky.

136

Fel'dman: ... I remember that we talked in more detail on the eve of the trip to **Germany** (Tukhachevsky was the head of the delegation). We spoke about overthrowing Soviet power by means of an armed uprising and if this was not successful in peacetime, then to hope for problems at the front that might lead to armed demonstrations inside the country. Our method of work would be supporting **Trotskyist** cadres, support for those commanders who had earlier belonged to the **Trotskyist** or Zinovievist opposition, from among whom it would be easier to recruit people; ...

137

Primakov ... At my question [to Tukhachevsky], who is your leader? Are you the leader, are you the boss, or does someone direct your work? He answered me that it was **Trotsky** who led his work, with whom he maintained contact, but he did not yet tell me the source of this contact. Tukhachevsky added that **Trotsky's** directive stated that the work of the military organization must be led extremely independently, not by any means to be in contact with the anti-Soviet groupings that exist in our country among civilian organizations.

138

Primakov: ... I was also interested (I considered myself not the least spoke in the wheel and had responsibilities, so I wanted to know everything) [and asked] Tukhachevsky several times about his contacts with civilian counterrevolutionary organizations. Only in 1933 or the beginning of 1934 did he tell me that he was in contact with Piatakov.

Contact with Piatakov helped carry out sabotage in the area of artillery armament from the viewpoint of lowering our orders. Tukhachevsky also said that there was also contact with the Rights. To my doubtful question – how with the Rights? From where? I knew that **Trotsky** was leading the conspiracy. Tukhachevsky answered that now the separation between the Rights and **Trotskyists** has been wiped away, and since this is useful for our general business, why not have contact with the Rights also?

I will talk later about my practical work, and for now will remain on these facts:

When in 1933-34 **Hitler** came to power, we were given an official directive to stress our coolness towards the **Germans** at banquets. Tukhachevsky told me that on **Trotsky's** directive, it was essential to let the **Germans** know that his attitude towards the Reichswehr remained just as good as earlier.

142

Fel'dman: ... I must return to **Trotsky's** directives. Later, when from **Trotsky's** first directives, about which Mikhail Nikolaevich [Tukhachevsky] informed me, he went on to discuss the preparation for the defeat of the Red Army, he said to me that he was doing this according to a new directive from **Trotsky**, adding that all means are good in the struggle to achieve our aims, in the struggle against Soviet power.

Here I must tell the court that my collaborators, my former colleagues, if I may express myself in this way, are very squeamish in their confessions about terror and espionage.

Citizen Primakov, here you are claiming that aside from the armed uprising in Leningrad you did not undertake anything. It's strange that you do not mind speaking about an armed uprising and drowning in blood many thousands of workers, peasants, and collective farmers, but you cannot speak frankly about terror. Tukhachevsky told me in 1936 that in carrying out **Trotsky's** directive about having recourse to terror, and in particular in relation to Voroshilov, he gave such a directive to Primakov in 1936.

146

Fel'dman... In this way, summing up, I must say that everything we did were actions that served the interests of the **fascist**s and their agent **Trotsky**, whose will we were carrying out.

There were talks, as I have explained, about a palace coup. When contact with **Trotsky** had been set up through Putna, who had been transferred to London, there began talks about defeatism, and methods of terror and espionage appeared – all this in order to overthrow Soviet power and guarantee **Trotsky's** coming to power. **Trotsky** did not have real forces numbering in the thousands besides those that you see here and therefore whatever **Trotsky** dictated to us, the **German General Staff** was dictating. That's the way I see it and that's the way we should put it.

147

Fel'dman: ... Whether **Trotsky** would come to power together with Rykov or Enukidze, we did not discuss this question and it played no role for us. What was important was to overthrow Soviet power.

147

Fel'dman: ... Speaking of **Trotskyist** cadres in the Far Eastern Region, there were many of them, but I did not know any members of the conspiracy. As for <u>Lapin</u> and the others who have been mentioned here, they were assigned to the Far East without my knowledge.

149

Putna: I did not have any direct contact with civilians concerning the conspiracy. I know only one person whom I knew to be a member of the general **Trotskyist** center – Mrachkovskii. I thought that I could meet with him if the occasion required it, but we never did meet. I did not have any direct talks concerning civilian matters.

152

Iakir, last words: ... I have already said that I had a long, good, honorable life before that moment when I fell into the abyss, fell into the hands of the enemy, fell into the hands of the vilest of vile enemies that progressive humanity has, into the hands of that murderer, that agent of **German fascism**, **Trotsky**.

I want you to believe that I, if I am not left with my physical forces, will die in complete tranquility and in the understanding that I die with the most legal justification, that I have committed more [crimes] that I could redeem with my death, and that you believe me in this, that I die with a curse against **Trotsky**, **German fascism**, and with my last word of love toward the army, towards you, towards my Party, towards Stalin, and towards my motherland.

153

Tukhachevsky, last words:

I wish to draw a conclusion for myself from this vile work that has been done. I wish to draw the conclusion that under the conditions of the victory of socialism in our country every grouping becomes an anti-Soviet group and every anti-Soviet groups becomes one with the vilest **Trotskyism**, with the vilest current of the Rights. And since there is no base for these forces within our country, then whether they wish it or not, these groups slide further, into contact with **fascism**, into contact with the **German General Staff**. This is the downfall of this counterrevolutionary work that was in its essence directed **towards the re-establishment of capitalism in our country.**

154

I want to say that I went through the civil war as an honest Soviet citizen, as an honorable Red Army soldier, as an honorable commander of the Red Army, that I fought for Soviet power without sparing any effort, and after the civil war I did likewise. But the road of the group, that put me on the road of foul Right opportunism and of three-times cursed **Trotskyism**, that led to contact with **German fascism** and the **Japanese** general staff, all this had not killed in me the love for our army, love for our Soviet country, and while doing this foul counterrevolutionary business, I was also two persons.

155

Uborevich last words:

... in 1935 I committed a military crime when I accepted the defeatist instructions of Tukhachevsky and for that I, as a soldier, if I had a thousand lives, would not be able to redeem my guilt with them. I beg the Party, the Soviet people, and the army forgiveness for my last and greatest crimes.

The trial has freed me from the nightmares of conspiracy and the diabolical directives of Tukhachevsky, -- that is to say, of **Trotsky**, and the **German General Staff**. I die now with my previous faith in the victory of the Red Army. They will prepare the Red Army strongly towards these victories. That is all!

156

Kork, last words:

I wish to say that, while I took the path of treason, of vile betrayal, the path of committing crimes for which there is no name, yet within me the whole time there continued to live something else. I gradually became convinced of the profound delusion in which I found myself since 1931. I did not

157

believe in the correctness of the Party's general line, did not believe in the correctness of Stalin's line, I was shot through with doubts and gave in to the vile slander of the Rights and the even viler activities of the **Trotskyists**, when the Rights and **Trotskyists** fused into one whole and plotted the most criminal acts that can come into a person's head.

160

Eideman, last words

I ask the court to believe one thing, that before I joined this organization I honorably, without any hesitation, gave all my strength to my native country. I lived together with the Party, I lived together with the whole country. I began to slide downwards, to become corrupted, during the years of hardship, during the years of the transitional period of 1930 and 1932. I did not go to the Party with these doubts and waverings. I kept everything to myself. I began to become corrupted. Keeping within myself these waverings and the corruption, I fell into the hands of the most damned implacable enemy of the people – **Trotsky**.

161

I feel now that I have returned back onto Soviet land, I can now say without hesitation that I accept this harsh verdict so that with the last bit, the last minutes of my life, the last hours of my life to cover with curses that vile enemy of the people, **Trotsky**, agent of **German fascism**, because of whom I too became an agent of **German fascism**.

162

Putna, last words:

The seed of corrupting **Trotskyism** was sown in me by those people who drew me to **Trotskyism** comparatively early. I followed gradually and steadily almost the whole path of **Trotskyism** from the beginning of the factionalism against the Party leadership through the transition to illegal methods of struggle against the Party, through the transition to instruction more shameful, more vile, and arrived in the camp of the enemies of the Party, the state, the Red Army, and the country as a whole in 1931.

...

This process was at first also rather painful for me, but I became stuck so far in the vile rut of **Trotskyist** decay, in my struggle against our country and leadership, so deeply, and so consistently, that my normal human courage, human bravery were not enough to tear me out of this rut.

163

Many people know that I was a different person, and for me now there is no other solace except that I was once a different person. And now, in a very short time, in my own internal feelings, I have returned to my former self. I believe that in a sick organism, one that is decaying, struck down as though by poisonous gases, in an organism rotted by **Trotsky**, who led me into service to the **German General Staff** and to that coalition, in this organism, evidently, there remain still some pockets that have not completely died, that have given me the physical and moral strength to tell the investigation and the court everything that I know about this criminal activity.

164

Primakov, last words:

In my last words, citizen judges, I must tell the final truth about our conspiracy, and the final truth consists in this, that in the history of our revolution, and in the history of other revolutions, there has not been such a vile conspiracy

165

as ours, neither in its goals, not in its membership, not in the means that the conspiracy chose for itself. Of whom does the conspiracy consist, whom did the **fascist** flag of **Trotsky** join together? It joined together all the counterrevolutionary elements that we had. All of them, from the rags of the old officers' groups, to the **Trotskyist** group, with its vile terrorist directives, with its practice of struggle against the Party, though the remains of the Zinovievists, everything that was counterrevolutionary in the Red Army – all were gathered into one place, under one flag, under the **fascist** flag in the hands of **Trotsky**. That is the main thing.

What means did this conspiracy choose that are unequaled in history? All means, from the blackest betrayal, from treason, from the preparation of the defeat of one's own country through sabotage, through espionage, through terror, directed against the brain and heart of our country. These are the means that the conspiracy chose. For what goal? **For the restoration of capitalism**. What does the achievement of this goal mean, and by what path can this goal be reached, acting as our conspirators acted? There was one path: **it was necessary to shatter the dictatorship of the proletariat, but only a fascist dictatorship could shatter it**. But this **fascist** dictatorship would be created in the form of a half-dozen Napoleons, but only that one Napoleon would become the boss who was beneficial to the **German General Staff**. Because if the Red army were defeated and bled to death, the country would be deprived of force. So who then would be boss if not **Hitler's** staff? And who would establish power in the country besides **Hitler's** general staff" That was the goal to which our conspiracy was moving. It was moving towards a **fascist** dictatorship, since from the half-dozen Napoleon's would be chosen one who was chosen by the path of treasonous defeatism, the path of its vile preparation for the enemy.

167

The second group to which I belong is the **Trotskyist** group. If the first group acted by means of betrayal, the second, **Trotskyist** group is the most cursed group in the conspiracy because it has travelled the most vile path, has the most vile school and has as its leader **Trotsky**, who demanded the **fascist** banner.

168

Two more words about myself. I must say directly that I, a former communist and former soldier of the revolution, thanks to the fact that I was made into a **Trotskyist**, that I travelled the whole path with them since 1932, I arrived in the **fascist** camp and I in despair see that I have arrived at a place than which there is nothing worse in the world.

Bibliography

"Editorial Perspective. In This Issue." *Science & Society* 82, No. 4 (October, 2018), p. 475.

"Pokazaniia Tukhachevskogo M.N. ot 1 iiunia 1937 goda." *Molodaia Gvardiia* 9 (1994), 129-136. (MG 9)

"Pokazaniia Tukhachevskogo M.N. ot 1 iiunia 1937 goda." *Molodaia Gvardiia* 10 (1994), 255-266. (MG 10)

Biulleten' Oppozitsii. 1929-1940. At http://web.mit.edu/fjk/www/FI/BO/index.shtml and http://www.1917.com/Marxism/Trotsky/BO/index.html

Broué, Pierre. "Ante Ciliga (1898-1992)," *Cahiers Léon Trotsky* no. 50, 1993, 121-122.

Broué, Pierre. "Le GPU à la chasse aux trotskystes." *Cahiers Léon Trotsky* 70 (2000), 89-98.

Broué, Pierre. "Compléments à un article sur les trotskystes en U.R.S.S" *Cahiers Léon Trotsky* 24 (1985) 63-72.

Broué, Pierre. "L'historien devant la vie. Charles A. Beard et les procès de Moscou." *Cahiers Léon Trotsky* 19 (1984), 68-77.

Broué, Pierre. "Party Opposition to Stalin (1930-1932) and the First Moscow Trial." In John W. Strong, ed. *Essays on Revolutionary Culture and Stalinism.* Columbus, OH: Slavica Publishers, 1990, pp. 98-111. (Broué, POS)

Broué, Pierre. "Trotsky et le bloc des oppositions de 1932." *Cahiers Léon Trotsky* 5 (Jan-Mar 1980), pp. 5-37. (Broué 1980)

Broué, Pierre. "Liova le 'fiston'." *Cahiers Léon Trotsky* 13 (1983), 5-24.

Broué, Pierre. *Léon Sedov. Fils de Trotsky, Victime de Staline.* Paris: Editions Ouvrières, 1993.

Chuev, Feliks I. *Molotov: Poluderzhavnyi Vlastelin.* Moscow: OLMA-PRESS, 1999.

Chuev, Feliks I. *Sto sorok besed s Molotovym.* Moscow: "Terra",1991.

Cohen, Stephen F. *Bukharin and the Bolshevik Revolution 1888-1938.* New York: Oxford University Press, 1973.

Cohen, Stephen. "Bukharin na Lubianke." *Svobodnaia Mysl'* 21, No. 3 (2003), 58-63.

Dimitrov, Georgi. *The diary of Georgi Dimitrov, 1933-1949.* Ed. Ivo Banac. New Haven : Yale University Press, 2003.

Enzensberger. Hans Magnus. *Hammerstein oder der Eigensinn. Eine deutsche Geschichte.* Berlin: Suhrkamp, 2008.

Ferr, Grover (Furr). *Antistalinskaia Podlost'.* Moskva: Algoritm, 2007.

Ferr (Furr), Grover, Vladimir L. Bobrov, *Pravosudie Stalina. Obzhalovaniu nt podlezhit!* Moscow: Eksmo, 2010,

Furr, Grover and Vladimir L. Bobrov. "Stephen Cohen's Biography of Bukharin: A Study in the Falsehood of Khrushchev-Era 'Revelations.'" *Cultural Logic* 2010. At https://ojs.library.ubc.ca/index.php/clogic/article/view/191531

Furr, Grover and Vladimir L. Bobrov. "Nikolai Bukharin's First Statement of Confession in the Lubianka." *Cultural Logic* 2007. At https://ojs.library.ubc.ca/index.php/clogic/article/view/191745

Furr, Grover and Vladimir L. Bobrov. "Marshal S.M. Budyonny on the Tukhachevsky Trial. Impressions of an Eye-Witness" (in Russian). *Klio* No. 2 (2012), pp. 8-24.

Furr, Grover. "Evidence of Leon Trotsky's Collaboration with Germany and Japan." *Cultural Logic* (2008). At http://clogic.eserver.org/2009/Furr.pdf (Evidence)

Furr, Grover. "New Light On Old Stories About Marshal Tukhachevsky: Some Documents Reconsidered." *Russian History* 13, No. 2-3 (Summer-Fall 1986; actually published in 1988), 293-308.

Furr, Grover. "The Moscow Trials and the "Great Terror" of 1937-1938: What the Evidence Shows." At http://msuweb.montclair.edu/~furrg/research/trials_ezhovshchi na_update0710.html

Furr, Grover. *Blood Lies. The Evidence that Every Accusation Against Joseph Stalin and the Soviet Union in Timothy Snyder's* Bloodlands *Is False.* New York: Red Star Publications, 2014. (Furr, Blood Lies)

Furr, Grover. *The Fraud of the Dewey Commission. Leon Trotsky's Lies.* New York: Red Star Publishers, 2018.

Furr, Grover. *Khrushchev Lied: The Evidence That Every "Revelation" of Stalin's (and Beria's) Crimes in Nikita Khrushchev's Infamous "Secret Speech" to the 20th Party Congress of the Communist Party of the Soviet Union on February 25, 1956, is Provably False.* Kettering, OH: Erythrós Press & Media LLC, 2011. (Furr, Khrushchev Lied)

Furr, Grover. *Leon Trotsky's Collaboration with Germany and Japan: Trotsky's Conspiracies of the 1930s, Volume Two.* Kettering, OH: Erythrós Press & Media, LLC, 2017. (Furr Collaboration)

Furr, Grover. *The Moscow Trials as Evidence.* New York: Red Star Publishers, 2018. (Furr Trials)

Furr, Grover. *The Murder of Sergei Kirov. History, Scholarship and the Anti-Stalin Paradigm.* Kettering, OH: Erythrós Press and Media, LLC, 2013. (Furr Kirov)

Furr, Grover. *Stalin: Waiting For ... The Truth! Exposing the False-hoods in Stephen Kotkin's Stalin. Waiting for Hitler, 1929-1941.* New York: Red Star Publishers, Corrected Edition April, 2019.

Furr, Grover. *Trotsky's "Amalgams": Trotsky's Lies, The Moscow Trials As Evidence, The Dewey Commission. Trotsky's Conspiracies of the 1930s, Volume One.* Kettering, OH: Erythrós Press & Media, LLC, 2015. (Furr Amalgams)

Furr, Grover. *Trotsky's Lies.* Kettering, OH: Erythrós Press & Media, LLC, 2019. (Furr, Trotsky's Lies).

Furr, Grover. Yezhov Vs. *Stalin: The Truth About Mass Repressions and the So-Called 'Great Terror' in the USSR.* Kettering, OH: Erythros Press & Media LLC, 2018 (2016

Getty, J. Arch. "To the Editors." *Kritika: Explorations in Russian and Eurasian History* 5, 1 (Winter 2004), 233-235.

Getty, J. Arch and Oleg V. Naumov. *The Road to Terror: Stalin and the Self-Destruction of the Bolsheviks, 1932-1939.* New Haven: Yale University Press, 1999. (Getty & Naumov)

Getty, J. Arch. "Trotsky in Exile: the Founding of the Fourth International." *Soviet Studies* XXXVIII, no. 1 (January 1986), pp. 24-35. (TIE)

Getty, J. Arch. *Origins of the Great Purges: The Soviet Communist Party Reconsidered, 1933-1938.* New York and Cambridge: Cambridge University Press, 1985.

Getty, J. Arch. post to H-RUSSIA list Nov. 24 1998. At http://tinyurl.com/getty-trotsky-lied

Getty, J. Arch, and Oleg V. Naumov. *Ezhov : the rise of Stalin's "iron fist."* New Haven : Yale University Press, 2008.

Gould, Stephen Jay. "Dinosaurs in the Haystack" *Natural History* 101 (March 1992): 2-13. At http://www.inf.fu-berlin.de/lehre/SS05/efs/materials/Dinosaur-Leviathan.pdf

Harvard Trotsky Archive, Houghton Library, Harvard University. (TA)

Hilger, Gustav. *Wir und der Kreml: Deutsch-Sowjetische Beziehungen 1918-1941 : Erinnerungen eines deutschen Diplomaten.* Berlin: Athenaum, 1955.

Holmström, Sven-Eric. "New Evidence Concerning the 'Hotel Bristol' Question in the First Moscow Trial of 1936." *Cultural Logic* (2009).   At https://ojs.library.ubc.ca/index.php/clogic/article/view/191550/188662

Humbert-Droz, Jules. *Mémoirs de Jules Humbert-Droz. De Lénin à Staline, Dix Ans Au Service de L' Internationale Communiste 1921-31.* Neuchâtel: A la Baconnière, 1971. (Humbert-Droz)

Izvestiia'TSK KPSS. Moscow: Izd. TSentral'nogo komiteta KPSS, Izd. TSentral'nogo komiteta KPSS, 1989-1991 (Izv TsK KPSS)

Junge, Marc. *Bucharins Rehabilitierung. Historisches Gedächtnis in der Sowjetunion 1953-1991. Mit einem Dokumentenanhang.* Berlin: BasisDruck Verlag, 1999.

Keeran, Roger. "Khrushchev Lied But What Is The Truth?" (review of Furr, *Khrushchev Lied*). *Marxism-Leninism Today* November 23, 2011. At https://mltoday.com/khrushchev-lied-but-what-is-the-truth/

Kotkin, Stephen. *Stalin. Waiting for Hitler, 1929-1941*, New York: Penguin, 2017.

Larina, Anna. *Nezabyvaemoe.* Moscow: Izd-vo APN, 1989.

Littlepage, John D. "Red Wreckers in Russia." *Saturday Evening Post* January 1, 1938, 10-11, 54-55.

Littlepage, John D. and Demaree Bess. *In Search of Soviet Gold.* New York: Harcourt, Brace, 1938; London: George Harrap & Co. Ltd, 1939.

*Lubianka. Stalin i Glavnoe Upravlenie Gosbezopasnosti NKVD. 1937-1938.*M.: "Materik," 2004. (Lubianka 1937-1938)

Lubianka. Stalin i NKVD-NKGB-GUKR "Smersh." 1939 – mart 1946. Moscow: MDF, 2006 (Lubianka 1939-1946)

Lubianka. Stalin I VChK-GPU-OGPU-NIKVD. IAnvar' 1922 – dekabr' 1936. Moscow: IDF, 2003 (Lubianka 1922-1936)

Main, Steven J. "The Arrest and 'Testimony' of Marshal of the Soviet Union M.N. Tukhachevsky (May-June 1937)." *Journal of Slavic Military Studies* 10, No. 1 (March 1997), 151-195. (Main)

Petrov,Nikita, Mark Jansen. *"Stalinskii pitomets" – Nikolai Ezhov.* Moscow: ROSSPEN, 2008.

Politbiuro i Lev Trotskii. Tom 2. Ed. Oleg B. Mozokhin. Praha : Sociosféra-CZ, 2013. (PiLT2)

Posner, Gerald "author of an anti-conspiracy account of the Kennedy assassination, on efforts to obtain C.I.A. documents relating to the assassin." *The New York Times.*"Quotation of the Day" of October 17, 2009.

Protsess Bukharina 1938. Dokumenty. M: Mezhdunarodniy Fond „Demokratiia" i Fond Stivena Koena i Katriny Vanden Khiuvel, 2013.

Reabilitatsia: Politicheskie Protsessy 30-x - 50-x gg. Moscow, 1991. (R-PP)

Reabilitatsiia. Kak Eto Bylo. Febral' 1956 – nachalo 80-kh godov. T. 2. Moskva: "Materik," 2003. (RKEB 2)

Reabilitatsiia. Kak Eto Bylo. Seredina 80-kh godov – 1991. Dokumenty. T. 3. Moskva: "Materik," 2004. (RKEB 3)

Reabilitatsiia: Kak Eto Bylo. Mart 1953 – Fevral' 1956 gg. Dokumenty Prezidiuma TsK KPSS i Drugie Materialiy. Moskva: Mezhdunarodnyi Fond "Demokratiia," 2000. (RKEB 1)

Reitlinger, Gerhard. "Last of the War Criminals." *Commentary* 27, 1 (January, 1959), 30-42.

Report of Court Proceedings in the Case of the Anti-Soviet "Bloc of Rights and Trotskyites" Heard Before the Military Collegium of the Supreme Court of the U.S.S.R. Moscow, March 2-13, 1938...Verbatim Report. Moscow: People's Commissariat of Justice of the U.S.S.R., 1938. (1938 Trial)

Report of Court Proceedings in the Case of the Anti-Soviet Trotskyite Centre. Heard Before the Military Collegium of the Supreme Court of the U.S.S.R. Moscow, January 23-30, 1937....Verbatim Report. Moscow: People's Commissariat of Justice of the U.S.S.R., 1937. (1937 Trial)

Report of Court Proceedings. The Case of the Trotskyite-Zinovievite Terrorist Center. Moscow: People's Commissariat of Justice of the U.S.S.R., 1936. (1936 Trial)

Sayers, Michael, and Albert E. Kahn, *The Great Conspiracy: The Secret War Against Soviet Russia.* Boston: Little, Brown & Company, 1946. (Sayers & Kahn)

Schwartz, Stephen. "Ante Ciliga (1898-1992): A Life at History's Crossroads." *Revolutionary History:* Unpublished Articles, 34, at https://web.archive.org/web/20010411013259/http://www.revolutionary-history.co.uk/supplem.htm

Shakhtinskii protsess 1928 g. Podgotovka, provedenie, Itogi. Kniga 1. M.: ROSSPEN, 2011,

Sokolov, B.V. *Mikhail Tukhachevskii. Zhizn' I Smert' 'Krasnogo Marshala'.* Smolensk, 1999

Stenogramma Sudebnogo Zasedaniia Spetsial'nogo Sudebnogo Prisutstviia Verkhovnogo Suda Soiuza SSR ot 11 IUnia 1937 goda ... M., 1937. RGASPI. f. 17. op. 171. d. 392. (Tukhachevsky trial transcript) At http://istmat.info/node/59108

Weber. O. "How Not to Prepare For Underground Conditions of Revolutionary Work." *The Communist International.* July 1, 1932.

Wheatcroft, Stephen. "Agency and Terror: Evdokimov and Mass Killing in Stalin's Great Terror," *Australian Journal of Politics and History*: Volume 53, Number 1, 2007, 20-43.

Writings of Leon Trotsky, 1929-1940. Various volumes.

Zhukov, Iurii. "Tainy 'Kremlevskogo dela' 1935 goda i sud'ba Avelia Enukidze" *Voprosy Istorii* No. 9 (2000), 83-113.

Index

Ol'berg, Pavel, brother of Valentin Ol'berg, Trotskyist conspirator, 80

Ol'berg, Valentin P., Trotskyist conspirator, defendant in the First Moscow Trial of August, 1936, 10, 65, 66, 70, 77, 78, 79, 80, 81, 82, 83

Ordzhonikidze, Grigorii K. (\„Sergo"), Commissar for Heavy Industry, close associate of Stalin, 26, 122, 124, 125

Ota, Tamekichi, Japanese ambassador to the USSR, 108, 110, 136, 137, 138, 145, 146, 211

Peshekhonov, Russian fascist conspirator, 91, 92, 93

Peterson, R.A., 26

Piatakov, Georgii L. (Yuri), Trotskyist conspirator, defendant in Second Moscow Trial, 5, 9, 11, 53, 86, 87, 88, 89, 93, 95, 96, 99, 101, 102, 104, 105, 107, 110, 113, 114, 115, 116, 118, 119, 120, 122, 123, 124, 125, 126, 127, 128, 130, 131, 132, 133, 135, 137, 138, 139, 140, 141, 142, 143, 145, 146, 147, 148, 149, 150, 159, 160, 161, 164, 166, 170, 171, 187, 188, 192, 195, 205, 223, 229, 230, 231, 232, 233, 239, 240, 242

Politburo, 25

Prendergast, Kevin, Inter-Library Loan Librarian,

Sprague Library, Montclair State University, 4

Primakov, Vitalii M., Soviet military commander, co-conspirator of Tukhachevsky, 128, 148, 150, 151, 160, 161, 162, 164, 166, 169, 170, 171, 172, 173, 222, 231, 239, 240, 241, 242, 243, 247

Putin, Vladimir V., President of Russian Federation, 177, 178

Putna, Vitovt K., Soviet military commander, co-conspirator of Tukhachevsky, 128, 148, 150, 151, 158, 159, 160, 164, 165, 166, 167, 168, 170, 171, 172, 222, 229, 232, 235, 236, 237, 238, 239, 243, 244, 247

Radek, Karl B., Trotskyist, defendant in the Second Moscow Trial of January, 1937, 9, 46, 58, 70, 72, 90, 100, 102, 105, 115, 116, 118, 127, 130, 131, 132, 134, 138, 144, 145, 148, 149, 150, 204, 205, 206, 207, 208, 209, 210, 211, 212, 213, 215, 222, 223

Rakov, Vasilii N., Trotskyist conspirator, 101

Rakovsky, Khristian G., Trotskyist, defendant in Third Moscow Trial of August, 1938, 100, 110, 128, 131, 148, 149, 222

Rappoport-Dar'in, Boris S., Trotskyist conspsirator, 59, 94, 103

Rehabilitations, 28, 151

Made in the USA
Columbia, SC
19 May 2024

35870292R00159